I0242508

A TEXT BOOK OF

BIOINFORMATICS

(CODE NO. 414451 ELECTIVE IV)

FOR
SEMESTER – II

FINAL YEAR (B.E.) DEGREE COURSE IN INFORMATION TECHNOLOGY

As Per Syllabus of Savitribai Phule Pune University

A. J. Patankar
M. E. (Computer)
H.O.D. & Asst. Professor
Dept. of Information Technology
D. Y. Patil College of Engineering
Akurdi, Pune - 411044

Nitin B. Tangade
B. E. (IT)

Miss Priti P. Dudde
B. E. (IT)

NIRALI PRAKASHAN
ADVANCEMENT OF KNOWLEDGE

N1399

BIOINFORMATICS **ISBN : 978-93-5164-376-0**

First Edition : November 2014

Published By :

NIRALI PRAKASHAN
Abhyudaya Pragati, 1312, Shivaji Nagar,
Off J.M. Road, PUNE - 411005
Tel - (020) 25512336/37/39, Fax - (020) 25511379
Email : niralipune@pragationline.com

Printed By :
Repro Knowledgecast Limited
Thane

PREFACE

Today, there is a need of knowing essentials of Bioinformatics as this is the field used in drug discovery and DNA analysis. Bioinformatics knowledge is now essential requirement for Information Technology sector.

This book is intended to serve both as a textbook for short bioinformatics courses and as a base for a self-teaching endeavor. It is designed for the students of Fourth Year Degree Course in (B.E.) Information Technology, strictly as per the syllabus (2008 course) of Savitribai Phule, Pune University.

So it will be helpful for scoring in examination. Publication of this book in such a short period required a very dedicated and active cooperation of the publisher.

We gratefully acknowledge this co-operation from Shri Dineshbhai Furia , Shri Jignesh Furia and Shri M. P. Munde and team namely Mrs. Neeta Kulkarni (DTP), Miss Sarika Shinde (Proof-Reading) and Mrs. Pratibha Bele (Diagrams).

Our special thanks to our family members, friends and all those who directly or indirectly supported us in this project. The frontiers of knowledge are boundless and fathomless.

Any suggestions and feedback shall be appreciated and acknowledged.

Pune **Authors**

SYLLABUS

Unit I : Introduction **(8 Hrs.)**

Introduction, Historical overview, Bioinformatics Applications, Bioinformatics Major databases, Molecular biology

Unit II : Data Visualization & Statistics **(8 Hrs.)**

Sequence Visualization, Structure visualization, statistical concepts, micro arrays, imperfects data, quantitative randomness, data analysis, tool selective,

statistics of alignment, clustering and classification.

Unit III : Data Mining and Pattern Matching **(8 Hrs.)**

Methods & Technology overview, infrastructure, pattern recognition & discovery, machine learning, text mining & tools, dot matrix analysis, substitution matrics, dynamic programming, word methods, multiple sequence alignment, tools for pattern matching.

Unit IV : Modeling, Simulation & Collaboration **(8 Hrs.)**

Drug discovery, fundamentals, protein structure, System biology, Collaboration & Communications, Standards, Issues.

Unit V : Bioinformatics Tools **(8 Hrs.)**

Introduction, Working with FASTS, Working with BLAST, FASTA & BLAST Algorithms & Comparison.

Unit VI : Further Scope **(8 Hrs.)**

Introduction to environmental biotechnology, introduction to generic engineering.

CONTENTS

❍ ❍ ❍

UNIT I

BIOINFORMATICS

1.1 INTRODUCTION

Bioinformatics is the field of science in which biology, computer science, and Information technology merges to form a single discipline. It is the emerging field that deals with the application of computers to the collection, organization, analysis, manipulation, presentation, and sharing of biologic data to solve biological problems on the molecular level.

- According to Frank Tekaia, Bioinformatics is the mathematical, statistical and computing methods that aim to solve biological problems using DNA and amino acid sequences and related information.

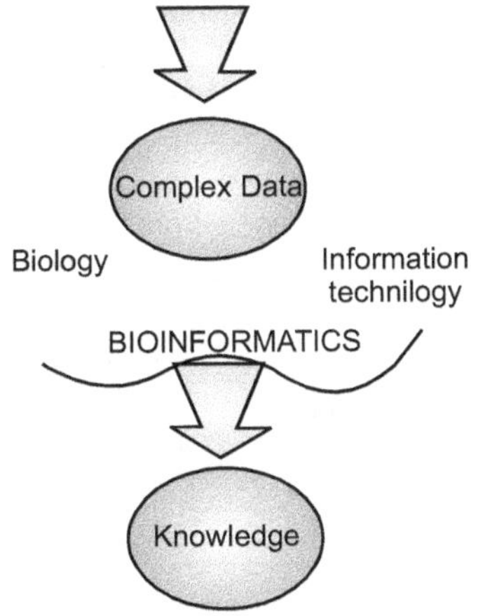

Fig. 1.1 : Concept of Bioinformatics

- Bioinformatics is a scientific discipline that has emerged in response to accelerating demand for a flexible and intelligent means of storing, managing and querying large and complex biological data sets.
- The ultimate aim of Bioinformatics is to enable the discovery of new biological insights as well as to create a global perspective from which unifying principles in biology can be discerned.
- Over the past few decades rapid developments in genomic and other molecular research technologies and developments in information technologies have combined to produce a tremendous amount of information related to molecular biology.
- At the beginning of the genomic revolution, the main concern of bioinformatics was the creation and maintenance of a database to store biological information such as nucleotide and amino acid sequences.

- Development of this type of database involved not only design issues but the development of an interface whereby researchers could both access existing data as well as submit new or revised data.
- More recently, emphasis has shifted towards the analysis of large data sets, particularly those stored in different formats in different databases. Ultimately, all of this information must be combined to form a comprehensive picture of normal cellular activities so that researchers may study how these activities are altered in different disease states.
- Therefore, the field of bioinformatics has evolved such that the most pressing task now involves the analysis and interpretation of various types of data, including nucleotide and amino acid sequences, protein domains, and protein structures.
- The development of genetic engineering technique is a big step forward in our understanding of genetic constitution of living things to enhance medical capabilities and the emergence of recombinant DNA technology or genetic engineering.

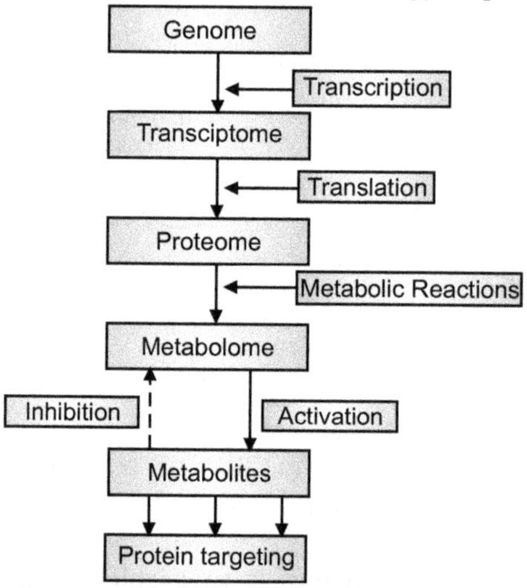

Fig. 1.2 : Flow of genetic information from genome to phenotype

- Basics of our study are DNA, RNA and protein. The process of replication, transcription, translation and protein targeting mediate and control the expression of genetic information.
- The goal of molecular biology is to understand the mechanism, specificity and regulation of these processes.
- Human genome projects were aimed at determining the base sequence of entire genome in human which involved sequencing of 3 billion base of DNA.

1.2 HISTORICAL OVERVIEW

In 1920's Bioinformatics was traced. A. J. Latka and V. Valtera introduced mathematical model of halt-preinteraction. This perhaps achieved the dynamic equilibrium.

- It was the age of computer development which allowed the 3-D structure of protein and DNA or amino acid sequence. Every human body is made of various amino acids and protein sequences. We can also call them as RNA and DNA.
- The genetic information of each species is saved in the DNA and RNA. So perhaps making the database of all the sequences of proteins and amino acids will produce a huge database. In addition to it the rate at which biological data is produced is very rapid. Thus to store, analyze and retrieve task has managed by the computers.
- Biological data is complex to stastical analysis which informs about information on the protein and to their expression in the call encoded by DNA. DNA representation can be represented by turning machine a mathematical model of a device that changes its internal state and reads from, writes on and moves a potentially infinite tape all in accordance with its present state.
- Polymers are the biologically important molecule, which ordered in chains of simpler molecular molecules called monomers. Many monomers all together forms macromolecule. The macromolecule of DNA or protein can be treated as computationally as letters to put together. In pre-programmed arrangements to carry messages or do work in cell.
- Also in bioinformatics we are going to collect the data for its manipulation, analyses and then transmitting the same with the help of computers, so we can say this science as computational bioinformatics.
- To see the overview of bioinformatics we are going to find out the relationship of molecular biology and bioinformatics with computer science and other sciences.
- For doing these operations, there will be many methods need to be applied which are computer based like pattern matching, simulation, visualization also the statistical tools being used.

1.2.1 Detailed Point Wise Overview

1.2.1.1 Killer Application

In killer application where designer drug are manufactured for a particular type of patients can start with tissue sample of that patient. Then by studying the microarray its patterns will be recognized will references, therapy medical relevance, gene expressions and then the drugs are designer for that particular patients.

Advantages

- High throughput screening
- Medically relevant information gathering.
- Custom drug synthesis.

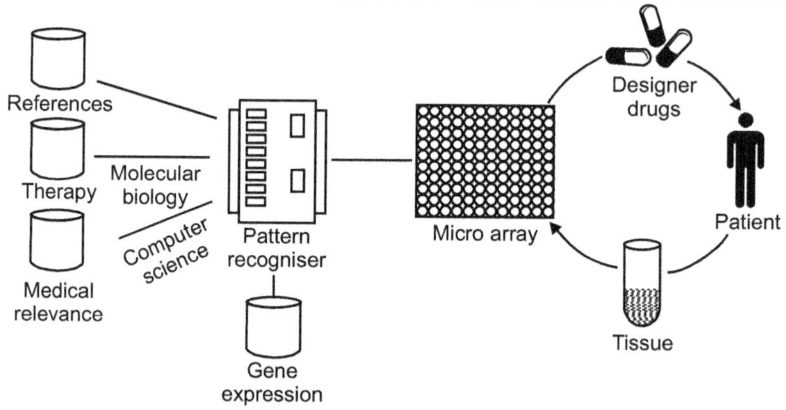

Fig. 1.3 : The killer application

(1) High Throughput Screening

With the help of computer enabled microarray technology it becomes affordable for the patient otherwise which was very costly.

(2) Medically Relevant Information Gathering

The databases of genes and medical symptoms can give us good therapy for the diseases. This is because the computer system can automatically matched the patients genetic profile with other databases related to each case.

(3) Custom Drug Synthesis

This is again related to drug database for a particular patients with the use of this synthesis of specific drugs can recommended for the proteins.

1.2.1.2 Parallel Universes

As a challenge in the Bioinformatics is to keep with the latest technology in both the molecular biology and computer discoveries. Both these development where initially independent but with the time of development in Bioinformatics they became inseparable and interdependent.

- The initial stages of 20th century the advances in chromosome therapy were taking place whereas in electronics, the transatlantic wireless communication took place. Similarity electronic amplifier and wrist watches.
- At the time of 1920 penicillin was discovered by Alexander Flemings whereas in case of electronics Intergraph. FM Radio was developed and also the architecture of hypothetical turing machine took place. This is as good as translation of RNA to proteins.
- As in 1940's synthetic antibiotics was developed whereas on electronic side FM Radio broadcast TV and electronic analog computer. With the analog computer developed after world war two the Claude Shannon published the paper on communication therapy.

- Round about 1950's the structure of DNA was developed and at the same time the development of the transistor and the commercial computer became digital within this only the artificial intelligent with computer science took place which was very helpful in the development of GPS programs [General problem solver programs].
- In the early of 1970's the development of RDBMS and OO programming's took place. This give rise to the timely use in molecular biology to correctly science the quantity of DNA data.
- In 1980's the development in the field of Artificial Intelligence took place. In 1985 Polymerase Chain Reaction (PCR) method of amplifying DNA sequence took place in molecular biology.
- In 1990's World Wide Web (WWW) came into existence which helped researchers in working with genomic data. In 1994 the first genetically modifies food (GM Food) came into market at the same time DVD were introduced in consumer market.
- With the 21st century development in both the field like computer science and molecular biology took very fast with distributed computer systems the capacity of super computers doubled and SEIT (Search for extraterrestrial intelligence) introduced. Similarly in molecular biology simulation of protein fold took place.
- With such development the computer speed and storage increased to very large capacity and in biology blue gene design took place to take care of Celera genomics to decade human genome.

1.2.1.3 Watson's Definition

The central idea of molecular biology was originally defined by James Watson. In this DNA gives us the synthesis of proteins with the help of RNA as a mediator. So, the focus of Bioinformatics is documenting, controlling and modifying.

This process which is a high level structure perspective. This is the basis for genetic engineering, it also helps in mapping the human genome and we can diagnose and treat the genetic diseases.

- Genetic engineering is modifying the process so that the new proteins are synthesized and these new proteins can become the basis for new drugs for plants and animals. DNA is a duplicated through replication and then transcribed to RNA and then ultimately translated to protein and this information transferred process is the basic force of Bioinformatics which is also very complex.
- DNA is archive of individual's genetics information of genome. This is the form of sequences of four different nitrogenous basis on a sugar phosphate backbone are as follows
    a. Adenine (A)
    b. Thymine (T)
    c. Cytosine (C)
    d. Guanine (G)

They are in the form of double helix mirror in a predefined manner. In human cell DNA is having twenty three pairs of chromosome in a compress manner and well organized. Each member of the pair is inherited from each parent.

- In the process of RNA synthesis within the cell nucleus DNA is transcribed to single standard nuclear RNA (nRNA). This is being processed to form mature messenger (mRNA). These are small nuclear RNA's (SNRNA) is involved in the process of maturation.
- This matured nRNA is a transported through the nuclear membrane to the cytoplasm where the translation of mRNA to protein occurs. This is with the aid of ribosomes. This ribosomes contains variety of different proteins and a collection of all such assorted RNA molecules is known as ribosomal RNA (rRNA).
- Information is transmitted in transcription and translation process with the help of transfer RNA (tRNA). This is done with three letter words and alphabet of four letters so there are three base sequences and $4^3 = 64$ possible codons three of which are used as stop codons one is used as start codons and the remaining codons are used as redundant representation of amino acids, the codons can be CCC, CCT, CCA and CCG.

Top Down Versus Bottom Up Approach

While making use of molecular biology and computer science for the betterment of human being. The two approaches can be followed

a. Top down approach
b. Bottom up approach

In top down approach the external factors are controlled like stress, environmental time and the lifestyle whereas this approach is taken by clinicians whereas the microbiologist can take approach with bottom up treatment. In this the principles are being worked with from the start. These principles include heredity, pathogens, trauma, parasites, Nutrition.

- The approaches with either of these may be neither correct nor incorrect. Even the simultaneous approach is considered in every field.
- A bottom up approach starts at the most detailed level and is always having big picture from the details, as both top down and bottom up are interrelated.
- The simultaneous approach helps in so many ways. If we consider the public health and molecular biology. This may require the bottom up approach like it was in smallpox vaccines whereas if we consider problem generated by smoking the top down approach is better alternative as it is an individual related problem another example is sickle-cell anemia where the bottom up approach is more effective similar the case of malaria.
- While taking care of these approaches well finding new drugs the interrelationship is always studied where the information flow perspective can be useful.

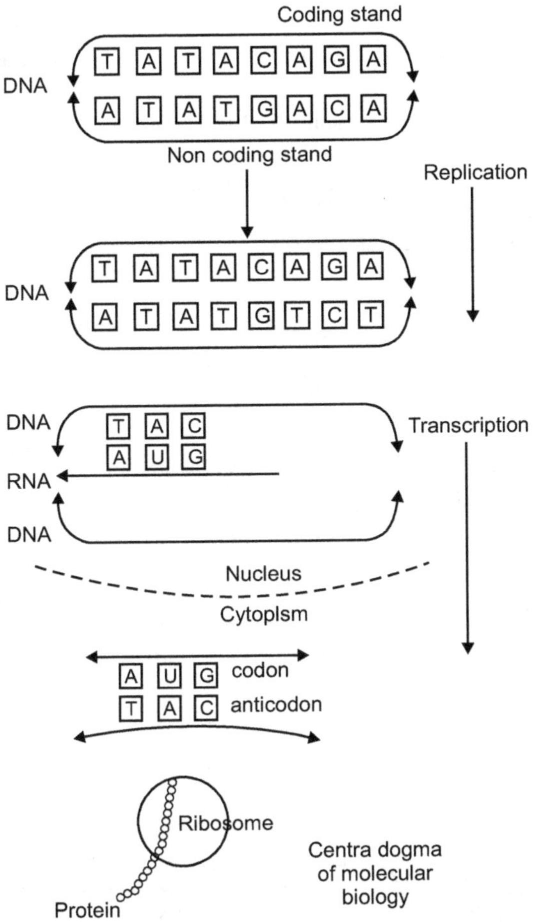

Fig. 1.4 : Top down versus bottom up approach

Information Flow

In microbiology when we think of DNA to protein there is a process of information flow. This information flow process can always be compared with Shannon's information theory. Just like this information transition DNA also carries out the process of replication from the original DNA.

- In which the messages are represented by combination of Adenosine, Tyrosine, Guanine and Cytosine (ATGC). These messages transmitted and second DNA is replicated. There are possibilities of noise in the system which may upset the information transfer process. This may generate imperfect DNA.

- Considering the central idea of information theory we can apply computer based numerical technique to model and evaluate the underlying process and this may use data achieving the effective flow process than error control the degree of uncertainty in the transmission.
- Information theory applies equally to the replication, transcription and the overall process of converting nucleotide sequences in DNA to protein.

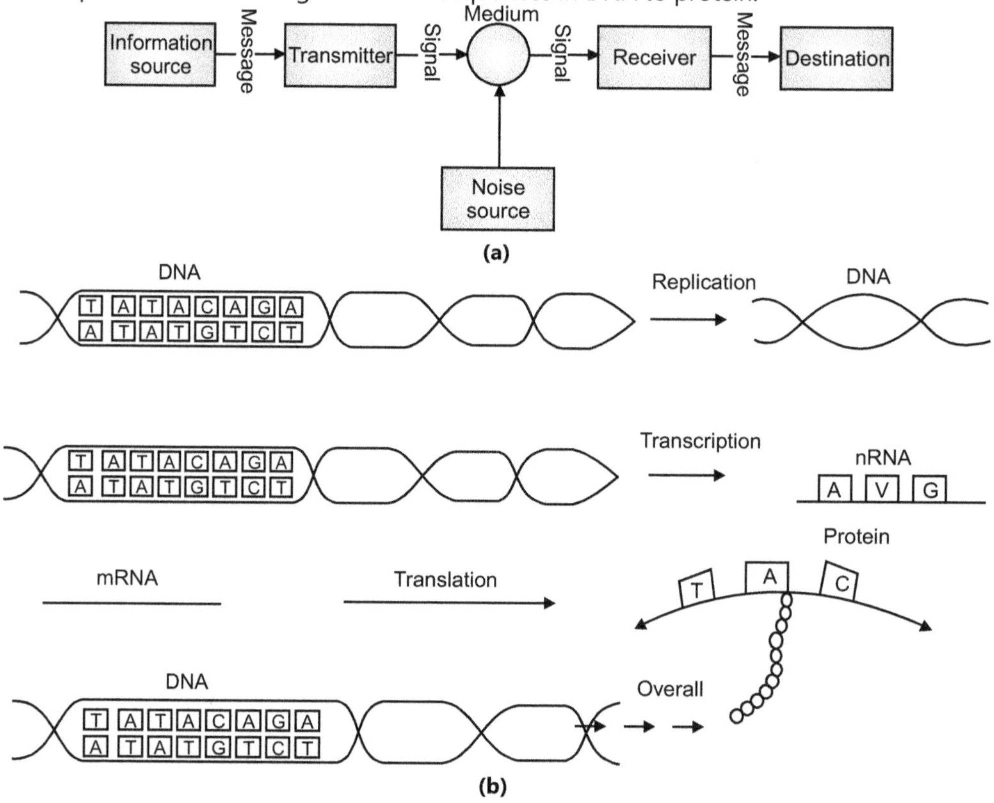

Fig. 1.5 : Information flow in microbiology

The information flow the processing of data is carried out and we must convert this data into knowledge and metadata.

Data

Data is the facts in the form of numbers and identifies from the observations or experiments.

Metadata

Metadata is data about data this gives the high level categories of the data describes and summaries related to data.

Information

Information is the data with explanation, interpretation related to particular object or event or process.

Knowledge

Knowledge is a combination of metadata and the awareness of the context in which metadata can be successfully applied. This is uniquely a human process we can convert data into information with the help of program. While processing this data into information and metadata and then afterwards into knowledge different perspective are there with molecular biologist and clinicians.

Convergence

As we have seen the co-evaluation of computer science and molecular biology. They are linked the main role of computer in Bioinformatics is for controlling, information archives, asynchronous communication devices and numerical processes whereas in molecular biology while prototyping the DNA sequence processes this information is useful.

- In automated gene sequencing process and purified genomic or complimentary DNA. We used the computer mediated information with this the data can characterized as
    a. Valuable
    b. Plentiful
    c. Incomplete
    d. Of questionable quality

These Characteristics of Data can be Described as Follows

(a) Valuable

As the data sequencing is valuable it can be decided whether they are worth for archiving or not for future use.

(b) Plentiful

The data generated in a single gene sequencing run can be with thousands of data points and for sequencing a whole gene it can be millions of data points.

(c) Incomplete

Although the data is plentiful they are often considered incomplete as the nucleotide sequence of a genome may be nearly complete. There may be major gaps in data on the proteins.

(d) Of Questionable Quality

Although the sequencing process is under computer control there are limits, for data accuracy, reputability, precision and reliability. There can be potential errors which may affect the quality of data and can give inconsistency in pattern matching.

1.3 BIOINFORMATICS

Bioinformatics is the field of study of how the information is represented and transmitted in biological systems, right from molecule level.

- Bioinformatics is the acquisition, storage, arrangement, identification, analysis and communication of information related to biology. Example, folic acid provides to the children in school because of weaknesses. This provision is providing by government and this is because of Bioinformatics.
- This is the new filed where the technologies of different fields are being used like computer science biological information of human genome along with other life sciences. Biotechnology contains the living things along with biomedical engineering, therapeutics and drugs. This also takes helps of nano science, nano engineering and computing.
- Bioinformatics will also take care of cloning for crops livestock and animal. This will also use for genetically modified fruits for higher sheflives, less pesticides, to grow faster in critical climate conditions and also supply all sources of vitamins, proteins and other nutrients.
- Biotechnology will also be used to create drugs to control human diseases to produce designer drugs for good effects in medicines. It also affects not only science but cultural and economic challenge also.
- Biotechnology area is complex, uncertain and full of unprecedented scale. To take of this innovative computational solutions are required to have in depth solutions it must go up to molecular biology.
- To take advantage of microbiology with computer science many parallel faces are used through the concept of genetics with Mendel's work. As a Bioinformatics is multidisciplinary characteristics which reference to computer science having computer visualization use of large databases, the methods of pattern matching etc. are applicable.
- Bioinformatics is a management information system for molecular biology and has many practical applications. Bioinformatics is conceptualizing biology in terms of molecules and applying informatics technique to understand and organize the information associated with these molecules on a large scale.
- Bioinformatics is the branch of science which uses the applications of information technology and computer science into the field of molecular biology. It was Paulin Hogweg who invented the term Bioinformatics in 1979 to study the processes of information technology into biological systems.
- The science of Bioinformatics actually develops algorithms and biological software of computer to analyze and record the data of genes, proteins, drug ingredients and metabolic pathways. As biological data is always in raw form and there is a need of certain storage house in which the data can be stored, organized and manipulated.

- Biological software and databases provide the scientists this opportunity so that the data can be extracted from these database easily and can be used by the scientists. The mathematical, statistical and computational methods that aim to solve biological problems using DNA and amino acid sequences and related information.
- Bioinformatics is an interdisciplinary scientific field that develops methods for storing, retrieving, organizing and analyzing biological data. A major activity in Bioinformatics is to develop software tools to generate useful biological knowledge.
- Bioinformatics is a distinct science from biological computation, the latter being a computer science and computer engineering subfield using bioengineering and biology to build biological computers, whereas Bioinformatics simply uses computers to better understand biology.
- Bioinformatics is similar to computational biology and has similar aims to it but differs on scale: whereas Bioinformatics works with basic biological data (e.g. DNA bases), i.e. it works on the small scale paying attention to details.
- Computational biology is a subfield of computer science which builds large-scale general theoretical models of biological systems seeking to expand our understanding of them from an abstract point of view, just as mathematical biology does with mathematical models.
- Bioinformatics as a science can provide input to all previously mentioned scientific fields, as the recording and processing of detailed biological data is the first step towards doing something with them.
- Bioinformatics uses many areas of computer science, statistics, mathematics and engineering to process biological data. Complex machines are used to read in biological data at a much faster rate than before.
- Databases and information systems are used to store and organize biological data. Analyzing biological data may involve algorithms artificial intelligence, soft computing, data mining, image processing, and simulation.
- Bioinformatics has emerged out of the inputs of specialists from several different areas such as biology, biochemistry, biophysics, molecular biology, biostatistics and computer science. Specially designed algorithms and organized computer databases are at the core of all Bioinformatics operations.
- Algorithms, that are necessarily complex, make voluminous data easy to handle for defined purposes, in an amazingly short time, a process that is humanly impossible. The requirements of such an activity make heavy and high level demands on both the hardware and the software capabilities of computers.
- With several divergent claimants, it is rather difficult to decide which areas of knowledge and information genuinely constitute Bioinformatics.

- It may be helpful to identify areas that are not normally considered as Bioinformatics, as for example:

  (a) Structure Determination by Crystallography and NMR,

  (b) Ecological Modeling of Populations of Organisms,

  (c) Genome Sequencing Methods (genetic mapping),

  (d) Radiological Image Processing (Human Structure Scans),

  (e) Artificial Life Simulation such as Artificial Immunology and life Security,

  (f) Organism Phylogenies based on non-molecular data,

  (g) Computerized Diagnosis based on Genetic Analysis (Pedigrees),

  and a few others, though all these constitute computer processing of biological data.
- By convention, which no one explains why so, only genomics (study of the total molecular sequencing of one set of all genes of an organism) and proteomics (amino acid sequences and the three dimensional structure related to function of proteins) constitute Bioinformatics.
- Thus, Bioinformatics is concerned with compounds of high molecular weight (HMW), particularly the nucleic acids and proteins. In recent times, cheminformatics (or chemoinformatics; study of low molecular weight, LMW, compounds), glycomics (study of carbohydrates), metabolomics (study of metabolic pathways in organisms) and drug design through Bioinformatics, are also being projected as legitimate areas of Bioinformatics.

1.4 APPLICATION AREAS OF COMPUTERS IN BIOINFORMATICS

There is a considerable overlap in the technologies associated with each application area.

Table No. 1.1 : Application areas of computers in Bioinformatics

Application Area	Associated Technology
Process control	Equipment control, Robotics, Automatic data collection
Archiving	Database, It infrastructure, Vocabulary
Numerical processing	Pattern matching, Simulation, Data mining, Search engines, Statistical analysis, Visualization
Communication	Desktop publishing, Web publishing, Internet

(1) Process Control

In typical gene sequencing machine we can use the control of embedded computer, it will be used for timing. The overall process and record it that of fluorescing color's as the dyes on the DNA fragments which gets excited by the laser and this can be controlled by computers which is just not possible manually.

Control is possible with computer science with the help of digital electronics which can also take care of complexity and logic with the help of numerical processing, archiving and communication.

(2) Archiving

The gene sequencing machine with which processing of DNA fragments is carried out which generates volumes of data so it must be stored properly for the variety of uses. This can be added to national databases for use of microbiologist researchers as we know the transfer of data from DNA to RNA and to proteins relies on information infrastructure and the data archives which again relies with IT (Information Technology).

Archiving is useful for the processing of data for molecular biologist and linking them together to reduce the gap of information as fast as possible. This can be used for publishing the different issues and finding of experiments.

(3) Numerical Processing

The numerical processing technology is use for sequence analysis, microarray data analysis and site prediction to gene finding, protein structure prediction and phylogenetic analysis. In all these different methods of numerical processing are used for pattern matching, simulation, data mining, statistics, cluster analysis and decision trees.

With numerical processing applications like pattern matching speed is most important which is possible with the help of computer hardware. The speed is also required and critical visualization sequence alignment, sequence prediction of biological data.

(4) Communication

The computer is having asynchronous communication media with different servers, email systems etc. They are real time and independent of the clock. The data in any biological database is considered permanent like the sequencing of protein structure information needs the proper communication sequence for creating and storing the gene data.

So the standards are established GEML (Gene Expression Markup Language) for such language there is collaboration between national center for biotechnology information and standard university and European Bioinformatics institute.

1.4.1 Bioinformatics Application

Bioinformatics joins mathematics, statistics and computer science and information technology to solve complex biological problems. These problems are usually the molecular level which cannot be solved by other means. This interesting field of science has many applications and research areas where it can be applied.

- Information search and retrieval
- Genetic related applications
- Sequence analysis
- Linkage analysis
- Phylogenetic analysis
- Prediction of protein structure
- Genome annotation
- Comparative genomics
- Health and drug discovery
- Proteomics
- Pharmacogenomics

(a) Information Search and Retrieval

Information search and retrieval is one of the most powerful applications of bioinformatics. eBLAST: is an application which is used to compare a query set of sentences with a database of text identify the text in dB that is most important for solving the query. It uses various algorithms to solve the related from abstract in MEDLINE to identify.

(b) Genetic Related Applications

Three types of computation:

- Analysis of a single sequence to assess similarity with known genes.
- Identification of features as binding sites or derives evolutionary relationship through phenogenetic trues.
- Complete gene analysis to determines gene families and determine chromosomal location in genes.

(c) Sequence Analysis

- The application of sequence analysis determines those genes which encode regulatory sequences or peptides by using the information of sequencing. For sequence analysis, there are many powerful of tools and computers which perform the duty of analyzing the genome of various organisms.
- These computers and tools also see the DNA mutations in an organism and also detect and identify those sequences which are related. Shotgun sequence techniques are also used for sequence analysis of numerous fragments of DNA. Special software is used to see the overlapping of fragments and their assembly.
- With these applications we can align two sequences, align multiple sequences, and perform phylogenic analyses. One reason we would do this is to determine what parts of the sequences are conserved from one species to the next.
- Another reason would be to see how much an organism has diverged from other organisms simply by comparing their DNA sequences. The more similar two gene sequences are to one another, the more closely the organisms are related.

- And the more dissimilar the two sequences, the farther the two genes are in relation. With this application we can compare sequences to determine how organisms have diverged possibly as a result of evolution.
- Single sequence alignments : Compares desired sequence to a database with many sequences in it for similarity. Aligning tow - Compare two sequences with one another for similarity and % identity.
- Multiple sequence alignments : Compare multiple sequences for similarity so that we may conclude % identity of sequence. Analogous to phylogenic studies. Restriction enzyme mapping – Determine cut sites in a sequence.
- Entelechon GmbH's Sequence inversion : This program takes a sequence and can invert it or output the complimentary strand. Instructions are included at the site and very simple to use.Oligo-Primer Properties Calculator - This program will calculate the melting point temperature and the OD of your oligo.

(d) Linkage Analysis

- Linkage analysis is to identify the chromosomal location of genes which can be used to identify implication of disease. Geneological research and linkage analysis involves the analysis of a large amount of data.

(e) Phylogenetic Analysis

- Phylogenetic analysis is the process to determine the evolutionary relationships between organisms. Phylogenetic trees determining evolutionary relationships include matching patterns in nucleic acid and protein sequences.

(f) Prediction of Protein Structure

- It is easy to determine the primary structure of proteins in the form of amino acids which are present on the DNA molecule but it is difficult the secondary, tertiary, quaternary structures of proteins.
- For this purpose either the method of crystallography is used or tools of Bioinformatics can also be used to determine the complex protein structure.

(g) Genome Annotation

- In genome annotation, genomes are marked to know the regulatory sequences and protein coding. It is a very important part of the human genome project as it determines the regulatory sequences.
- In the context of genomics, annotation is the process of marking the genes and other biological features in a DNA sequence. The first genome annotation software system was designed in 1995 by Owen White, who was part of the team at The Institute for Genomic Research that sequenced and analyzed the first genome of a free-living organism to be decoded, the bacterium Haemophilus influenzae.

- White built a software system to find the genes (fragments of genomic sequence that encode proteins), the transfer RNAs, and to make initial assignments of function to those genes.
- Most current genome annotation systems work similarly, but the programs available for analysis of genomic DNA, such as the GeneMark program trained and used to find protein-coding genes in Haemophilus influenzae, are constantly changing and improving.

(h) Comparative Genomics

- Comparative genomics is the branch of Bioinformatics which determines the genomic structure and function relation between biological species.
- For this purpose, inter genomic maps are constructed which enable the scientists to trace the processes of evolution that occur in genomes of different species. These maps contain the information about the point mutations as well as the information about duplication of large chromosomal segments.

(i) Health and Drug Discovery

- The tools of Bioinformatics are also helpful in drug discovery, diagnosis and disease management, complete sequencing of human genes has enabled the scientists to make medicines and drugs which can target more than 500 genes.
- Difficult computational tools and drug targets has made the drug delivery easy and specific because now only those cells can be targeted which are diseased ormutated. It is also easy to know the molecular basis of a disease.

(j) Proteomics

- Proteomics is the large-scale study of proteins, particularly their structures and functions. Proteins are vital parts of living organisms, as they are the main components of the physiological metabolic pathways of cells.
- The term proteomics was first coined in 1997 to make an analogy with genomics, the study of the genome. The proteome is the entire set of proteins, produced or modified by an organism or system. This varies with time and distinct requirements, or stresses, that a cell or organism undergoes.
- Proteomics is an interdisciplinary domain form on the basis of the research and development of human genome project; it is also emerging scientific research and exploration of the proteomes from the overall level of intracellular protein composition, structure, and its own unique activity patterns.
- Proteomics involves the sequencing of amino acids in a protein, determining its three-dimensional structure and relating it to the function of the protein.

- Before computer processing comes into the picture, extensive data, particularly through crystallography and NMR, are required for this kind of a study.
- With such data on known proteins, the structure and its relationship to function of newly discovered proteins can be understood in a very short time. In such areas, Bioinformatics has an enormous analytical and predictive potential.
- Metabolic proteins such as haemoglobin and insulin have been subjected to intensive proteomic investigation

(k) Pharmacogenomics

- Pharmacogenomics (a portmanteau of pharmacology and genomics) is the study of the role of genetics in drug response. It deals with the influence of genetic variation on drug response in patients by correlating gene expression or single-nucleotide polymorphism with drug absorption, distribution, metabolism and elimination, as well as drug receptor target effects.
- Pharmacogenomics may be used interchangeably with the term pharmacogenetics, which focuses on the effects of candidate genes in drug response.

1.5 MAJOR DATABASES

- Genome sequencing and the many other large scale research projects have generated an explosive growth in biological data. There are many specialized databases. A database is a collection of structured, searchable and up-to-date data.
- In Bioinformatics there are literally hundreds of public, free accessible databases. The data are usually deposited in databases and assigned a unique identifying number for quotation in publications.
- Most of these are not source data, their contents have been extracted from other databases by a process of filtering, transforming and manual correction and annotation.
- A biological database is a large, organized body of persistent data, usually associated with computerized software designed to update, query, and retrieve components of the data stored within the system.
- A simple database might be a single file containing many records, each of which includes the same set of information. For example, a record associated with a nucleotide sequence database typically contains information such as contact name; the input sequence with a description of the type of molecule; the scientific name of the source organism from which it was isolated; and, often, literature citations associated with the sequence.

Public Versus Private Databases

- Most of the databases are **public**. This means they are free accessible for everybody everywhere in the world. But in recent years it has become more and more common that **private** companies sequence genomes of commercially or scientifically interesting organisms.

- Because of the need for companies to make a profit they typically do not make their sequence data available to the public free of charge, which means that if you want to gain access to the information contained in these databases it comes with a cost.
- Academics normally are not able to pay the money required for accessing these databases and they are mainly used by the pharmaceutical and biotech industries. This means that some sequence information is available to everyone, whereas a lot of sequence information is only available to the big industries.
- Sometimes, databases that have been public turn private. For example, on the 1st of June 2002 the former public genome database of **Saccharomyces cerevisiae** (yeast) and **Caenorhabditis elegans**, two of the most widely studied eukaryote model organism, changed from a free to a chargeable service.

There are Following Types of Database

- Nucleotide databases
- Protein sequence databases
- Structure databases
- Microarray databases
- Mutant databases
- Pathway databases
- Literature databases

(a) Nucleotide Databases

- There are three major nucleotide databases EMBL (European Molecular Biology Laboratory), GenBank (National Center for Biotechnology Information) and DDJB (DNA databank of Japan). EMBL, GenBank and DDBJ collaborate and synchronize their databases will contain the same information.
- As a sequence is only submitted to one of them. There is a very short lag-time as these databases communicate with one another on a daily basis. As a result, the rough data are identical, although the format in which they are stored and the nature of annotation, very slightly among them.
- Most data is generated from genome sequenced organisms such as Homo sapiens, Caenorhabditis elegans, Mus musculus and Arabidopsis thaliana.
- Many of these species also have special databases that combine the genome sequence and its annotation with other data related to the species in a genome database.
- The rate of growth of nucleotide databases has been following an exponential trend, with a doubling time now estimated to be 9 to 12 months.

GenBank (Genetic Sequence Databank)

- GenBank is developed and maintained by the National Center Biotechnology Information (NCBI) at the National Institutes of Health (NIH). GenBank is the primary nucleic acid public database for which genomic data is directly submitted from individual laboratories and large scale sequencing projects by and for the scientific community.

- GenBank is one of the fastest growing repositories of known genetic sequences. It has a flat file structure that is an ASCII text file, readable by both humans and computers. In addition to sequence data, GenBank files contain information like accession numbers and gene names, phylogenetic classification and references to published literature.
- It contains all known nucleotide and protein sequences with supporting bibliographic and biological annotation. The database contains over 55,000 different organisms and is accessible through EntreZ.
- GenBank together with the DNA Data Bank of Japan (DDBJ) and the European Molecular Biology Laboratory (EMBL) comprise the international nucleotide sequence database collaboration.

EMBL

- The EMBL Nucleotide Sequence Database is a comprehensive database of DNA and RNA sequences collected from the scientific literature and patent applications and directly submitted from researchers and sequencing groups. Data collection is done in collaboration with GenBank (USA) and the DNA Database of Japan (DDBJ).
- The major contributors to the EMBL database are genome project groups and individual authors. Access to the most recent data and services is free via internet and WWW interfaces. The EBI's Sequence Retrieval System (SRS) is a network browser for databanks in molecular biology, which integrates and links the main nucleotide and protein databases.
- For sequence similarity searching several tools (like FASTA and BLAST) is accessible which allows external users to compare their own sequences against the most currently available data in the EMBL Nucleotide sequence database and SWISS-PROT (See Protein Sequence Databases). The databases of GenBank and DDBJ are quite similar to the access of the EMBL nucleotide database.

(b) Protein Sequence Databases

- Protein sequence databanks collect additional information about proteins, like ligands, subunit association, disulphide bridges, catalitic activity, family, etc. Most of the information is collected from literature. These databases arise by translation of nucleic acid sequences. There are several protein sequence databases. Two of the most important are PIR International and SwissProt.

PIR International

- PIR (Protein Information Resource) produces and distributes the PIR-International Protein Sequence Database (PSD). It is the most comprehensive and expertly annotated protein sequence database. The PIR serves the scientific community through on-line access, distributing magnetic tapes, and performing off-line sequence identification services for researchers.

- The PIR was the very first sequence database, setup at the National Biomedical Research Foundation (Georgetown University, Washington DC, USA). In 1988 the PIR joined with two other groups: the Munich Information Center for Protein Sequences (MIPS) in Germany and the Japan International Protein Information Database (Tsukuba).

The PIR maintains several databases about proteins:

- PIR-PSD : About protein sequence
- iProClass : Classification of protein according to structure and function
- ASDB : Annotation and similarity database;
- P/R-NREF : A database of sequence and annotations of proteins of known structure deposited in the Protein Data Bank
- RESID : A database of covalent structure modifications (like disulphide bridges)
- The PIR also has created **IESA** : a site for information where you can do several kinds of **calculations** on your protein. You can do calculations on annotations, motifs, statistical analysis, gene family classification, similarity searches. There are several links to other databases, including bibliographic databases, as well.

SWISS-PROT

- This is a protein sequence database that provides a high level of integration with other databases and also has a very low level of redundancy (means less identical sequences are present in the database).

The Swiss Prot Database Consists the Description of the following Items

- Function of the protein, post-translational modifications, domains and sites, secondary structure, quaternary structure, similarities to other proteins, diseases associated with deficiencies in the protein, variants and many descriptions more.
- In order to provide high quality annotation, it is only important to provide a good integration between nucleic acid sequences, protein sequences and protein tertiary structures as well as with specialized data collections.
- SwissProt is currently cross-referenced with 30 different databases. Cross-references are provided in the form of pointers to information related to SwissProt entries and found in data collections other than SwissProt.
- As a non-redundant database, the SwissProt tries to maintain minimal redundancy, where in cases of conflicts between various sequencing reports they are indicated in the feature table of the corresponding entry.

(c) Structure Databases

- Structure databases archive, annotate and distribute sets of atomic coordinates to visualize three dimensional structures. There are several structure databases. Structure databases contain specific information about stereochemical analysis, like bond lengths and angles, X-ray cristal structures and NMR spectroscopic data. The best established database for biological macromolecular structures is the Protein Data Bank, also known as PDB.

Protein Data Bank

- The PDB is an American database started in 1971 by the late Walter Hamilton at Brookhaven National Laboratories at Long Island, New York. It is now managed by the Research Collaboratory for Structural Bioinformatics (RCSB) at Rutgers University.
- It is based in the San Diego Supercomputer Center in New Jersey, California and at the National Institute of Standards and Technology in Maryland. The Protein Data Bank contains three dimensional structures about proteins, nucleic acids and some carbohydrates. Most of the data of the PDB is generated by X-ray crystallography and NMR.

(d) Microarray Databases

- Microarrays allow snapshots to be made of expression levels for thousands of genes in a single experiment. Microarrays are typically used to measure the abundance of mRNA. The amount of information generated by a microarray-based experiment is sufficiently large that no single study can be expected to mine each nugget of scientific information.
- The amount of finished microarray experiments grows rapidly, and because of that the massive amounts of valuable functional genomics data are already generated. The Microarray Informatics Team at the EBI was established in May 2000 to address this problem of managing and analyzing this data. They found that systems were needed for the management and storage of microarray data and the use of ontologies are crucial to managing and sharing these data.

Array Express

- The microarray data can be accessed through Array Express which is a public database for microarray based gene expression data. Array Express is the micro array database setup by the EBI. It exchanges information with the NCBI and DDBJ micro array database every week.

(e) Mutant Database

- A mutant database is a database that contains all kind of information about all kind of naturally and laboratorium made mutants. There are already several of them. An insertion may reveal gene function via a gene knock-out or a gene knock-up (over-expression and mis-expression) or the expression patterns of promoters or enhancer elements.
- The finding of the function of a gene with an insertion is called insertional mutagenesis. Most of the mutant databases are from Arabidopsis, but databases of other crops are already made.

Arabidopsis Thaliana Insertion Database (ATIDB)

- The ATIDB is collaboration between the American Cold Spring Harbor Laboratory and John Innes Center from the UK. The ATIDB was designed as a public tool for genome researchers and other biologists to find Arabidopsis breeding lines of Arabidopsis created with insertional mutagenesis and to facilitate the study of their distribution on the World Wide Web.

(f) Pathway Databases

- A pathway database (DB) is a DB that describes biochemical pathways, reactions, and enzymes. For the modeling and simulation of a biopathway, suitable information selection from public biopathway databases, such as Kyoto Encyclopedia of Genes and Genomes (KEGG) and BioCyc are useful.

KEGG

- KEGG is a database with associated software suitable for making simulations of behaviour of the cell or the organism from the information out of the genome. KEGG is specialized in a pathway database, and a ligand database. They can be used to find and visualize information from data and knowledge on protein interactions and chemical reactions.
- These reactions can be responsible for various cellular processes. Second, KEGG attempts to reconstruct protein interaction networks for all organisms whose genomes are completely sequenced. KEGG provides enzyme data with links to pathways, genes, diseases (OMIM database), motif and PDB (Protein Data Bank) structures.

BioCyc

- BioCyc is another collection of Pathway/Genome Databases. Each database in the BioCyc collection describes the genome and metabolic pathways of a single organism, with the exception of the MetaCyc database, which is a reference source on metabolic pathways from many organisms.
- Researchers can use BioCyc databases to visualize the layout of genes within a chromosome, or of an individual biochemical reaction, or of a complete biochemical pathway.
- The structures of chemical compounds can be displayed in pathways and reactions. The navigation capabilities of the software allow a user to move from a display of an enzyme to a display of a reaction that the enzyme catalyses, or to the gene that encodes the enzyme.
- The interface supports a variety of queries, such as generating a display of the map positions of all genes that code for enzymes within a given biochemical pathway. As well as being used as a reference source to look up individual facts,

- BioCyc databases support computational studies of the metabolism, such as design of novel biochemical pathways for biotechnology, studies of the evolution of metabolic pathways, and simulation of metabolic pathways.
- BioCyc is linked to other biological databases containing protein and nucleic-acid sequence data, bibliographic data, protein structures, and descriptions of different strains.
- One of the databases of BioCyc is called MetaCyc. This MetaCyc metabolic pathway database contains literature-derived metabolic pathway data for 160 species. It describes metabolic pathways, reactions, enzymes, and substrate compounds. MetaCyc is a collaborative project between SRI International, the Carnegie Institution, and Stanford University.

(g) Literature Databases

- Literature or bibliographic databases contain scientific articles or abstracts of them. Searches usually give the author's name, title, publication and date (citation information). Some also provide abstracts of the article. There are several high quality databases, but the most used is called PubMed.

PubMed

- The most used literature database is PubMed. PubMed is a project developed by the U.S. National Center for Biotechnology Information at the National Library of Medicine, located at the National Institutes of Health. It provides access to over 12 million MEDLINE citations back to 1966 and also to additional life science journals.
- PubMed integrates articles with other information retrieval tools, such as links to web sites providing full text articles. It also has an option to retrieve related articles. This gives you a clear option to get several articles about one topic. There is also a search tool to do general searches for web sites that do not correspond to articles published in journals.
- PubMed is a very useful and complete database because almost all scientific journals publish their table of contents or the issues themself on websites. Coverage is worldwide, but most of the articles or their abstracts are in English.

1.6 MOLECULAR BIOLOGY

- Molecular biology is the understanding of biological processes at the molecular level. The understanding is built through the use of physic-chemical laws. Molecular biology is amalgamation of genetics and biochemistry.
- Biological processes involve biomolecules (lipids, nucleic acids, carbohydrates, proteins etc.) that form biological structures (organelles, membranes, tissues, etc.).
- These biomolecules are present in the organism because of the expression of information residing in the genetic material (DNA). Molecular biology is therefore an information science.

- The major characteristics of nucleic acids and proteins : the two most fundamental biomolecules are given in Table 1.2

Table 1.2 : Basics of the biomolecules-nucleic acids and proteins

Macro-molecule	E.G.	Backbone of the Structure	Repeating Unit	Number of Units	Role
Nucleic acid	DNA	Phosphodie-ster bonds	Deoxyribonucleotides (A, C, G, T)	10^3-10^8	Genome
	RNA	Phosphodie-ster bonds	Ribonucleotides (A, C, G, U)	10^3-10^5 10^3-10^4 10^2-10^3	Genome Messenger Gene product
Protein	Myoglobin, Haemoglobin, GPCRs, etc.	Peptide bonds	Amino acids (A, C, D, E, F, G, H, I, K, L, M, N, P, Q, R, S, T, V, W, Y)	10^2-10^3	Gene product

- Molecular biology deals with the biological activity at the "molecular" level. The basic level is the atomic level, which leads to the higher level designated as network level (metabolic pathways).
- Biological processes can be studied at all these levels. This concept of multiple levels of biological process understanding is shown in Fig. 1.6.

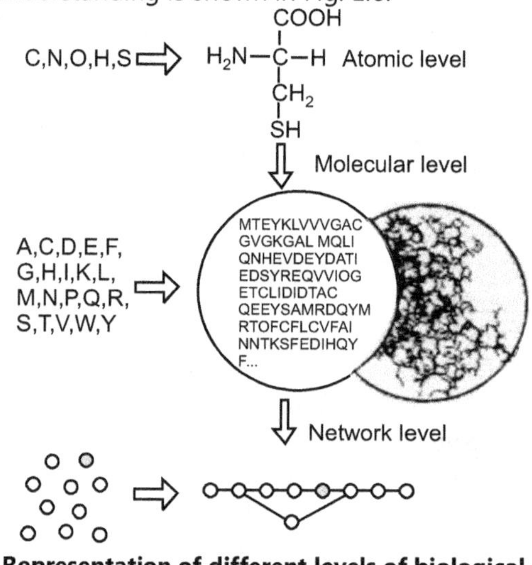

Fig. 1.6 : Representation of different levels of biological processes

1.7 CENTRAL DOGMA OF MOLECULAR BIOLOGY

- Central dogma can be stated as "DNA makes RNA makes protein". The processes related to central dogma replication, transcription, translation. The creation of multiple copies of DNA itself is called replication. The schematic central dogma is shown in Fig. 1.7.

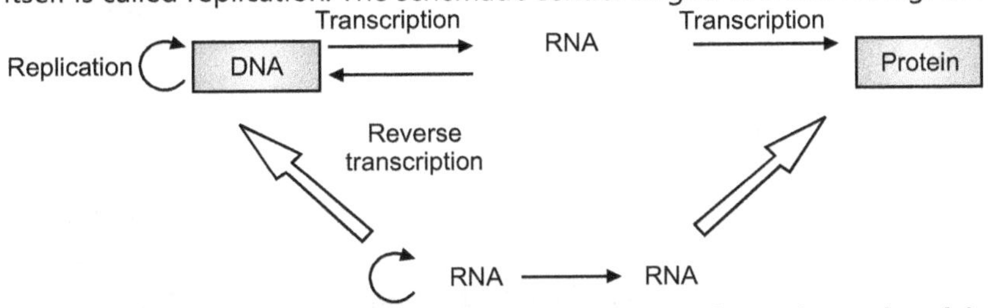

Fig. 1.7 : The central dogma is about the flow of biological information and explains the expression of the biological information into functional units.

- As mentioned above, the biomolecules playing critical role in the central dogma are the nucleic acids and proteins. Nucleic acids play various roles and they have various functional sites that enable them to play those roles.
- There are other molecules that interact with this information flow system. The molecules, their roles and the summary of the process are summarized in table 1.3.

Table 1.3 : Molecules participating in information flow and the functional sites

Molecule	Role	Functional Sites	Interacting Molecules
DNA	Replication Transcription	Replication origin Promotor Enhancer Operator & other prokaryotic regulators	Origin Recognition complex RNA polymerase Transcription factor Repressor, etc.
RNA	Post-transcriptional Processing Translation	Splice site Translation initiation site	Spliceosome Ribosome
Protein	Post-translational Processing Protein sorting Protein function	Cleavage site Phosphorylation and other modification sitesATP binding sites Signal sequence, localization signals DNA binding sites Ligand binding sites Catalytic sites	Protease Protein kinase, etc. Signal recognition particle DNA Ligands Various other molecules.

Various terms that are commonly used in relation to the central dogma, are briefly explained below in the following sections.

Nucleic Acids : DNA and RNA

- All plants, animals, bacteria and some viruses contain genetic information in the form of DNA. DNA contains the instructions for making proteins. It is a blueprint of information composed of a linear array of nucleotides, each of which has a base plus a deoxyribose sugar and a phosphate.
- There are four types of bases: cytosine (C), thymine (T), adenine (A) and guanine (G). DNA is in the form of a double helix. Unlike DNA, RNA is single-stranded. It contains ribose instead of deoxyribose in its sugar-phosphate backbone, and uracil (U) instead of thymine (T) in its pyramidine bases.
- It can be assembled from ribonucleotides using DNA as a template. Transcription preserves the whole information content of the DNA sequence that is transcribed on to RNA, since RNA has the same base-pairing characteristics. There are three major classes of RNA: messenger RNA (mRNA), transfer RNA (tRNA) and ribosomal RNA (rRNA).

DNA Replication

- DNA replication involves unwinding of the two strands of paternal DNA duplex, with each strand serving as the template for the synthesis of new strand, complementary to and wound about parental strand.
- Expression of genetic information in DNA involves transcription of the DNA sequence into RNA (messenger RNA), then translation of mRNA sequence into the protein sequence.

Genes

- A gene is a segment of DNA representing nucleotides required for the production of a functional protein or a functional RNA molecule. A gene includes not only the actual coding sequences but also adjacent nucleotide sequences required for the proper expression of genes.

Genome

- Genome constitutes the total genetic material of an organism. The human genomeis highly complex and contains about three billion nucleotides. The human genome has been sequenced recently; there are several other organisms that have been sequenced already.

Chromatin

- The eukaryotic chromosome is composed of DNA and proteins, together called chromatin. The proteins include positively charged basic proteins called histones as well as non-histonic the basic structural unit of chromatin are nucleosome, which is a complex of DNA with a core of histones.

SUMMARY

- The field of science in which biology, computer science, and information technology merge into a single discipline.
- Bioinformatics is an essential component of modern biology and not independent of it. Bioinformatics is not an area of information technology and cannot be restricted to biotechnology alone.
- In 1920's Bioinformatics was traced. A. J. Latka and V. Valtera introduced mathematical model of halt-preinteraction. In killer application where designer drug is manufactured for a particular type ofpatients can start with tissue sample of that patient.
- As a challenge in the Bioinformatics is to keep with the latest technology in both the molecular biology and computer discoveries. Both these development where initially independent but with the time of development in Bioinformatics they became inseparable and interdependent.
- The central idea of molecular biology was originally defined by James Watson. Bioinformatics joins mathematics, statistics and computer science and information technology to solve complex biological problems.
- The Bioinformatics applications are Information search and retrieval, Genetic related applications, Sequence analysis, Linkage analysis, Phylogenetic analysis, Prediction of protein structure, Genome annotation, Comparative genomics, Health and drug discovery, Proteomics, Pharmacogenomics.
- Biological databases are libraries of life sciences information, collected from scientific experiments, published literature, high-throughput experiment technology, and computational analyses.
- There are following types of database:Nucleotide databases, Protein sequence databases, Structure databases, Microarray databases, Mutant databases, Pathway databases, Literature databases.
- Molecular biology is the understanding of biological processes at the molecular level. The understanding is built through the use of physic-chemical laws. Molecular biology is amalgamation of genetics and biochemistry.
- Central dogma can be stated as "DNA makes RNA makes protein". The processes related to central dogma replication, transcription, translation.

QUESTIONS

MAY 2012

1. (a) Define Bioinformatics. Explain Bioinformatics applications related to the following areas **[10]**
   (i) Phylogenetic Analysis, (ii) Genome Annotation, (iii) Proteomics, (iv) Drug Discovery.

Ans. : Please refer section 1.4.

(b) Classify and explain major databases in Bioinformatics giving examples of each database. **[8]**

Ans. : Please refer Section 1.5.

OR

2. (a) Explain central dogma of molecular biology with neat diagram. Explain how is it an information science. **[8]**

Ans. : Please refer Section 1.6.

(b) State and explain various data retrieval tools in Bioinformatics. Explain the steps for data mining and knowledge discovery of biological databases. **[10]**

Ans. : Please refer Section 1.4

MAY 2013

3. A What is the scope of Bioinformatics? Explain Bioinformatics applications related to the following areas **[10]**

(i) Information search & retrieval. (ii) Microarrays

(iii) Sequence Assembly (iv) Pharmacogenomics

Ans. : Please refer Section 1.4.

4. Explain with neat diagram the central dogma of molecular biology. Explain the molecules participating in Information flow and the various functional sites. **[8]**

Ans. : Please refer Section 1.7.

OR

5. A Discuss the public Bioinformatics databases which are accessible via the internet with appropriate examples. **[10]**

Ans. : Please refer Section 1.5.

6. Explain Data Life Cycle for clinical data management with respect to following steps: **[8]**

(i) Data creation and acquisition, (ii) Use, (iii) Modification, (iv) Archiving data disposal

Ans. : Please refer Section 1.4.

MAY 2014

1. (a) Define Bioinformatics. Discuss in detail any four Bioinformatics applications. **[10]**

Ans. : Please refer Section 1.4.

(b) Explain various protein databases used in Bioinformatics for analysis and developing applications.

Ans. : Please refer Section 1.5.

OR

2. (a) Discuss the application areas of computers in Bioinformatics with their associated technologies. **[8]**

Ans. : Please refer Section 1.4.

(b) Explain with neat diagram the Central dogma of molecular biology. How can molecular biology be considered as an information science.

Ans. : Please refer Section 1.6, 1.7.

UNIT II

DATA VISUALIZATION AND STATISTICS

2.1 VISUALIZATION

- Visualization in bioinformatics is to render the 3D of protein structure and modeling the interactions of protein and protein in real time. To have visualization of this type requiring high end computing where computer and grid computing is being used.
- The development of modern acquisition technologies for biological processes comes along with a vast amount of data. This data may result from experimental measurements as well as simulations of processes of single molecules, the expression of genes, or models of complete populations.
- Analysis of such data is challenging, as it is oftentimes fraught with uncertainty and errors, heterogeneous, and high-dimensional. Therefore, modern and adequate visualization techniques are essential ingredients for the analysis of such data.
- Bioinformatics has to develop visualization technique which can be easily used and can give support for long terms and will also be useful in developing the next generation hardware and software.
- In visualization it will be graphical representation of data with meaning and context. Molecular biology has a lot of confusing data so it becomes essential to visualize getting the correct information or correcting pictures of data available.
- In bioinformatics majority of data is in abstract from and this makes essential to have the visualization technique. Protein structure prediction and protein to protein interaction are the essential thing visualize. It can give us physical location of the genes on the chromosomes.

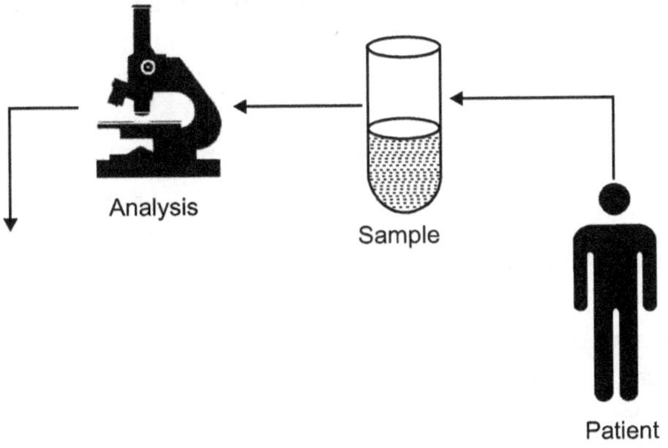

Fig. 2.1 : Visualization aids to tabular clinical laboratory

There are two types of visualization

(a) Sequence visualization

(b) Structure visualization

(a) Sequence Visualization

- In sequence visualization we have to work with nucleotide sequences which can gives us gene maps i.e. high level graphic representation of specific sequences residing on chromosomes.
- This requires along with some of low level machine programming language. The high level programming language are also essential like c++, basic or HTML etc.
- Artemis is a DNA sequence visualization and annotation tool that allows the results of any analysis or sets of analyses to be viewed in the context of the sequence and its six-frame translation.
- Artemis is especially useful in analyzing the compact genomes of bacteria, archaea and lower eukaryotes, and will cope with sequences of any size from small genes to whole genomes. It is implemented in Java, and can be run on any suitable platform. Sequences and annotation can be read and written directly in EMBL, GenBank and GFF format.

(b) Sequence Mapping

When it comes to visualizing nucleotide sequences, the amino acids, proteins, chromosome segments and genes.

- Gene maps provide a high level view of relative and absolute gene and nucleotide sequence location.
- Gene mapping application is done at NCBI (National Center for Biological Information) which is represented on web based map viewer. NCBI's map viewer program integrates physical and genetic map information for specific sequences, proteins and genes.
- The web based map viewer program provides a composite interface to several of NCBI's online databases. The nucleotide sequences are depicted graphically in map viewer through composite of genetic, cytogenetic, physical and radiation hybrid map and all these are having its particular use with relative position order of gene and sequence of chromosome.
- These are having variety of application in research of DNA with chromosomes for its coding. This genetic map gives the distance between genes and markers. Markers are variation at single genetic locus due to mutation or alteration.
- Markers (path) include Single Nucleotide Polymorphisms (SNPs) which gives individual mutation points. The map creation also depends on methodology used. It can be cytogenetic mapping or high resolution sequence based physical mapping.
- This uses Sequence Tagged Sites (STSs). Valuable mapping technique provides connection between physical and genetic map. This involves radiations hybrid mapping (RH) mapping and Simple Sequence Length Polymorphisms (SSLPs).

- RH mapping gives us distance between genetic markers and SSLP gives us both genetic markers and basis for sequence mapping. Accuracy of mapping technique depends on computational method.
- The sequence mapping uses up of chromosome at random fragment and then cloned with bacteria to make Bacterial Artificial Chromosome (BAC).
- Each BAC's is broken at random into fragments that can be handled by a sequence machine less than around.
- Structural bioinformatics is the branch of bioinformatics which is related to the analysis and prediction of the three-dimensional structure of biological macromolecules such as proteins, RNA, and DNA.
- It deals with generalizations about macromolecular 3D structure such as comparisons of overall folds and local motifs, principles of molecular folding, evolution, and binding interactions, and structure/function relationships, working both from experimentally solved structures and from computational models.

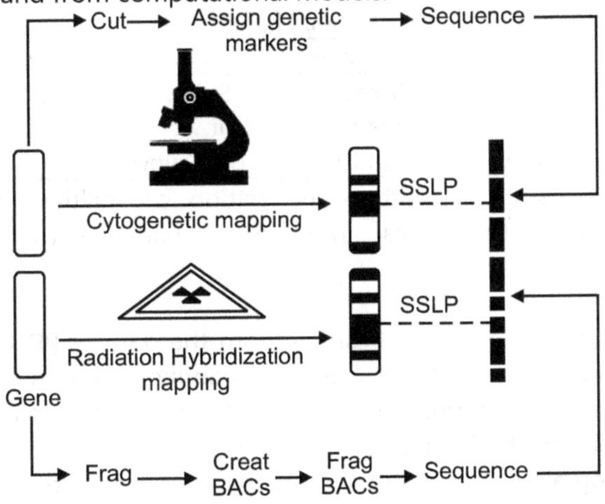

Fig. 2.2 : Gene mapping process

- The term structural has the same meaning as in structural biology, and structural bioinformatics can be seen as a part of computational structural biology.
- 3D structure visualization is essential for structure of proteins so that we can find out where the days might modulate their activity. Even this visualization in 3D can help us in identifying the proteins produced by given cell or tissue and how they interact.
- Without 3D it was being done by time taking method of protein purification and X-ray crystallography.

- 3D visualization of protein structure is essential as protein are dynamic entities they change their shape and association with other molecules as a function of temperature, chemical interaction, PH value and other changes due to environment.
- Only the sequence of nucleotide visualization gives us very little knowledge of protein structure valuable in comparing protein structure prediction.

2.1.1 Visualization Tools

Visualization requires different tools which can be used from the available one or needs to be developed in bioinformatics. There are tools for micro-array devices return in computer languages like c++ and some other graphical user interfaces used with commercial database in genes. There are certain visualization tools as per given table 2.1.

Table 2.1

No.	Visualization Tools	Examples
1	Nucleotide Location	Map viewer
2	Protein Structure	SWISS_PDBviewer, WebMol, RasMol, Protein Explorer, MolMol, Chimera, VMD, MidasPlus, PayPymol, Chime
3	User Interface	Third party browser, VRML, Java Applets, C++
4	General purpose software	Microsoft Excel, Strata vision 3D, Max 3D, 3D Studio, Ray Dream Studio, Star view, SAS/Insight, Minitab, Matlab
5	General purpose hardware	Haptic devices, Data gloves

Visualization tools leverage the pattern recognition capabilities of the viewer's visual apparatus as opposed to the logical, intellectual capabilities that can be more easily saturated.

Rendering Tools

- Imaging work in bioinformatics is basically from the data of PDB (Protein database) or MMDB (Molecular modeling Database). Rendering data is computationally very expensive. There are certain protein structure rendering programs which are available as a free download like RasMol, Cn3D, SWISS_PDBViewer and Chimera.
- The rendered program for protein structure should be easy to use, must be powerful, must be speedy and should giving special features, cost factor should also be considered along with hardware requirements, documentation and support etc.
- Rendering output is still more complex with great computational load and requiring more time for each image.
- The results of wide variations in the display of rendering system can be from the same PDB data where with MMDB data which uses ANS.1(Abstract Syntax Notation Number One) gives the consistent result but may not be to the great accuracy even MMCIF(Macromolecular Crystallographic Information Format) is one of the rendering in genes for protein structure.

Display the Structure File

	File Format			
	PDB		MMCIF	
Complete with coordinates "Header only"	HTML	TEXT	-	TEXT
(no co-ordinates)	HTML	TEXT	-	-

Download the Structure File:

	File Format	
Compression	PDB	MMCIF
None	X	X
Unix compressed	X	X
GNU zipped("gzipped")	X	X
Zipped	X	X

Fig. 2.3 : Structure explorer from protein Database (PDB).

2.2 STATISTICS

- We can explore the practical considerations by applying statistical techniques to modern bioinformatics. This gives us range and complexity of issues for controlling the variability with microarray experiments and other bioinformatics work.
- This statistical study also gives us concept of randomness and variability over microarray experimental process.
- Statistical techniques for analyzing biological data: probability and statistical estimation theory; sampling theory; stochastic models for biological processes; multiple linear regression; logistic regression; applied multivariate analysis including discriminant functions, factor analysis, principal components, cluster analysis.
- Applications and computer-based data analysis are stressed. Knowledge of calculus and statistics is assumed.
- "Basic" section gives us the microarray experiments the fundamental statistical concept relation. "Quantifying Randomness" gives us how the randomness and variability are assigned to devices and process.
- "Data Analysis" discusses the experimental output data and its evaluations. "Tool Selection" examines the criteria for statistical analysis tool selection. "Statistics of Alignment".
- "Clustering and classification" section gives us the practical applications of the statistical concept.

2.2.1 Statistical Concepts

- Statistics in bioinformatics ranges from clinical diagnosis and descriptive summaries also the gene hunting and nucleotide alignments. This helps us in treating genetic diseases on disease prevalence for clinical and genetical testing for positive or negative results.
- Statistics can estimate population characteristics. Statistical work can quantify the magnitude of error while estimating the parameters.
- In statistic it is important to consider the basic concept of randomness and the probability related to bioinformatics. Stochastic system involves the random behavior (Stochastic: - Quantity wise data collection for taking the decision).
- Processes like mutation (selection with sort of data) chance making random environment procedure and the relative contribution of parents to the genotype is offspring that give itself to statistical interpretation.
- Statistics can be used with different observations and format mathematical proofs. There are different models we can say the first model is Mendel's work, next is pannet squares which come after 50 years of Mendel's work.
- These statistical methods provide the basis for modern genomic and proteomic lab automation.

Application of Statistics in Bioinformatics

- Clinical Diagnosis
- Descriptive Summaries
- Equipment Calibration
- Experimental Data Analysis
- Gene Expression Prediction
- Gene Hunting
- Gene prediction
- Genetic Linkage Analysis
- Laboratory Automation
- Nucleotide Alignment
- Population Studies
- Protein Function Prediction
- Protein Structure Prediction
- Quantifying Uncertainty
- Quality Control
- Sequence Similarity

2.3 MICROARRAYS

- Microarray offer an efficient method of gathering a data which is used to determine the expression patterns of tens of thousands of genes in only a few hours.
- Microarray method allows the researchers to examine the mRNA from different tissues which may be in a normal disease states and this will helps to determine which genes and environmental conditions * are responsible for the disease.
- Even this method can be used to determine which genes are expressed in which tissue and at what time during embryonic development process flow diagram give us spotting.
- This method is widely used in gene expression analysis.
- A DNA microarray consists of a solid surface, usually a microscope slide, 1 onto which DNA molecules have been chemically bonded.
- The purpose of a microarray is to detect the presence and abundance of labeled nucleic acids in a biological sample, which will hybridize to the DNA on the array via Watson–Crick duplex formation, and which can be detected via the label.
- In the majority of microarray experiments, the labeled nucleic acids are derived from the mRNA of a sample or tissue, and so the microarray measures gene expression.
- The power of a microarray is that there may be many thousands of different DNA molecules bonded to an array, and so it is possible to measure the expression of many thousands of genes simultaneously.
- The mathematics, statistics and computing you will need to design microarray experiments; to acquire, analyze and store your data; and to share your results with other scientists.
- One of the features of microarray technology is the level of bioinformatics required: it is not possible to performa meaningful microarray experiment without bioinformatics involvement at every stage.

2.3.1 Microarray Spotting Process Flow Method

- In spotting microarray method several microarrays are created on membrane. This is in a gel matrix and this is on the side of microscope with low fluorescence glass. These are used as substrate when they are coated with non-fluorescing compound.
- Where DNA sequence can easily adhere than the solution having the expressed gene is applied to the treated face of each slide. This is done with robot controlled micro pens or sprayers and then the slides are heated and dried.
- While experimenting the loosely attached DNA can migrate from one spot to another the next step is to see the microarray with know cDNA probe.
- To create a probe tissue sample is harvested by laser capture micro dissection or by some other method than mRNA from few cells are isolated, purified, amplified, processed and labeled with fluorescent nucleotides. This is known as cDNA.

- This is also compared with similar processed cDNA. The populated microarrays is an excited by laser and resultant fluorescence at each spot is measured. For the statistical method where tens of thousands of data point giving relative gene activity need to be analyzed.
- Because of random variation the final data must be prepared in meaningful way. Microarray results can be studied with the help of gene expression charts the ID line gives us variability in spotting.
- The microarray data is arranged in the form of expression matrix. The expression matrix format is readable by humans. The color version of expression matrix is more useful.

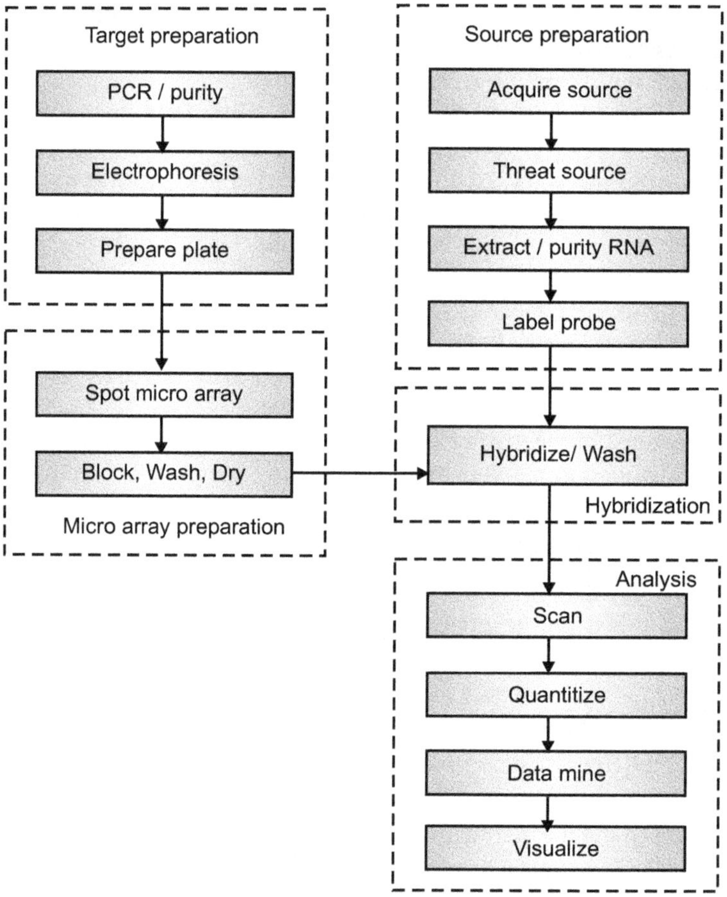

Fig. 2.4 : Microarray spotting process flow

2.3.2 Method of Affymetrix

- The microarray preparation and analysis can also be based on photolithography the process which is used for chip making. This IC fabrication method used for microarray is commercialized by affymetrix.
- Affymetrix arrays use light to convert the protective group on the terminal nucleotide into a hydroxyl group to which further bases can be added. The light is directed to appropriate features using masks that allow light to pass to some areas of the array but not to others.
- This technique is known as photolithography and was first applied to the manufacture of silicon chips. Each step of synthesis requires a different mask, and each mask is expensive to produce.
- However, once a mask set has been designed and made, it is straightforward to produce a large number of identical arrays. Thus Affymetrix technology is well suited for making large numbers of "standard" arrays that can be widely used throughout the community.

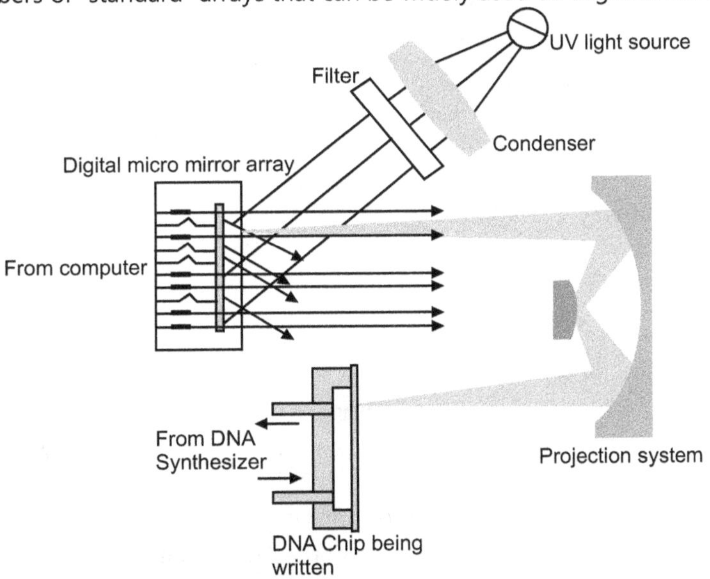

Fig. 2.5 : Maskless photodeprotection

- This technology is similar to Affymetrix technology in that light is used to convert the protective group at each step of synthesis. However, instead of using masks, the light is directed via micro mirror arrays, such as those made by Texas Instruments.
- These are solid-state silicon devices that are at the core of some data projectors: an array of mirrors is computer controlled and can be used to direct light to appropriate parts diagram for Maskless photodeprotection.

- This system also uses light-mediated deprotection. However, instead of using a physical mask, the array is synthesized using a computer-controlled micro mirror array.
- This consists of a large number of mirrors embedded on a silicon chip, each of which can move between two positions: one position to reflect light, and the other to block light.
- At each step, the mirrors direct light to the appropriate parts of the array. This technology is used by Nimblegen and Febit.

There are four laboratory steps in using a microarray to measure gene expression in a sample

1. Sample preparation and labeling
2. Hybridization
3. Washing
4. Image acquisition

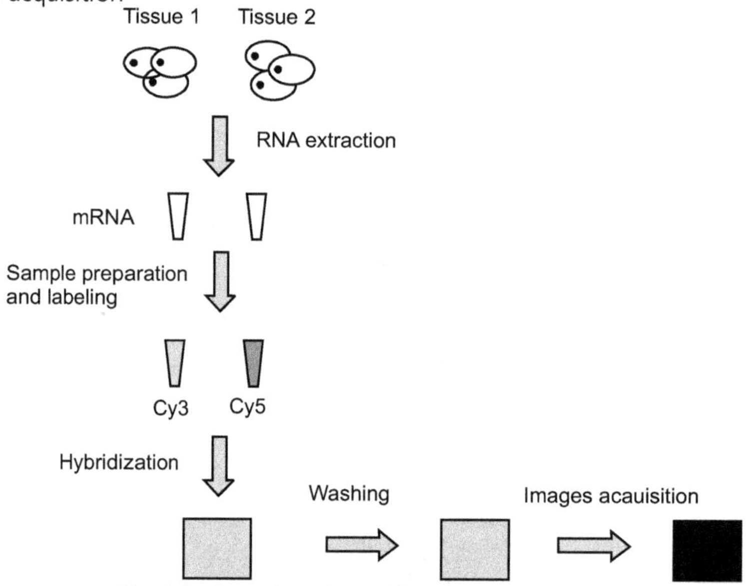

Fig. 2.6 : Steps in using a microarray

- Diagram for Steps in using a microarray. The first step is to extract the RNA from the tissue(s) of interest.
- With most technologies, it is common to prepare two samples and label them with two different dyes, usually Cy3 (green) and Cy5 (red).
- The samples are hybridized to the array simultaneously and incubated for between 12 and 24 hours at between 45 and 65°C. The array is then washed to remove sample that is not hybridized to the features.

Sample Preparation and Labeling

- There are a number of different ways in which a sample can be prepared and labeled for microarray experiments. In all cases, the first step is to extract the RNA from the tissue of interest.
- This procedure can be difficult to reproduce, and there is much variability among the individual scientists performing the extraction the labeling step depends on the technology used. For the Affymetrix platform, one constructs a biotin-labeled complementary RNA for hybridizing to the GeneChip.
- The protocols are very carefully defined by Affymetrix, 4 so every Affymetrix laboratory should be performing identical steps.
- This has the advantage that it is easier to compare the results of experiments performed in different Affymetrix laboratories, because the procedures they will have followed should be the same.
- Although it is possible to hybridize complementary RNA to other types of microarrays, it is much more common to hybridize a complementary DNA to these arrays. In the past, the DNA has been radioactively labeled, but now most laboratories use fluorescent labeling, with the two dyes Cy3 (excited by a green laser) and Cy5 (excited by a red laser).
- In the most common experiments, two samples are hybridized to the arrays, one labeled with each dye; this allows the simultaneous measurement of both 4 See the reference to the Affymetrix manual at the end of the chapter samples.
- In the future, it is possible that more than two labeled samples could be used. There are three common ways to make labeled cDNA. The most common method is direct incorporation by reverse transcriptase.
  - The mRNA is primed with a poly-T primer:
  - The next most common method is indirect labeling.
  - The third and least common method for labeling is by random primed labeling using the Klenow fragment of DNA polymerase.

Hybridization

Hybridization is the step in which the DNA probes on the glass and the labeled DNA (or RNA) target form hetero duplexes via Watson–Crick base-pairing. Hybridization is a complex process that is not fully understood. It is affected by many conditions:

- Including temperature
- Humidity
- Salt concentrations
- Formamide concentration
- Volume of target solution and operator.

There are Two Main Methods for Hybridization

- Manual
- Robotic.

Washing

After hybridization, the slides are washed. There are two reasons for this. The first is to remove excess hybridization solution from the array. The second reason is to increase the stringency of the experiment by reducing cross-hybridisation.

Image Acquisition

The final step of the laboratory process is to produce an image of the surface of the hybridized array. The hetero duplexes on the array, where the target has bound to the probe, contain dye that fluoresces when excited by light of an appropriate wavelength. The slide is placed in a **scanner**, which is a device that reads the surface of the slide.

2.3.3 Comparison of Spotting and Affymetrix Process

Table 2.2 : Microarray fabrication comparison. Spotting is more variable than the affymetrix process

Sr. No.	Factor	Spotting	Affymetrix
1	Source of variability	Mechanical Pin Positioning Bonding of cDNA to slide reagent purity environment.	Mask Positioning Mask Fenestrations Reagent Purity Environment
2	Repeatability	Moderate/low	High
3	Layout design time	Low	High
4	Analysis possible	Qualitative	Quantitative
5	Inter-Array Variability	High	Low
6	Modification time	Low	High
7	Intellective Property	Public domain	Proprietary

2.4 IMPERFECT DATA

- Databases collecting a huge amount of information pertaining to real world processes, for example industrial ones, contain a significant number of data which are imprecise, mutually incoherent, and frequently even contradictory. It is often the case that databases of this kind often lack important information.

- All available means and resources may and should be used to eliminate or at least minimize such problems at the stage of data collection. It should be emphasized, however, that the character of industrial databases, as well as the ways in which such bases are created and the data are collected, preclude the elimination of all errors.
- It is, therefore, a necessity to find and develop methods for eliminating errors from already-existing databases or for reducing their influence on the accuracy of analyses or hypotheses proposed with the application of these databases.

  There are at least three main reasons for data preparation

  (a) The possibility of using the data for modeling

  (b) Modeling acceleration, and

  (c) An increase in the accuracy of the model
- Various data preparation tasks (characterized by means of numerous methods, algorithms, and procedures). Apparently, however, no ordered and coherent classification of tasks and operations involved in data preparation has been proposed so far.

This has a number of reasons, including the following:

(a) Numerous article publications propose solutions to problems employing selected individual data preparation operations, which may lead to the conclusion that such classifications are not really necessary.

(b) Monographs deal in the minimal measure with the industrial data, which have their own specific character, different from that of the business data

(c) The fact that the same operations are performed for different purposes in different tasks complicates the job of preparing such a classification.

(d) Imperfect *data* are prevalent in health informatics and biomedical engineering. Therefore, data analysis and modeling tools in real world applications must be able to represent, recognize and process imperfect data.

(e) Several studies have aimed to classify the different types of data imperfections and their possible sources. Incompleteness, imprecision, inconsistency and uncertainty are some of the problems associated with data imperfection.

(f) In data-driven application domains, such as bioinformatics and medical informatics, these types of problems may originate from unreliable data acquisition sources, faulty sensors, data collection errors and the lack of data representation standards.

(g) Ronald Pearson's book discusses the detection of different types of imperfect data, their potential sources, implications and methods to treat them. It mainly focuses on three types of data imperfections

  (1) Outliers

  (2) Missing data

  (3) Misalignments

- As in every other physical system, the data generated by a microarray experiments are imperfect. One way to conceptualize these imperfections is as noise in the communication channel. This noise due to the limitations of the equipment reagents, tissue sample and deficiencies in the overall process.
- Some of this noise is unavoidable and can at best only be reduced. However, the glass likes the coating that allows DNA to adhere to the slide, fluoresces slightly when it is excited by the laser light used to read spots on the microarray.
- The background noise level is directly proportional to the ambient temperature, in that all conductors operated above absolute zero produce thermal or Johnson noise.
- Variations in the preparation of a microarray can make the accuracy of results questionable. For example : In preparing a glass slide for spotting, slight variations in the volume of substrate deposited on the slide, or variations in the chemistry of the substrate, can severely compromise subsequent analysis.
- Some applications of microarray expression data, like genetic mapping, are associated with binary measurements (either present or absent).
- Most applications benefit from consistent volumes of materials deposited precisely on the microarray so that at least rudimentary qualitative measurements can be made.
- Sources of variability in microarray spot analysis include the stability of the spotting technology used to create the microarray and the stability of the environmental conditions.
- For example : The reproducibility and accuracy of the robotic assembly that determines the location and volume of DNA material deposited at each spot are critical factor.
- The environment, including humidity, temperature and amount of particulate matter in the air, can add additional variables that must be considered.
- For example : If the relative humidity is too high, then the samples in the microarray evaporate as fast as expected. Because of unavoidable variability in the spotting process, active areas on the microarray are commonly printed in triplicate to private an internal control.
- Variability in microarray experimental results is also a function of the methods used in the data acquisition phase of microarray experiment. For example : Two most popular methods of capturing data from a microarray are

  (a) Scanning

  (b) Spotting

(a) Scanning

- A laser illuminates each point in the microarray separately. Variability in the data is commonly due to inaccuracies in positioning the laser over each area where spot is expected.

In addition, there is a tradeoff between the diameter of the excitatory laser beam and the relevance of the fluorescence data.

A beam that is only slightly larger than the expected spot size (high specificity) theoretically provides the least amount of extraneous fluorescence noise, assuming that the spot in the microarray is in expected location, with the reading laser superimposed over the spot.

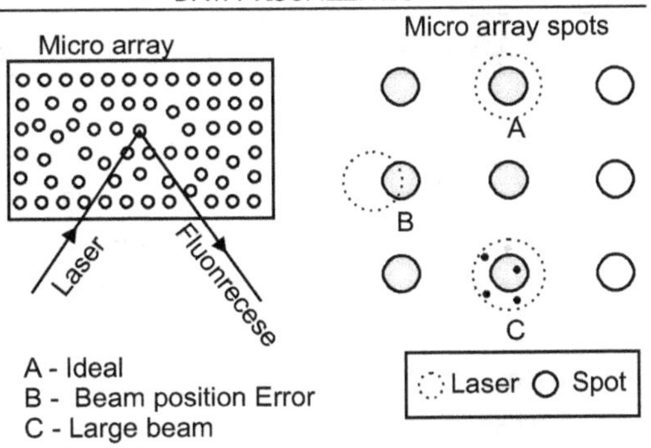

Fig. 2.7 : Sources of variability in reading microarray spots through spotting

- The ideal situation (A) is when the excitatory laser beam is tightly focused on a single microarray spot. However, archiving this level of perfection requires accurate positioning of both the spot and the reading equipment.
- If beam position is off the mark (B), gene expression data will be underrepresented. Using a larger beam than absolutely necessary (C) incorporates a full spot in the analysis, even if the spot placement isn't ideal.

(b) Spotting

- The spotting process may result in erroneous output signal interpretation, depending on the statistical method used to analyze spot intensity.
- Variations in spot shape and derivations from expected spot location result in errors in intensity reading of spot fluorescence. Starring and scanning are both susceptible to variations in spot shape.
- In starring, a mask is used to limit the extent of the area read on the captured image, even though the excitatory laser beam covers many spots at once.
- The opposite is true of scanning, in that the image capture device is respective to fluorescence signals from anywhere on the microarray.

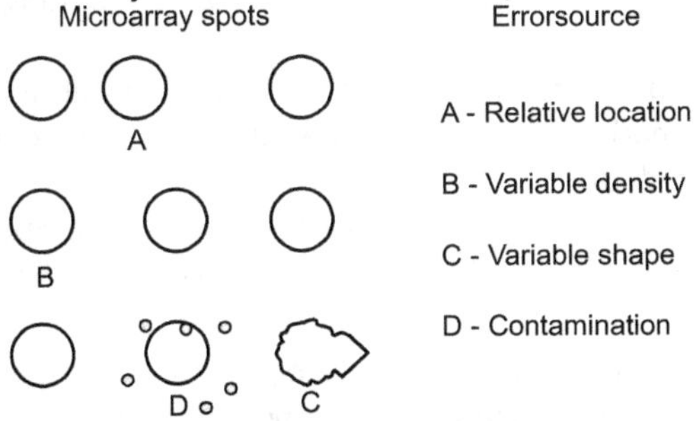

Fig. 2.8 : Common sources of variability associated with microarray preparation. These sources of error affect both the spotting and starring methods of microarray reading

2.5 QUANTITATIVE RANDOMNESS

Basics

One of the key statistical concepts highlighted by the microarray experiment is that data are inherently noisy and that randomness is inherent in any sampling process. Randomness is inherent in, and a necessary component of biological system.

- Randomness is an integral component of working of biological systems. Mutation and the distribution of maternal and paternal genetic material during meiosis are biological process that reflects the dependence of biodiversity on the randomness of biological process.
- Every measurement system introduces noise, random variability into the desired signal. This noise can be minimized by controlling the external environment.

For example :

- By reducing the ambient temperature in a system designed to make very low-level measurements or by reducing the bandwidth of the system, using statistical techniques.
- Statistical method can be used to filter data during the final analysis of gene expression experiment; reliance on statistical analysis of the final results alone isn't optimal.

For example :

- Analysis of intra-array spot fluorescence intensity can be used to control for contamination and other sources of variability in the overall process.
- The microarray experiment also illustrates how conventional mechanical systems are more variable than their electronic counterparts.
- One of the greatest potential sources of variability in the placement of cDNA solution on a prepared glass side microarray is the robotic assembly that performs the spotting of the microarray.
- The amount cDNA that actually adheres to the slide can vary widely as well as a function of the slide coating, the ambient environmental conditions, and the presence of contaminants.
- Estimating the variability contributed by the mechanical and biochemical systems through computer modeling or direct measurement provides an indication of the expected value of the data.
- Nanotechnology may eventually reduce the variability of computer-enabled mechanical system to the point that it is comparable to that of digital electronic circuitry.

Variability is Cumulative

- Whether the source is mechanical, biological or electronic variability is cumulative, in that noise introduced in the early stage of a system propagates and is amplified by later activity in the system.

- For example : extraneous genetic material commingled with the cDNA used to create a microarray will add to the fluoresce activity measured from each spot.
- Controlling variability is a key component of process management. Managing the chain of the processes in the microarray experiment involves controlling variability through computer-enabled statistical controls.

Approximation

- The microarray experiment also illustrates that statistical summary, probability-based predictions, and estimates of variability introduced by various processes are at best approximations.

Interface Noise

- Much of bioinformatics work involves interfacing mechanical, biological and electronic systems, each of which has its non-linearities, variability, and noise sources. Each interface introduces noise and variability in the overall process.

Assumptions

- Most statistical methods assume basic premises that hold regardless of specific applications in bioinformatics. One of the most popular statistical pattern classification methods is Bayes Theorem.
- His theorem is applied to such problems as determining the probability that disease is present given that a gene is shown to be expressed in microarray experiment, combines the prior probabilities of outcomes together with the conditional probabilities of various input features in order to reach conclusion.
- A basic assumption in many statistical analyses is that sample mean tends to approach the population mean, given a large enough sample size or enough smaller samples.

Sampling and Distributions

- Much of the statistics deals with obtaining as much information as possible from small samples. The question is how large sample is large enough considering it's usually unrealistic to measure every data element even if they are generated by a sequence machine or other automatic device.
- Popular distributions used in statistical analysis of discrete random variables include binomial, hypergeometric, and Poisson distributions.
- The distinctions between distributions of continuous and discrete variables are important because many statistical methods are valid only when used with data drawn from populations with specific distributions.

Hypothesis Testing

- Hypothesis testing, in which a hypothesis (often termed the "null hypothesis" because it is a negatively stated hypothesis that a researcher suspects is incorrect) is assumed to hold unless there is enough evidence is reject it, is another basic statistical method.

2.5.1 Quantifying Randomness

Randomness is commonly quantified in the equipment's published specifications document, which characterizes the equipment's performance in terms of accuracy, resolution (precision), repeatability, stability, and sensitivity.

Accuracy

The degree to which a data value being measured is correct-is usually expressed as plus or minus a percentage of the reading.

Resolution

Resolution, sometimes referred to as precision, is the ability of an expressed instrument to resolve small differences.

Sensitivity

The ability of a device to detect low-level signals-is function of the resolution and the amount of noise in the system.

Repeatability

The ability of an instrument or system to provide consistent results. Repeatability is related to stability, which is the ability of an instrument or device to provide repeatable results over time, assuming certain environmental conditions such as ambient temperature.

- Results of instrument may be inaccurate unless the instrument is properly calibrated. The accuracy of calibration standard limits the maximum accuracy of the equipment being calibrated.

2.6 DATA ANALYSIS

Computer scientists, banish from your mind any thought of assembly language. Sequencing can only be performed for relatively short stretches of a biomolecule and finished sequences are therefore prepared by arranging overlapping "reads" of monomers (single beads on a molecular chain) into a single continuous passage of "code". This is the bioinformatics sense of assembly.

- They can be mapped***---that is, their sequences can be parsed to find sites where so-called "restriction enzymes" will cut them. They can be compared, usually by aligning corresponding segments and looking for matching and mismatching letters in their sequences.
- Genes or proteins that are sufficiently similar are likely to be related and are therefore said to be "homologous" to each other---the whole truth is rather more complicated than this. Such cousins are called "homologs".
- If a homolog (a related molecule) exists, then a newly discovered protein may be modeled---that is the three dimensional structure of the gene product can be predicted without doing laboratory experiments.

- Bioinformatics is used in primer design. Primers are short sequences needed to make many copies of (amplify) a piece of DNA as used in PCR (the Polymerase Chain Reaction). Bioinformatics is used to attempt to predict the function of actual gene products.
- Information about the similarity and by implication the relatedness of proteins is used to trace the "family trees" of different molecules through evolutionary time. Molecular modeling / structural biology is a growing field which can be considered part of bioinformatics.
- There are, for example : tools which allow you (often via the Net) to make pretty good predictions of the secondary structure of proteins arising from a given amino acid sequence, often based on known "solved" structures and other sequenced molecules acquired by structural biologists.
- Structural biologists use "bioinformatics" to handle the vast and complex data from X-ray crystallography.
- Nuclear magnetic resonance (NMR) and electron microscopy investigations and create the 3-D models of molecules that seem to be everywhere in the media.
- (The definition given above is the one most frequently used in this context, but a gene can be said to be "mapped" when its parent chromosome has been identified, when its physical or genetic distance from other genes is established and---less frequently---when the structure and locations of its various coding components (its "exons") are established.

Customized Data Analysis

- The AltheaDx Bioinformatics team offers a wide range of bioinformatics analysis services for various research and clinical projects using industry leading bioinformatics tools. The main bioinformatics services include
  (1) PCR Data Analysis.
  (2) Gene Expression Microarray and RNA Sequencing Data Analysis
  (3) Genotyping Microarray Data Analysis
  (4) Next Generation DNA Sequencing Data Analysis
  (5) Bioinformatics Consultation

PCR Data Analysis

- Reference (house-keeping) genes can be recommended according to the experimental sample types

For real-time PCR assay:

1. Raw CT/CRT values will be reported.
2. Data can be normalized with reference genes and reported using the delta or delta-delta CT/CRT method.
3. PCR results can also be reported in copy number as referenced to target standard curves, for example, for the assessment of genomic amplifications.

4. SNP genotype and mutation analysis can be reported in raw data format as delta-CT/CRT between allele forms combined with genotype call.

- Data quality measurements will be reported.
- Discriminatory analysis to determine differentially expressed genes, e.g. t-test, ANOVA and ANCOVA.

Gene Expression Microarrays Data Analysis

- Data quality measurements will be reported
- Data normalization and summarization, e.g., MAS5.0 and RMA
- Inter-array correlation analysis
- Annotation of genes with gene symbol, gene description, gene function and public database identifiers etc.
- Discriminatory analysis to determine differentially expressed genes, e.g. moderated t-test, ANOVA and ANCOVA
- Multiple hypotheses testing correction
- Supervised and unsupervised (e.g. hierarchical) clustering of the gene expression data
- Gene ontology and KEGG pathway analysis
- Multiple dimensional scaling and principal component analysis

Predictive model based on machine learning language such as neural networks, support vector machine, shrunken centroid and decision tree

Genotyping Microarrays Data Analysis

- Data normalization and data filtering
- Genotype calling with confidence limits
- Association analysis and sample clustering
- Linkage of variants to phenotype data
- Comparison of expression and genotype data

Next Generation DNA Sequencing Data Analysis

- De novo genome and transcriptome assembly
- Variation detection for re-sequencing projects
- Variation detection from amplicon-based samples
- Digital gene expression analysis
- Chip-Seq analysis
- Customized data analysis

Microarray Data Analysis

- Once a fluorescence signal is detected, it has to be quantized or digitized before it can be manipulated statistically. The digitization or A-to-D conversion is performed at a fixed sampling frequency, with a converter rated at a certain dynamic range, measured in bit depth.

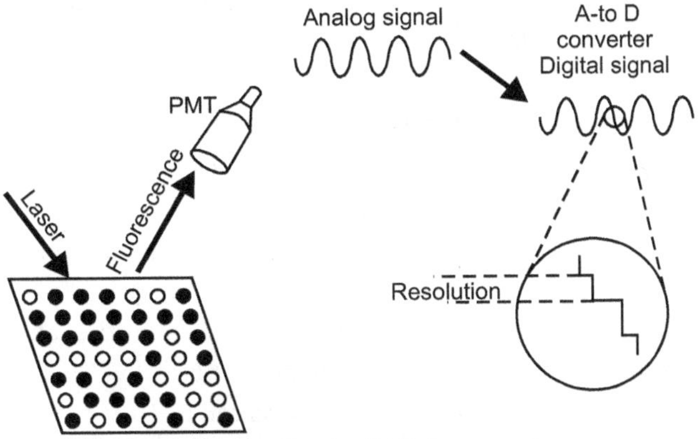

Fig. 2.9 : Analog to digital conversion

- For example: a 16 bit A-to-D converter can process a signal into one of (2^{16}) or 65,636 levels, a dynamic range of over 4 orders of magnitude which is generally considered as minimum for gene expression application.
- The dynamic range of the microarray experiment is limited by the resolution or bit depth of A-to-D conversion process. The output of the digitizer is typically a 16-bit TIFF (.tif) file is fed to the workstation for analysis and visualization.
- Analysis of the fluorescence data includes a check for microarray-to-microarray variability using a scatter plot. The most common methods of accomplishing microarray-to-microarray agreement are to rely on simple descriptive statistics such as mean, mode and median.

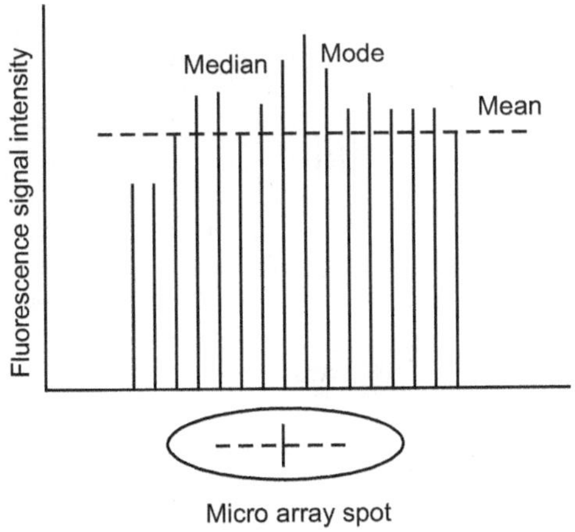

Fig. 2.10 : Microarray fluorescence statistical analysis

- The mean is the average pixel density over a spot, corresponding to the average fluorescence intensity. The mode is most likely intensity value represented by the highest peak in the fluorescence plot. The median is the midpoint in the intensity plot, is also resistant to outliers.
- Other measures of assessing spot intensity include the total pixel intensity the sum of all pixels corresponding to fluorescence in an area. However, the total intensity value is sensitive to the amount of DNA deposited on a spot microarray.
- The role of statistical analysis in reading the intensity value associated with each spot is to control for variability a challenge that isn't possible always.
  For example: when a microarray is contaminated, simple statistical analysis on individual's spots offers little in the way of reducing variability or noise.
- However, inter- and intra- microarray comparisons can be used to identify contamination and other sources of variability.
- Intra-microarray comparison, in which spotting is duplicated within the same microarray, allow the statistical analysis to control for variability in the spotting process at the expense of fewer gene expression experiments per microarray.
- Statistical analysis of the means of the relative fluorescence intensity can be used to programmatically identify a contaminated sample (far right) that can be discarded from the final gene expression analysis, thereby reducing variability in the experiment.

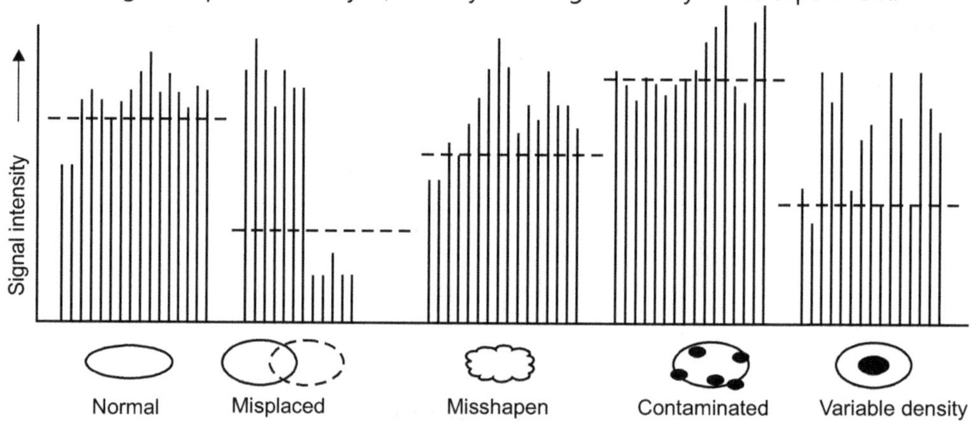

Fig. 2.11 : Microarray spot intensity distribution

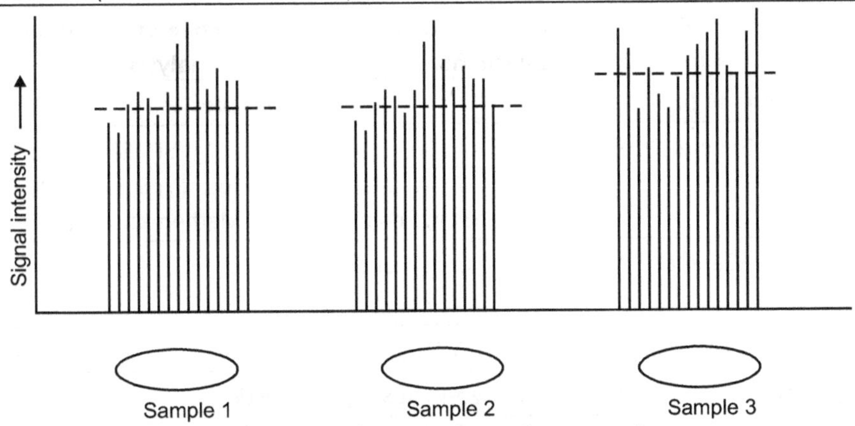

Fig. 2.12 : Intra microarray intensity comparisons

2.7 TOOL SELECTION

- Natural selection rejects with variable strength, mutations reducing the individual's capability to survive and reproduce. Evolutionary theory predicts that mutations producing disease will be under strong selective constraints.
- Selective strength at the codon level will determine if mutation frequency will increase, decrease or change randomly during evolution. This strength finally serves in the prediction of nonsynonymous single nucleotide polymorphisms (nsSNPs) producing disease in humans.
- By using comparative genomics data and maximum likelihood phylogenetics approaches we demonstrate that mutations on residues showing low rates of evolution are significantly associated to disease and not to human genetic polymorphisms.
- An arbitrary decision to use median spot fluorescence intensity instead of a mean or mode measurement.

  For example: can drastically alter gene expression analysis. Ideally the selection of a statistical method reflects the researcher's knowledge of the underlying biological principles as well as the inherent limitations of the statistical methods used to analyze the data.
- Selecting the statistical methods and tools most appropriate for a problem requires an understanding of the assumptions of the available statistical methods, the underlying biology, the data requirements, the validity of the overall experiment design, and computational requirements.
- With the proliferation of malfunction calculators, dedicated statistical analysis software packages which is shown in table 2.3.

Table 2.3 : Statistical analysis tools. This sample is representative of the thousands of tools available on the market for statistical analysis

Type of Tool	Examples
Dedicated, General-Purpose	SAS, Mitlab, Decision Pro, MVSP, SimStar , NCSS, PASS, SISA, Statistica, S-Plus, R, Splus, SPSS, Perl, SigmaStat, Prism, Starview, Mathematica, ProStat
Ancillary, General-Purpose	Microsoft Excel
Bioinformatics-Specific	BLAST, VAST, BioConductor
Excel, Add-Ons	Analyze-it, XLStar, XLStatistics

- One way of assessing the performance of a set of statistical tools is to determine its sensitivity and specificity.
- A criterion for when to call a test abnormal, sensitivity is the percentage of actual positives that are counted as positive, whereas specificity is the percentage of actual negatives that are rejected.

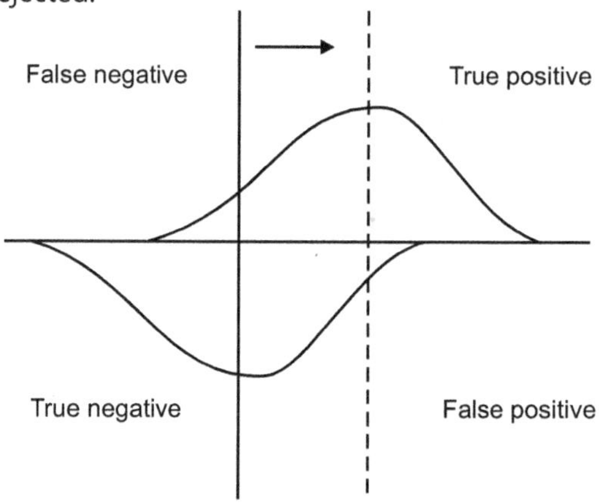

Fig. 2.13 : Sensitivity and specificity

- Both are a function of the number of true and false positives and negatives. Moving the cutoff value (vertical bar) to the right (dotted line) results in almost false positives at the expense of fewer true positives.
- Another way to evaluate the sensitivity and specificity of a statistical test is to determine its receiver operating characteristics. The ROC curve is a plot of tests sensitivity versus 1- specificity, or true-positive versus false-negative rate.

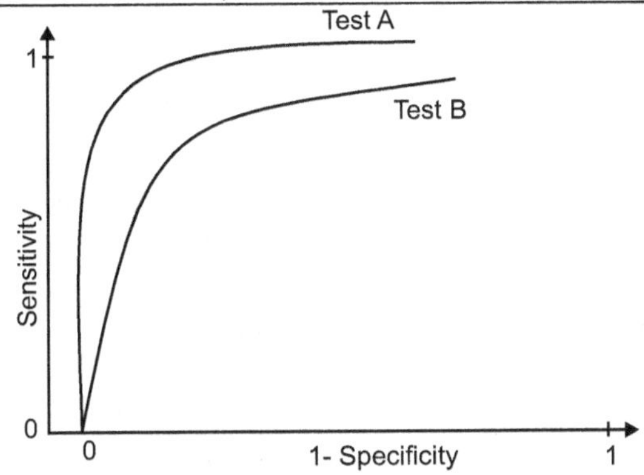

Fig. 2.14 : Receiver operating characteristics (ROC) curves. For the two tests shown here, Test A provides superior discrimination over Test B.

2.8 STATISTICS OF ALIGNMENT

- Much of the day-to-day work in bioinformatics involves using tools that utilize statistical principles to explore nucleotide and protein sequences, a review of some of the principles related to the statistics of alignment are in order.
- Because of good alignment of nucleotide sequences can occur by chance alone, statistical method often combined with heuristics is used to help determine the significance of an alignment.
- For example The blast algorithm computes the expected frequency of matching sequences that should occur in an alignment search in order to conduct more efficient search.
- In calculating an alignment score (s), the underlying question is usually" is the alignment score high enough to suggest homology?" The first part of answer is to determine how high a score could by chance alone.
- However, the challenge here is no mathematical theory adequately describes statistics of the scores that can be expected for global alignments. The situation is different for local alignment, because extreme value distribution adequately describes the expected distribution of random local alignment scores. By relating the observed direct score to the expected distribution, the statistical significance of alignment can be assessed.
- A statistic commonly used in alignment searches is the z-scores, which is a measure of the distance from the mean, measured in standard deviation units. If each sequence to be aligned is randomized and an optimal alignment is made, the result is a series of

scores (s) for the alignment of two sequences, with a mean (μ) and stand deviation (δ) : $Z = \frac{s - \mu}{\delta}$

- The advantage of z-score over simple percentage score is that it corrects for compositional biases in the sequence and accounts for the varying length of sequences. The problem with z-score to access whether an alignment occurred by chance is that a z-score assumes a normal distribution.

Distribution have different usages in Bioinformatics Statistical Work

Binomial Distribution

Spotting stretches of DNA with unusual nucleotide sequences and pairwise sequence comparisons.

Normal Distribution

Modeling continuous random variables, with applications such as the statistical significance of pairwise sequence comparison.

Multinomial Distribution

Spotting stretches of DNA with unusual content, distinguishing test for introns by composition, and quantifying relative codon frequency.

Relying solely on purely mathematical methods for statistical analysis without incorporating heuristics on knowledge of the underlying biology can often lead to incorrect conclusion.

- For example : A run of pure C-G sequences in a sequences in a sequence to be aligned will likely match many C-G-rich regions in a sequence to be aligned will likely match many C-G rich regions in a sequence database.

2.9 CLUSTERING AND CLASSIFICATION

- Two statistical operations commonly applied to microarray data are clustering and classification. Clustering is purely data driven activity that uses only data from the study or experiment to group together measurements. Classification in contrast, uses additional data, including heuristics, to assign measurements to group.
- Cluster analysis or clustering is the task of grouping a set of objects in such a way that objects in the same group (called a cluster) are more similar (in some sense or another) to each other than to those in other groups (clusters).
- It is a main task of exploratory data mining and a common technique for statistical data analysis, used in many fields, including machine learning, pattern recognition, image analysis, information retrieval, and bioinformatics.
- Cluster analysis itself is not one specific algorithm, but the general task to be solved. It can be achieved by various algorithms that differ significantly in their notion of what constitutes a cluster and how to efficiently find them.

- Popular notions of clusters include groups with small distances among the cluster members, dense areas of the data space, intervals or particular statistical distributions.
- Clustering can therefore be formulated as a multi-objective optimization problem. The appropriate clustering algorithm and parameter settings (including values such as the distance function to use, a density threshold or the number of expected clusters) depend on the individual data set and intended use of the results.
- Cluster analysis as such is not an automatic task, but an iterative process of knowledge discovery or interactive multi-objective optimization that involves trial and failure. It will often be necessary to modify data preprocessing and model parameters until the result achieves the desired properties.
- Cluster analysis was originated in anthropology by Driver and Kroeber in 1932 and introduced to psychology by Zubin in 1938 and Robert Tryon in 1939 and famously used by Cattell beginning in 1943 for trait theory classification in personality psychology.
- The notion of a cluster, as found by different algorithms, varies significantly in its properties. Understanding these "cluster models" is key to understanding the differences between the various algorithms. Typical cluster models include

1. A "clustering" is essentially a set of such clusters, usually containing all objects in the data set. Additionally, it may specify the relationship of the clusters to each other, for example: a hierarchy of clusters embedded in each other. Clustering can be roughly distinguished as Hard clustering: each object belongs to a cluster or not soft clustering (also: fuzzy clustering): each object belongs to each cluster to a certain degree (e.g. a likelihood of belonging to the cluster).

- Two of the most common methods of clustering gene expression data are hierarchical clustering and k-means clustering.

Hierarchical Clustering

- Mathematically hierarchical clustering involves computing a matrix of all distances for each expression measurement in study. Merging and averaging the values of the closet nodes, and repeating the process until all nodes are merged into a single node.
- Data in the expression matrix can be clustered to an arbitrary depth. One of the many options of computing the matrix of distances involves evaluating the relative ranking of the measures of red and green fluorescence intensities taken from the expression matrix associated with a given microarray study.

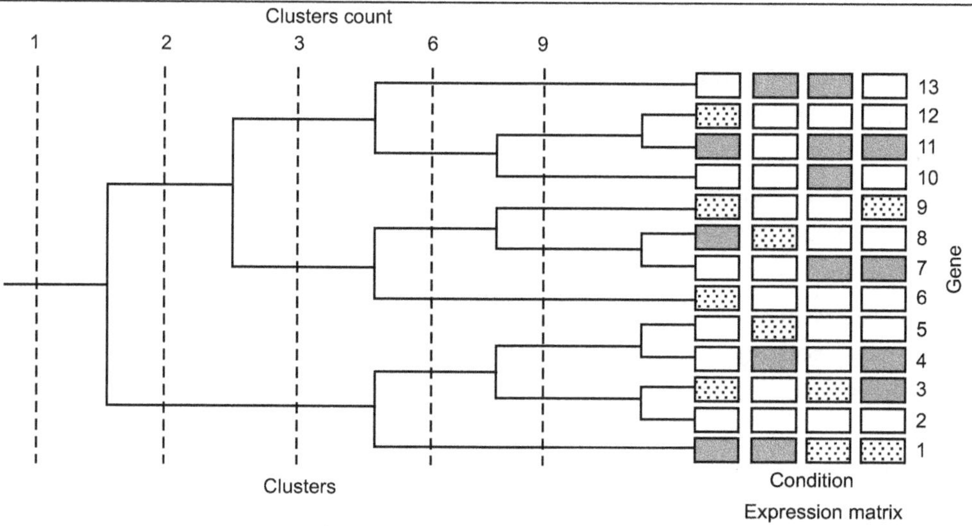

Fig. 2.15 : Hierarchical clustering

K-means Clustering

- It involves generating cluster centers in n dimensions and computing the distance of each data point to each of the cluster centers. The process is repeated until the positions of the cluster centers stabilize.

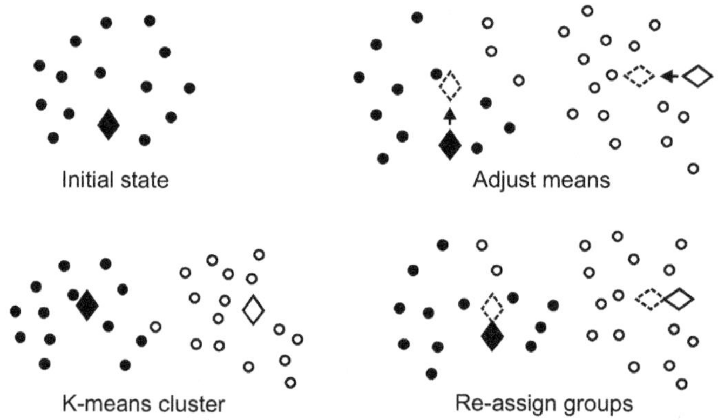

Fig. 2.16 : K-means clustering

- Items are assigned to the nearest cluster and the cluster centers (square) are recalculated. This process is repeated until the cluster centers don't change significantly.
- In the end, there are two clusters, one with filled circles and one with empty circle. Clustering microarray gene expression data is useful because it may provide insight into gene function.

- For example : if two genes are expressed in the same way, they may be functionally related. In addition, if a genes function is unknown but it is clustered with genes of known function, the gene may share functionality with the genes of known function.
- Common classification methods applied to gene expression data include the use of linear models, logistic regression, Bayes theorem, decision tree and support vector machines.
- For example : Consider using Bayes theorem to classify microarray data one of two groups illustrated in Fig. 2.17.

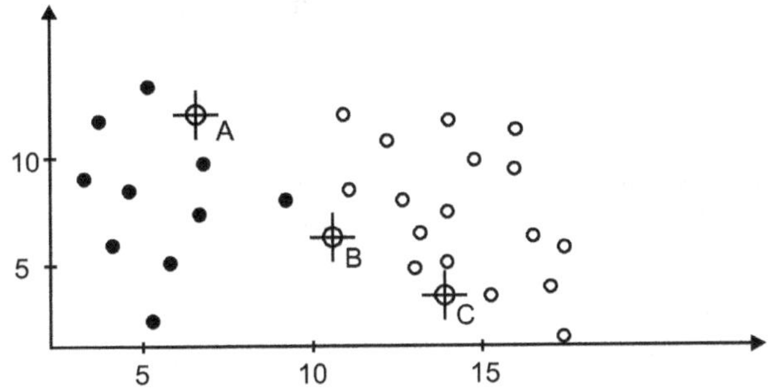

Fig. 2.17 : Example of bayes theorem

- The data points A, B and C can be classified using Bayes theorem. Using Bayes theorem to determine whether given a data point should be classified as a member of, for example : the open-circle group, the following equation applies:

  p(OpenCircles|XiYi) = p(OpenCircles|Xi) x p(OpenCircles|Yi)

  For the data point

  A(x=7, y=3), B(x=10, y=5) and C(x=14, y=3) the equations take the form:

  p(OpenCircles|XaYa) = p(OpenCircles|7) x p(OpenCircles|3)

  p(OpenCircles|XbYb) = p(OpenCircles|10) x p(OpenCircles|5)

  p(OpenCircles|XcYc) = p(OpenCircles|14) x p(OpenCircles|3)

- Visually the data point C can reasonably be classified as a member of open circle group. The probability of data point A is a member of open group is high. The main issue surrounds the cutoff probability for evaluating the equation.
- If probability must be high in order to accept the given data point is a member open-circle group then data point B may not be classified in the open-circle group, and may best be assigned to another group.
- Classification may refer to categorization, the process in which ideas and objects are recognized, differentiated, and understood.

Classification

- Classification may refer to categorization, the process in which ideas and objects are recognized, differentiated, and understood. Classification techniques, also known as clustering techniques, are important in bioinformatics as they allow the separating of various biological data with similar attributes into distinct sets.
- The size of biological data has been growing exponentially, with the doubling of information observed every 15 months. As a result, computer science and informatics techniques are used intensively in the processing and management of biological data.
- The most fundamental concept in bioinformatics is that most biological data share similar characteristics and can be separated into clusters. For instance, the genes of an organism can be classified into their functional groups or metabolic pathways. Proteins can also be classified based on the genes that are expressed.
- Classification or clustering techniques are necessary in the management of huge databases of genetic and biological data. There are two primary types of classification techniques in bioinformatics: the hierarchical and the k-Means classification techniques.

Hierarchical Classification

- The hierarchical classification technique organizes biological data into a tree data structure. Genes are expressed as nodes in the tree, while each sub-tree of nodes represents a cluster or grouping of genes. The tree could be either rooted or unrooted. A rooted tree is defined as a tree with just a single node at the top. In contrast, an unrooted tree has multiple topmost nodes.

k-Means Classification

- A more complicated classification technique is the k-Means classification, which attempts to find a set of centers that minimize the square error distortion among the data sets in multidimensional space.
- A cluster is classified by grouping related points to their nearest center. The Lloyd algorithm is often used in the k-Means classification technique. In this algorithm, data points are randomly arranged into separate clusters, which are subsequently optimized to produce the minimal local square error distortions.

SUMMARY

Visualization

- Visualization in bioinformatics is to render the 3D of protein structureand modeling the interactions of protein and protein in real time. To have visualization of this type requiring high end computing where computer and grid computing is being used.

There are Two Types of Visualization

- Sequence visualization
- Structure visualization
- In sequence visualization we have to work with nucleotide sequences which can gives us gene maps i.e. high level graphic representation of specific sequences residing on chromosomes.
- 3D structure visualization is essential for structure of proteins so that we can find out where the days might modulate their activity. Even this visualization in 3D can help us in identifying the proteins produced by given cell or tissue and how they interact.
- Statistics can estimate population characteristics. Statistical work can quantify the magnitude of error while estimating the parameters.

Application of Statistics in Bioinformatics

- Clinical Diagnosis, Descriptive Summaries, Equipment Calibration, Experimental Data Analysis, Gene Expression Prediction, Gene Hunting, Gene prediction, Genetic Linkage Analysis, Laboratory Automation, Nucleotide Alignment, Population Studies, Protein Function Prediction, Protein Structure Prediction, Quantifying Uncertainty, Quality Control, Sequence Similarity.
- Microarray offers an efficient method of gathering a data which is used to determine the expression patterns of tens of thousands of genes in only a few hours.
- In every other physical system, the data generated by a microarray experiments are imperfect.
- One way to conceptualize these imperfections is as noise in the communication channel.
- Randomness is an integral component of working of biological systems. Mutation and the distribution of maternal and paternal genetic material during meiosis are biological process that reflects the dependence of biodiversity on the randomness of biological process.
- An arbitrary decision to use median spot fluorescence intensity instead of a mean or mode measurement. For example: can drastically alter gene expression analysis.
- Clustering is purely data driven activity that uses only data from the study or experiment to group together measurements.
- Classification in contrast, uses additional data, including heuristics, to assign measurements to group.

QUESTIONS

MAY 2012

1. (a) What is structure visualization? Explain the various rendering tools in structure visualization. **[8]**

Ans. : Please refer Section 2.1 and 2.1.1

(b) Explain microarray spotting process flow in detail. How is microarray result analysis done? **[8]**

Ans. : Please refer Section 2.3.

OR

2. (a) Explain in detail the various methods of data mining for extracting patterns from data. **[8]**

(b) Differentiate between clustering and classification. Explain hierarchical and k-means clustering in brief. **[8]**

Ans. : Please refer Section 2.9.

MAY 2013

3. (a) A Define Microarray. Explain the sources of variability in Microarray preparation and reading. Explain how statistical analysis can be used to reduce variability. **[8]**

Ans. : Please refer Section 2.3.

(b) Explain in brief the data visualization techniques applicable to Bioinformatics. Discuss any two visualization tools with example. **[8]**

Ans. : Please refer Section 2.1. **OR**

4. (a) A Differentiate between clustering and classification. Discuss in brief the K-means clustering and Decision tree. **[8]**

Ans. : Please refer Section 2.9.

(b) List the various statistical analysis tools. What is meant by Sensitivity and Specificity of a tool? Explain in brief False Negative, True Negative, True Positive and False positive. **[8]**

Ans. : Please refer Section 2.7.

❍ ❍ ❍

UNIT III

DATA MINING AND PATTERN MATCHING

3.1 METHODS AND TECHNOLOGY OVERVIEW

Getting at the hard own sequence and structure data in molecular biology. Databases and functional data in the online biomedical literature are complicated by the size and complexity of the database.

- However exhaustively searching for the raw data and performing the transformation and manipulations on the data through manual operations is often impractical. In general we want to know what reside in a database and there is a need to extract it, the challenge is more of a translation problem.
- Camouflaged by the size and the complexity of a database, the millions of data points from genomic or proteomic studies are of little value. Only when these data are categorized according to a meaningful them are they useful in furthering our understanding of sequence, structure or function.
- Regardless of whether this categorization is at the base pair, chromosome, or gene level an organizing theme is critical because it simplifies and reduces the complexity of what could otherwise be a flood of incomprehensible data.
- For example: the individual database managed by the NCBI represents generally recognizable organizational themes that facilitate use of their content.
- At a higher level out understanding of health and disease is facilitated by the organization of clinical research data by the organization of clinical research data by organ system, pathogen, genetic aberration, or site of trauma.
- Ideally the creator and the users of the database share on understanding of the underlying organizational theme. These themes and tools used to support them, determine how easily databases created for one purpose can be used for other purpose.
- For example: In a relational database of gene sequences, the data may be arranged in tables, and user may need to construct Structured Query Language (SQL) statements to search for and retrieve data.
- If inherited disease organizes the relational database, it may not readily support an efficient search by protein structure. The challenge for researchers looking in the exponentially increasing quantities of microbiology data for assumed and unknown relationships can be formidable, even if the number of data elements and dimensionality are relatively small.
- Within a relatively small database, it may be practically impossible to specify a relationship query exactly. At issue is how best to support the formulation of a hypothesis based query.

- Even if technology is available that allows a researchers to specify any hypothetical query, the potential for discovering new relationships in data is a function of the insight and biases imposed by the researchers.
- These limitations may be problematic in relatively small databases; they may be intolerable in databases with billions of interrelated data elements. To avoid the computational constraints exhaustive searches for processes with a low likelihood of success.
- For example : In hunting for new genes, a good place to short, from a statistical perspective, is near sequences that tend to be found between introns and exons. However, even with heuristics, user-directed discovery is inherently limited by the time required to manually search for new data.
- To use computer-mediated data mining, the process of automatically extracting meaningful patterns from usually very large quantities of seemingly unrelated data. This isn't to see that data mining reduces the need for the researchers to establish a strategy or to evaluate the results of data mining session.
- When used in conjunction with the appropriate visualization tools, data mining allows the researcher to use her highly advanced pattern recognition skills and knowledge of molecular biology to determine which warrant further study.
- For example : mining the millions of data points from series of micro-array experiments might reveal several clusters of data, as visualized in a 3D cluster display. The researcher could then select data belonging.

3.1.1 Methods

Data mining isn't an endpoint, but is one stage in an overall knowledge discovery process. It is an iterative process in which preceding are modified to support new hypothesis suggested by the data.

The Knowledge Discovery Process involves following stages

(1) Selection and sampling of the appropriate data from the databases.

(2) Preprocessing and cleaning of the data to remove redundancies, errors and conflicts.

(3) Transforming and reducing data to a format more suitable for the data mining.

(4) Data mining.

(5) Evaluation of the mined data.

(6) Visualization of the evaluation results.

(7) Designing new data queries to test new hypothesis and returning to step 1.

(1) Selection and Sampling

Because of practical computational limitations and a priori knowledge, data mining isn't simply about searching for every possible relationship in a database. In a large database or data warehouse, there may be hundreds or thousands of valueless relationships.

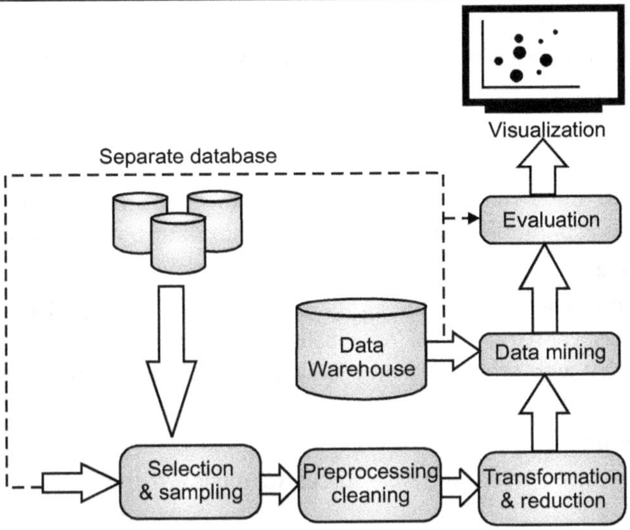

Fig. 3.1 : Data mining operations are shown here in the context of a larger knowledge discovery process

For example : a researcher interested in the relationship of SNPs which clinical findings can reasonably ignore the zip code of the tissue donor or the dates that the tissue samples were obtained. Because there may be millions of records involved and thousands of variables, initial data mining is typically restricted to computationally tenable samples of the holding in an entire data warehouse. The evaluation of the relationships that are revealed in these samples can be used to determine which relationships in the data should be mined further using complete data warehouse.

- With large, complex database, even with sampling, the computational resource requirements associated with non-directed data mining may be excessive. In this situation researchers generally rely on their knowledge of biology to identify potentially valuable relationships and they limit sampling based on these heuristics.

(2) Preprocessing and Cleaning

The bulk of work associated with knowledge discovered is preparing the data for the actual analysis associated data mining. The major preparatory activities listed below:

- Data characterization
- Consistency analysis
- Domain analysis
- Data enrichment
- Frequency and distribution analysis
- Normalization
- Missing value analysis.

(a) Data Characterization

It involves creating of high level description of the nature and the content of the data to be mined. This stage in the knowledge discovery process is primarily for the programmers and the other staff involved in a data mining project. It provides form of documentation.

(b) Consistency Analysis

It is the process of determining the variability in the data, independent of the domain. consistency analysis is primarily statistical assessment of data, based on data values.

(c) Domain Analysis

It involves validating data values in the larger context of the biology. That is domain analysis goes beyond simply verifying that a data value is a text string or an integer, or that it's statistically consistent with other data on the same parameter, to ensure that it makes sense in the context of the biology.

(d) Data Enrichment

It involves drawing from multiple data sources to minimize the limitation of a single data source.

(e) Frequency and Distribution Analysis

It places weights on values as a function of their frequency of occurrence. The effect is to maximize the contribution of common findings while minimizing the effect of rare occurrences on the conclusion made from the data mining output.

(f) Normalization

It involves transforming data values from one representation to another, using a predefined range of final values. The major issues in normalization are range, granularity, accuracy, precision, scale and units. The most common scales used in normalization process are listed below

Table 3.1

Scale	Example
Absolute	Count (3 amino acids)
Nominal	List of Protein Names (Lysine, Arginine, Tyrosine)
Ordinal	Process Phase (First, Second, Third)
Categorical	Types of amino acids (essential, non-essential)
Rank	Protein Folding (Primary, Secondary, Tertiary)
Interval	Time (Seconds)
Ratio	Weight (Micrograms)

(g) Missing Value Analysis

It involves detecting, characterizing and dealing with missing data values. One way of dealing with missing data values is to substitute the mean, mode or median values of the relevant data that are available.

(3) Transformation and Reduction

In transformation phase of knowledge discovery process, data sets are reduced to the minimum size possible through sampling or summary statistics. For example : Tables of data may be replaced by descriptive statistics, such as mean and standard deviation.

- Transformation involves translating one type of data to another through mathematical or operations. Transformation differs from the normalization process in the preprocess and cleaning phase of knowledge discovery in that purpose of the transformation isn't to allow the combination of data from multiple sources, but rather to directly support the data mining and knowledge discovery process.
- For example : Normalized data may be transformed from floating point to integer data to increase computer processor performance.

(4) Data Mining Methods

The process of data mining is concerned with extracting patterns from the data, typically using classification, regression, and link analysis, and segmentation or deviation detection.

(a) Classification involves mapping data into one of several predefined or newly discovered classes. In the former case, a set of predefined examples is used to develop a model that can be used develop a model that can be used to classify data called from data warehouse or database.

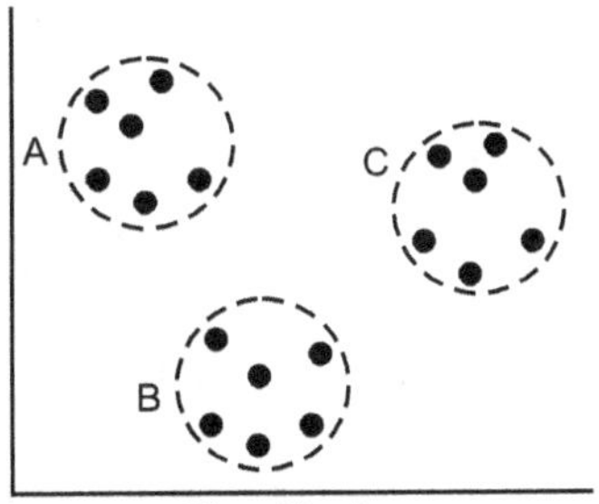

Classification

Fig. 3.2 : Classification

- In the latter case, the system develops its own models that it uses to classify data according to analysis of the data. The classification rule may specify minimum proximity to the center of a particular group, as defined by numerical range or statistical spread.

(b) Regression Method involves assigning data a continuous numerical variable based on statistical methods. One goal in using regression method is to extrapolate trends from a few sample of the data. The extrapolation formula is a simpler linear function of the form:

$$y = mx + b$$

Where, x and y are coordinates on the plot.

m is the slope of the line,

b is constant.

In practice, more complex extrapolation formulas are used to describe data trends.

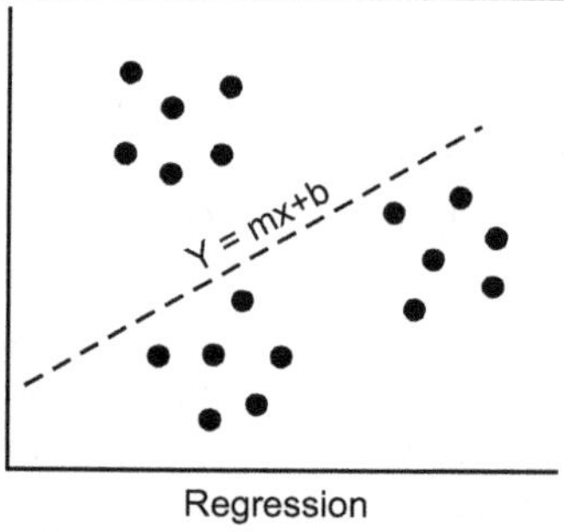

Fig. 3.3 : Regression method

(c) Link analysis evaluates apartment connection or links between data in the database or data warehouse. Link analysis highlights correlations in data that can suggest linkage but not causality.

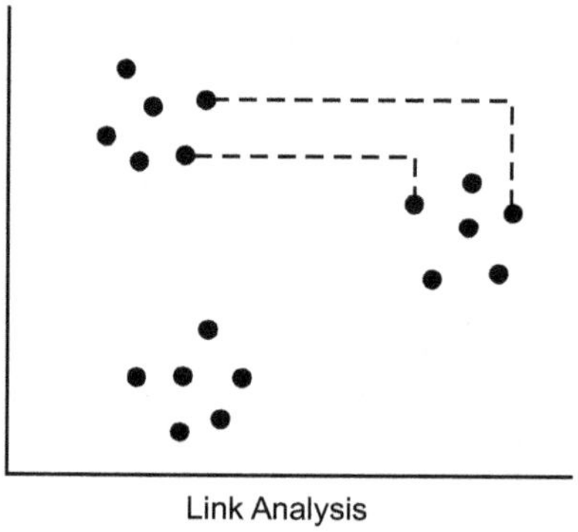

Fig. 3.4 : Link analysis

(d) Deviation Detection identifies data values that are outside of the norm, as defined by existing models or by evaluating the ordering of observations. The data may represent a particular sequence of amino acids or the molecular weight of a protein, or vital sign.

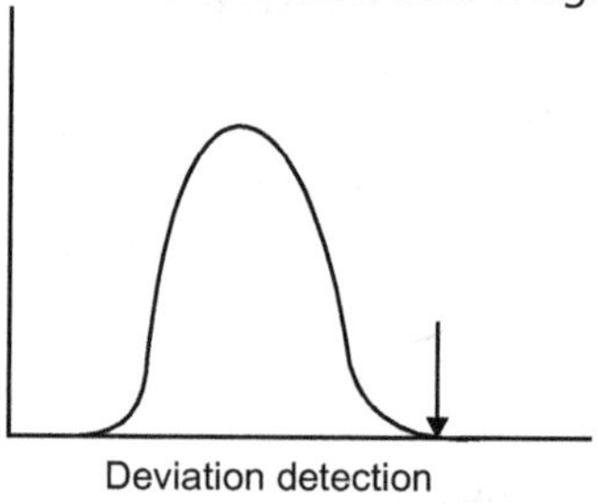

Fig. 3.5 : Deviation detection

(e) Segmentation identifies classes or group of data that behave similarly, according to some metric. Segmentation is a kin to link analysis applied to groups of data instead of individual data points. These methods of data mining are typically used in combination with each other, either in parallel or as a part of a sequential operation.

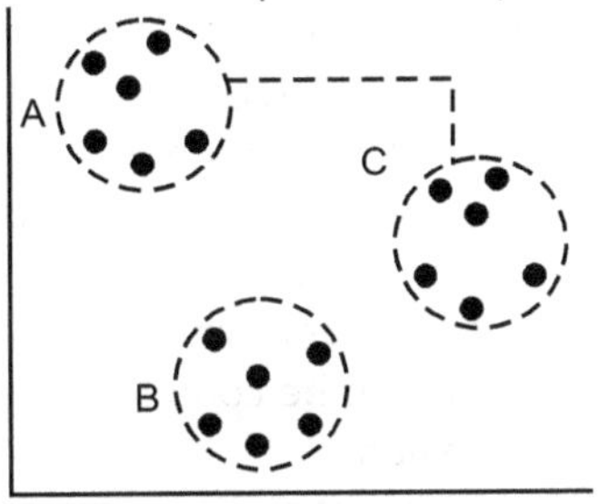

Segmentation

Fig. 3.6 : Segmentation

- For example : segmentations require classes to be defined through a classification process. Similarly, link analysis assumes that statistical analysis, including correlation coefficients, is available.
- Likewise deviation detection assumes that the data have been properly classified and evaluated statistically to define the "normal" model. There is variety of technologies available to support these methods.

(5) Evaluation

In this phase of knowledge discovery, the patterns identified by the data-mining analysis are interpreted. Typical evaluation ranges from simple statistical analysis and complex numerical analysis of sequences and structures to determining the clinical relevance of the findings.

(6) Visualization

Visualization of evaluation results is an optional stage in the knowledge discovery process, but one that typically adds considerable value to the overall system. Visualization can range from converting tabular listings of data to create 3D virtual reality displays that can be manipulated by haptic controllers.

(7) Designing New Queries

Data mining is iterative continual activities, in that there are always new hypothesis to test. Sometimes the new hypothesis are suggested by the data returned by the mining process, and other times the hypothesis originate the from other research. In either case, testing the new queries and revisiting the selection and sampling stage of the data-mining process.

3.1.1.1 Data Warehouse

- The relative timing of sequences in the knowledge discovery process depends on the source of the data is a data warehouse or one or more separate databases. The data warehouse is a central database in which data have been combined from a variety of non-compatible sources, such as sequencing machines, clinical systems, textual bibliographic databases, or national genomic databases.

- In the process of combining data from disparate sources, the data are selected, cleaned and transformed to support user driven analytical and data driven mining tools. Whereas data warehouse is a ready store of data to be mined at a time, using separate databases requires much more work on as needed basis.
- The processing upto the point of data mining may take hours or weeks, depending on the complexity and size of database involved in the process. The advantage using a data warehouse approach of data mining is time saving.
- Assuming that everything needed for data mining is available in the data warehouse, a typical mining operation may be able to be completed in a matter of hour. This ability to begin mining operators at any time at a cost.
- A data warehouse that is capable of efficiently supporting data mining is significantly larger and the associated data processing take much longer than in a simple database, one designed to provide a central, unified data repository that can be accessed through a single user interface.
- The reason for increase data warehouse size and increase in complexity of associated processing is the increasingly fine-grained data required for data mining support, as well as the need to incorporate contextual or metadata to support the data-mining process.
- For example : data mining requires controlled vocabulary, usually implemented as part of data dictionary, so that a single word can be used to express a given concept. Similarly extra attention to cleaning the data and other processing is necessary to maximize the odds that the conclusion based on data mining is valid.
- There is no guarantee that the data in data warehouse will be sufficient to support the desired data-mining activities. Additional data may be needed from the source databases, which then must also be cleaned, transformed, and stored, activities that obviate the advantage of data warehouse.
- One approach to guarding against this eventuality is to incorporate more data into the data warehouse when it is built, at the cost of increased complexity and size, with no guarantee that any of the additional data in the warehouse will ever be used in mining activities.
- The primary advantage of using a database approach to data mining is that resources are used on an as-needed basis. Only those data from the separate databases that are involved with a specific data-mining operation are processed.
- It may takes days or weeks in order to arrange for the appropriate processing in preparation for data mining. The resources required for just-in-time data mining are generally much less than those associated with data warehousing.
- Regardless of the data sources, knowledge discovery is an iterative process that involves feedback at each stage. This feedback can be used programmatically or can serve as the basis for human decision-making.

- For example : If processing and cleaning of data from a data warehouse results in an insufficient quantity of cleaned data, inappropriate data altogether, then the researcher may redefine the selection and sampling criteria to include more or different data.
- Although the methodology seems straightforward, data mining and the overall knowledge discovery process involve much more than the simple statistical analysis of data.

3.1.2 Technology Overview

- It provides an overview of the key technologies that can be applied to data mining, especially those capable of supporting the basic data-mining methods outlined earlier. Technology is an empowering agent that provides leverage to facilitate a well-designed data-mining initiative technology isn't solution in itself.
- Simply connecting a black-box to a database with a hope of it turning up fruitful information on previously hidden relationships in the data is unlikely at best.
- Given this caveat, data mining requires hardware and software infrastructure capable of supporting high-throughput data processing and a network capable of supporting data communication from the database to the visualization workstation.
- With a robust hardware and software infrastructure in place, processes such as machine learning can be used to automatically manage and refine the knowledge discovery and data-mining process.
- This work can be performed with minimal user interaction once a knowledgeable researcher has established the basic design of the system. The core technologies that actually perform the data mining, whether under computer control or directed by users, provide a means of simplifying the complexity and reducing the effective size of the database.
- This focus isn't limited to genome sequence and protein structures, but extends to the wealth of data hidden in the online literature. Advanced text-mining methods are used to identify textual data and place them in proper context.
- Although data mining was once relegated to internal research groups, the technology is readily available today through a variety of commercial and academic shareware tools.
- These tools range from shrink-wrapped, general-purpose software tool to bioinformatics specific commercial and academic system designed for highly specific data-mining applications.

3.2 INFRASTRUCTURE

- Data mining can be performed with little more than a laptop and connection to the internet. Although it is possible to work with such a system serious data mining work typically requires much more in terms of infrastructure.

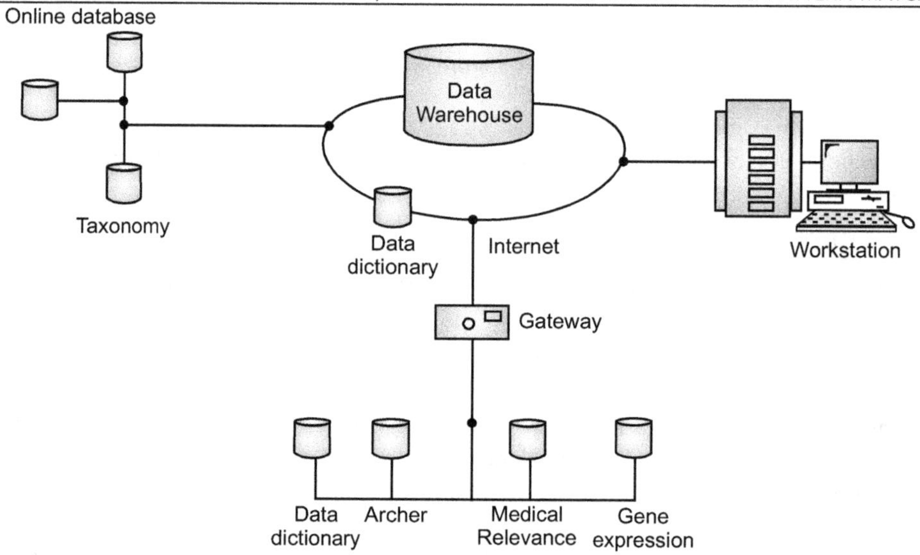

Fig. 3.7 : Centralized data-mining infrastructure

- In this example data warehouse, data dictionary, high bandwidth access to data on the internet, and a high performance workstation from the basis for an effective data-mining operations.
- A typical laboratory data mining infrastructure includes high-speed internet and intranet connective, a data warehouse with a data dictionary that defines a standard vocabulary and data format, several databases, and high performance computer hardware.
- Not shown are the software that support queries and searching and ensures data integrity and the data mining software. Data-mining operations take place on a workstation with high-speed connection to the data warehouse.
- However this centralized data-mining infrastructure is only one of several configurations possible. For example: A completing infrastructure involves distributing the data-mining operation to process specific workstations
- In this configuration, a server dots out data in a format appropriate to the process performed by a particular workstation. A server to specialized workstations distributes data from a central data warehouse or single database.
- The distribution refers to the processing not the data source. In this way overall throughput can be achieved, using inexpensive desktop hardware that is configured with the appropriate hardware and software tools to support a specific process.
- A distributed architecture also supports parallel processing, so that intermediate results from one workstation can be fed to another workstation. For example: link analysis performed on a one workstation can be fed the regression analysis results from another workstation.

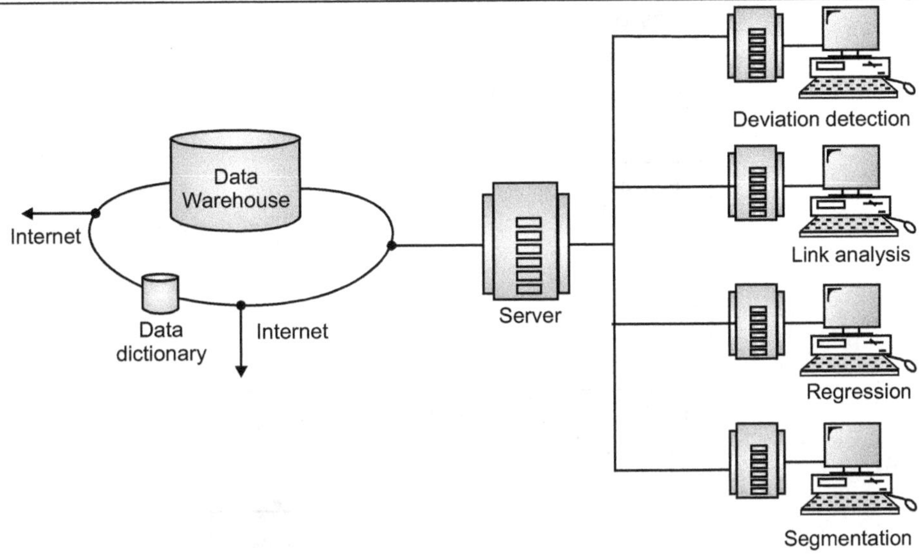

Fig. 3.8 : Distributed data-mining infrastructure

- The trend of distributed data mining using relatively inexpensive desktop hardware is largely a reflection of the economics of modern computing. Not only is the price-performance ratio of desktop hardware superior to that of mainframe computers, but the cost of desktop software licenses is typically several orders of magnitude less than that for mainframe computer systems.
- Of course time is the primary issue, then a mainframe computer optimized for data mining can provide superior performance compared to small networks of desktop computer.

3.3 PATTERN RECOGNITION AND DISCOVERY

- Data mining is the process of identifying patterns and relationship in data that often are not obvious in large, complex data sets. As such data mining involves pattern recognition and, by extension, pattern discovery.
- In bioinformatics, pattern recognition is most often concerned with the automatic classification of character sequence representative of the nucleotide bases or molecular structures, and of 3D protein structures.
- A servers to specialized workstations distributed data from a central data warehouse or single database. Distribution refers to the processing not the data source. The pattern recognition process start with an unknown pattern, such as a potential protein structure, and ends with a label for the pattern.

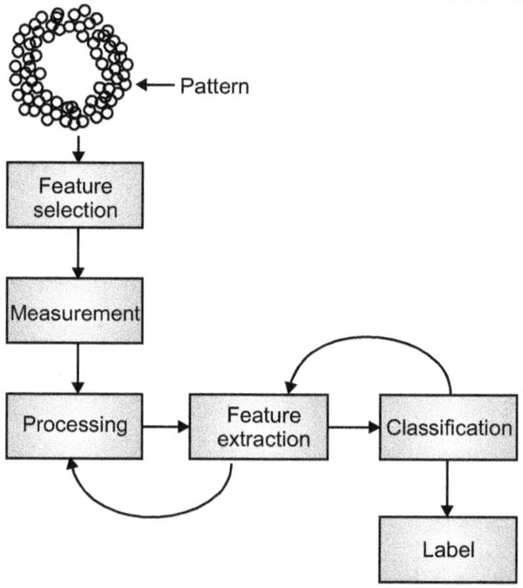

Fig. 3.9 : Pattern recognition and discovery process.

- Pattern discovery differs from pattern recognition in that feature selection determined empirically under program control. From an information processing perspective, pattern recognition can be viewed as a data simplification process that filter extraneous data from consideration and labels the remaining data according to a classification scheme.

The major steps in Pattern Recognition and Pattern Discovery are

(a) Feature Selection

- Given a pattern, the first step in pattern is to select a set of features or attribute from the universe of available features that will be used to classify distinguish the pattern from other data.
- When pattern recognition is directed at known patterns, the researcher defines a priori the features that will be used to distinguish the pattern from other data. Feature selection often takes the form of representative examples of the features that will be measured, such as the tertiary geometry of a protein. In pattern discovery which is more complex than simple pattern recognition, feature selection is under program control.
- Instead of a priori definition of pattern attributes defining a class or group of data that are similar to equivalent in some way, samples are classified programmatically into empirically established groups, based on groups or clusters in the unlabeled collection of sample.
- That is simple pattern recognition is assumption-driven, in that a hypothesis is developed and tested against the data. In pattern discovery, the extracted data serve as the seed of a new hypothesis.

- Clustering technique are used to group samples that are more similar to each other than to other groups, and that have a low internal cluster variability or scatter.

(b) Measurement

It involves converting the original pattern into a representation that can be easily manipulated programmatically. For example: 3D vector image of a protein might be represented as a series of 2D metrics. Depending on the underlying technology used to perform the pattern-matching operation.

(c) Processing

After the measurement process, the data are processed to remove noise and prepare for feature extraction. Processing typically involves executing a variety of error checking and correction routines, as well as specialized processes that depend on the nature of the data.

For example: Images may undergo edge enhancement and transformation to correct for size and orientation variations (normalization) in order to facilitate feature extraction.

(d) Feature Extraction

Feature extraction involves searching for global and local features in data that are defined as relevant to pattern matching during feature selection. Clustering techniques, in which similar data are grouped together, often form the basis of feature extraction.

(e) Classification and Discovery

In this phase data are classified based on measurements of similarity with other patterns. These measurements of similarity are commonly based on either a statistical or structural approach.

- In the statistical approach multidimensional space that is partitioned into regions associated with a classification. In the structural approach the structures of the exemplar patterns are explicitly defined.
- In either case similarity of the data to be classified is compared with the exemplar data to access closeness of association.

(f) Labeling

The pattern-recognition process ends when a label is assigned to the data, based on its membership in a class. The pattern recognition isn't unidirectional, but is iterative to the extent that failures at the classification and feature-extraction phase can be corrected by reevaluating the preceding phase.

- For example: If the feature extraction phase fails to identify relevant data, then the processing of the original image may need to be modified by removing extraneous data from consideration and by taking other, more relevant data, into consideration.
- Feature extraction and classification and discovery which represent the core of the pattern recognition and discovery process.

3.4 MACHINE LEARNING

- The pattern matching and pattern discovery components of data mining are often performed by machine learning techniques. Machine learning isn't a single technology or approach, but encompass a variety of methods that represent the convergence of several disciplines, including statistics, biological modeling, adaptive control theory, psychology, and artificial intelligence (AI). These include genetic algorithms and neutral networks. Similarly adaptive control theory parameters change dynamically to meet the current conditions and psychological theory, especially those regarding positive and negative reinforcement learning, heavily influence machine learning methods. AI techniques, such as pattern matching through inductive logic programming, are designed to derive general rules from specific examples. The spectrum of machine learning technologies applicable to data mining includes;

Table 3.2

Machine Learning Technologies	Data–Mining Methods				
	Classification	**Regression**	**Segmentation**	**Link Analysis**	**Deviation Detection**
Inductive logic programming	X	X			
Genetic algorithm	X	X	X		
Neural network	X	X	X		
Statistical method	X	X	X	X	X
Decision tree	X		X		
Hidden markov models	X				

- Regardless of the underlying technology, most-machine learning follows the general process outlined in above Fig. 3.10.
- Input data are fed to a comparison engine that compares the data with an underlying model. The result of an comparison engine then direct a software actor to initiate some type of change.
- This output whether it takes the form of change in the data or a modification of a underlying model, is evaluated by an evaluation engine, which uses the underlying goals of the system as point of reference. Feedback from the actor and the evaluation engine direct changes in the model. In this scenario, the goal can be standard patterns that are known to be associated with the input data. Alternatively the goals can be states, such as

minimal change in output companies with the systems previous encounter with the same data. The feedback loops capable of responding to feedback enable two types machine learning.

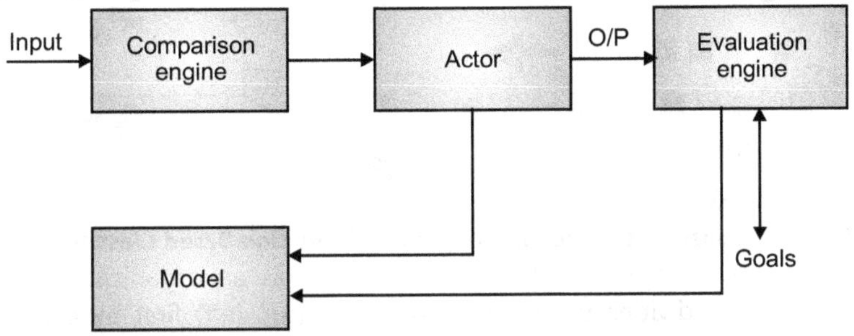

Fig. 3.10 : The machine learning process

Supervised: A system is trained with a set of examples, called the training set. The goals are specific outputs that are associated with each input. The performance of supervised learning system can be evaluated by presenting the system with a known testing set that is similar to the training set.

Unsupervised: There is no specific output associated with a given input, and the system must invent new categories and ways to classify input data. The machine learning system which is based on unsupervised learning it isn't know a priori whether the input data contains a biological significant pattern, where it is, or even what it looks like.

- One of the key issues in supervised learning is that the training set must be sufficiently large relatively to the number of categories or different output provided by the machine learning.
- When there are too many categories or recognized patterns that are consistent with the input data, the training data is said to be overfitted. Overfitted is the process of assigning undue importance to random variation in the data.
- Whether supervised or unsupervised the machine learning process requires bias. Bias is created by placing constraints on the data that can be examined, by using different underlying models, and by altering machine learning goals.

It can increase the efficiency of the machine learning process and provide more meaningful result.

(1) Inductive Logic Programming

- It uses a set of rules of heuristics to categorize data. A common heuristics to use change an attribute of the data that will subset the data according to the attribute. That is, an entropy-based classification system based on an individual algorithm works by incrementally dividing the data into largest possible spaces until all data has been assigned to a collection.

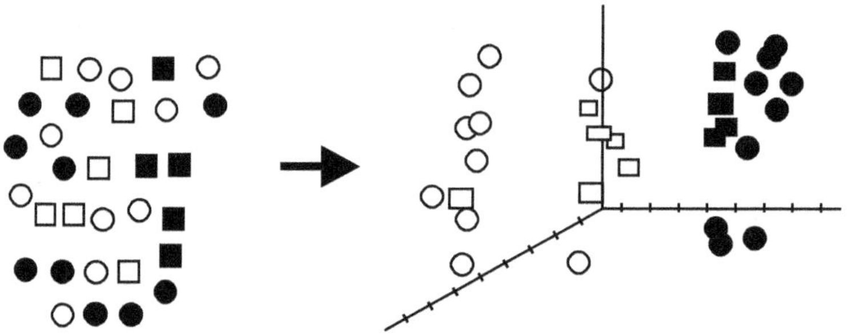

Fig. 3.11 : Consider the scenario depicted. (Induction Based Classification.)

- Using changes in entropy (a measure of disorder) as an organizational heuristic, the induction algorithm divides the unorganized data (top left) first by color and then by shape.

In the Fig. 3.11 data to be classified includes 20 circles, 10 squares and 16 of which white and 14 of which are black. With two dimensions to compare

- Shape
- Color
- An entropy-based inductive classifier bifurcates the shape first according to color because it provides the maximum change in entropy, resulting in one group of 14 black circles and 16 squares and one group of 16 white circles and squares.
- After dividing the shape by color, it's further subdivided by shape, as shown in Fig. 3.11. The alternative bifurcating the circles and squares initially by shape would have resulted in split of 10 to 20, which is less than the spread (increase in entropy) associated with a 14 to 16 split. In a typical bioinformatics data-mining problem, there may be 10 or more attributes to consider, according to entropy change or some other driving heuristic.

(2) Genetic Algorithm

- Genetic algorithm are based on evolutionary principles wherein a particular function or definition that best fits the constraints an environment survives to the next generation, and the other functions are eliminated. This iterative process continuous indefinitely, allowing the algorithm to adapt dynamically to the environment as needed. Genetic algorithm evaluates a large number of solutions to a problem that are generated at random.
- The members of the solution population with the highest fitness scores are allowed to" mate" with crossover and mutations creating the next generation. Figure 3.4 (b) typically illustrate the typical genetic operation. In this example possible solutions to a problem defined by the fitness function are represented by bit string. Each bit represents the presence or absence of some quality that is mapped to the real-world solution.
- If there is a need to represent gradations of quantities, then integrates or floating-point variables could be used instead of bit string. However, this example, 1z bits are used to represent the problem matrix.

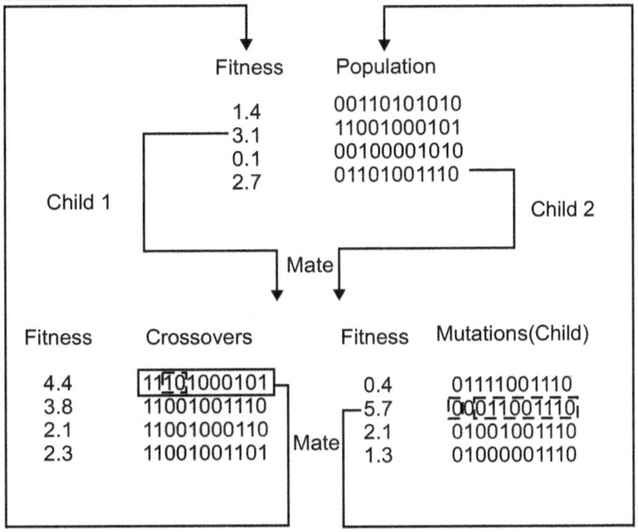

Fig. 3.12 : Genetic algorithm operations.

- When the algorithm is initialized, a population of bit string is generated, using random number generator. Although only four bit strings are shown here in the initial population, a typical population may include hundreds or even thousands of patterns.
- The larger the initial population, the more likely a high-scoring or "fit" solution will emerge, at the expense of computation time. From this initial population, two children are selected based on the two highest-scoring pattern.
- All other bit strings are discarded. These children are then allowed to "mate" with crossover (bottom, left) and point mutation (bottom, right). As in the initial population, there are hundreds or even thousands of crossover and mutations created, and each resulting bit string is ranked by the fitness function to identify two new children. There are various combinations of crossover and mutations possible. For example; the fittest two children from the crossover population can each be subject to point mutations at each position in their string.
- And the fittest children with mutations can be mated with the highest ranking crossover children or with the parents. In this way the string with the highest score from the fitness function is iteratively generated. The process can continue indefinitely or, as is normally done, terminated after a set number of generations. Both the encoding of bit string and the fitness function are domain-specific.
- For example : The first position in the bit string might represent the presence of particular amino acid in a protein, the presence of a hydrogen bond at a position on an alpha helix. Similarly, the fitness function can be as simple as positive and negative weightings for each of the 12 bits (for example 1s add positions are weighted with -1,

and 1s at even position are weighted with +1). For sequence analysis problem or as a complex trigonometric function for structure prediction problem.

(3) Neural Networks

- Neural networks are simulations loosely patterned after biological neurons. In molecular biology, they learn to associate input patterns with output patterns in a way that allows them to categorize new patterns and to extrapolate trends from data.
- In operation a neural network is presented with patterns on its input nodes and the network produces an output pattern, based on this learning. The power of neutral network is that they can apply this learning to new input pattern.
- For this reason, neural networks, like genetic algorithm are often referred to as a form of "soft " or "fuzzy" computing because the answer or pattern matching provided by these methods represent best guesses, based on the data available for analysis.
- Neural networks always produce an output when presented with an input pattern. However the resultant categorization isn't necessarily the best answer.
- The best answer computed using traditional algorithms, weeks of computing time on a desktop workstation. In comparison a neural network may be able to categories data in a few seconds using the same hardware.
- The inner workings of neural networks are independent of the problem domain, in that the same neural network configuration (with different training) can be used to recognize a nucleotide triplet, or a critical pattern on a patient EKG tracing or a potential mid-air collision when used with radar data. Its upto the researchers to determine what the input and output patterns represent. That said neural networks, like other fuzzy systems, work best in a narrowly defined domain in which input patterns are likely fail to classify the universe of known proteins, despite additional training. As increase in the umber and complexity of input pattern typically requires reconfiguring or rewriting a neural network with more layers and different interconnections.
- For example : simple 3-layer neural network shown in figure 3.4 (c) may have to be replaced by a four layer neural network with double the number of interconnections.
- As a result training time-the time required for a neural network to consistently associate an input pattern with an output pattern correctly may be extended form a few minutes to several hours, even on high-performance hardware. Recognition time should be relatively unaffected. One of the neural network is that the significance of the strength of the internal interconnection in unknown. As a result, as a pattern recognizer or categorizer, the neural can be treated as a black box. The challenge of using neural network to recognize and categorize data, especially novel data that haven't been presented to the system before is that validating the result and of communicating the rationale behind the results to the user.
- The greatest drawback of neural network is that it's practically impossible to access the significance of what's happening inside of a complex network. Even though "writing" of

the nodes may be known, the relevance of changes in the strength of the connections is difficult to access, even when the strength are known. As a result inner workings of a neutral network are difficult to validate.

- Because of pure neural network presents such a formidable validation challenge, many neural network data-mining systems are used in conjunction with rule-based expert systems that human-readable rules in the form. IF condition THEN outcome.
- These hybrid systems can categorize novel patterns and provide researchers with insight into the operation of the biological system.

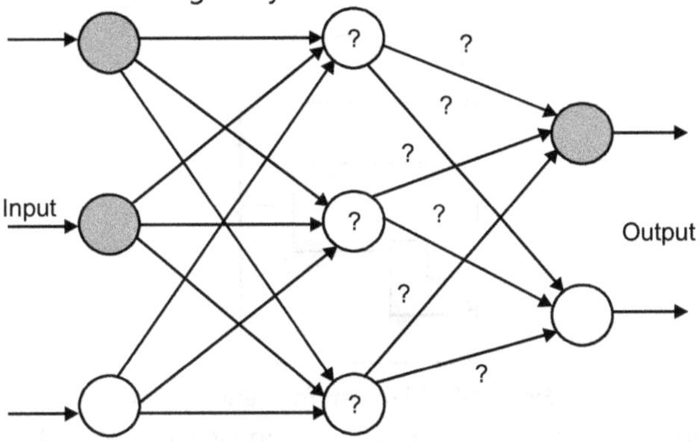

Fig. 3.13 : Neutral Network

(4) Statistical Methods

- The statistical methods used to support data mining are generally some form of feature extraction, classifications or clustering. Statistical feature extraction is concerned with recovering the defining data attributes that may be obscured by imperfect measurement, improper data processing, or noise in the data.
- A variety of statistical pattern-classification methods may be applied to data mining. Bayesian techniques that estimate the joint probability of distributions can also be used to assess this probability. Geometric classifiers are based on template matching in which the observed pattern is compare to geometric template that represents data in each category. Conceptual classifiers rely on biological heuristics to define categories, fuzzy logic techniques can be used to assign data to a class by degree.
- Statistical data-mining methods based on structural pattern representation attempt to describe complex patterns in terms of simpler patterns. They extract features from the data and represent the structural features as vectors that are used with statistically determined discriminant functions. Predictive modeling, which uses data within a database to predict other missing data, can be based on continuous numerical variables (regression) or, more frequently, on categorical data. The major challenge in predictive modeling is to select the input criteria that are most influential in defining missing data and in identifying the most appropriate transformation.

- Cluster analysis, also known as data segmentation, groups data into subsets that are similar to each other. Cluster analysis is a technique that can take a large amount of data about a number of objects and construct a simple, unique tree diagram that expresses those objects similarities and differences.
- It involves sorting data so that members of the same cluster are most alike and members of different clusters are least alike.
- The result of cluster analysis is commonly reported in human-readable form as a dendogram.

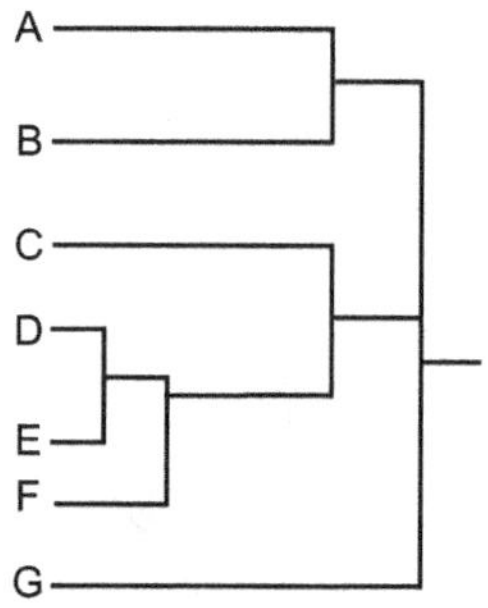

Fig. 3.14 : Diagram for dendogram

- In this dendogram group (D) and (E) are the most alike, as indicated by the shortest bracket. The next level of similarity between (F) and the (D)-(E) complex. In addition groups (A) and (B) are similar. Group (G) shares the least similarity with the other group. Cluster analysis may reveal associations and structure in data that, though not previously evident, are sensible and useful once found.

Cluster Analysis Include

- Metric based clustering
- Model based clustering
- Partition based clustering

Metric Based Clustering

The data are partitioned so that they are closer to the centroid or center of mass than they are to other data in the cluster.

Model Based Clustering

A hypothetical model for each cluster is defined and the data that best fit the model are considered part of that cluster. Problem with model based approach is over fitting by chance, a model may fit data that is irrelevant to it.

Partition Based Model

Which are generally cases of metric and model based methods use an ad hoc method of dividing the data space.

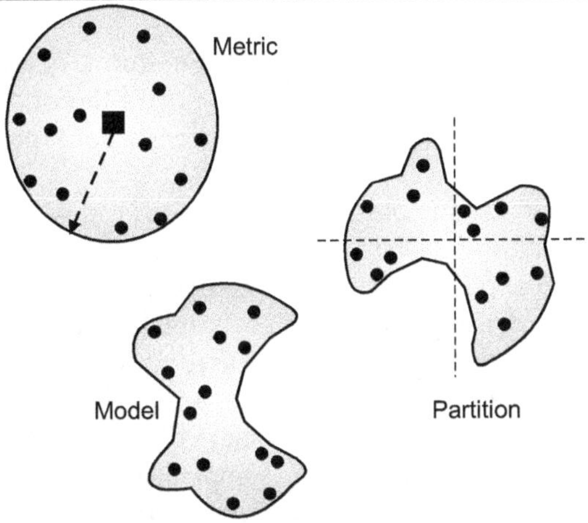

Fig. 3.15 : Diagram for cluster analysis methods

(5) Decision Tree

Decision trees are hierarchically arranged question and answers that lead to classification. As shown Fig. decision trees are formed by input nodes and tests on input data whose leaf nodes are categorize of those data.

In the following figure Prog A to Prog H results in numerical categories (1 to 8). An advantage of using decision tree in data mining is that they can be easily read and modified by human.

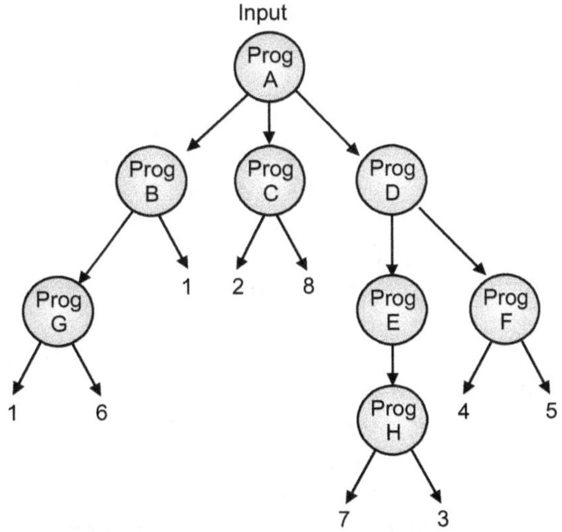

Fig. 3.16 : Diagram for decision tree

For example :

The result of Prog A may lead to Prog2, 3, 4. Once the Prog D is selected, the only options are characterize the input as belong to Prog E, or Prog F. The options from Prog E are to place the data into category 4 or category 5. The options from Prog F are to place the data into category 6 or category 7.

- The test can be binary in Prog B, or multi-variant as in Prog A. As illustrated in the figure, the terminal or leaf nodes needn't results in mutually exclusive categorization of the input data. Both Prog B and Prog G classify in category 1.
- A potential limitation of using decision tree is related to their inability to represent relative occurrences frequencies. In some cases this inability to represent relative frequency of occurrence can be used to advantage.
- For example : in classifying globins from a variety of species, multiple samples from the same or closely related species, multiple samples from the same or closely related species may skew the relative abundance of some properties over others.
- If these properties are represented as a decision tree, then the skew due to sample anomalies can be avoided.

(6) Hidden Markov Model

- A powerful statistical approach to constructing classifiers that deserves a separate discussion is the use of Hidden Markov Modeling. Hidden Markov Model (HMM) is a statistical model for an ordered sequence of symbols, acting as a stochastic state machine that generate a symbol each time a transition made from one state to the next.
- Transitions between states are defined by transition probability. In Markov process a process is move from one state to state depending on the previous n states.
- The process called an order n model where n is the number of states affecting the choice of next state. In first order Markov process the probability of a state is depending only on the directly preceding state. For understanding of HMMs, consider the concept of Markov chain, which is a process that can be in one of a number of states at any given time. In Markov chain each state generates an observation, from which the state sequence can be deduced.
- It is defined by the probabilities for each transition in state occurring, given the current state. That is, it is a non-deterministic system in which it is assumed that the probability of moving from one state to another doesn't vary with time.
- A HMM is a variation of Markov Chain in which the states in the chain are hidden. Like a neural network classifier, a HMM must be trained before it can be used. It establishes the transition probabilities for each state in the Markov Chain.
- When presented with the data in the database, the HMM provides a measure of how close the data patterns, sequence data. HMM based classifiers are considered approximations because of the often unrealistic assumptions that a state is dependent only on predecessors and that this dependence is time-independent.

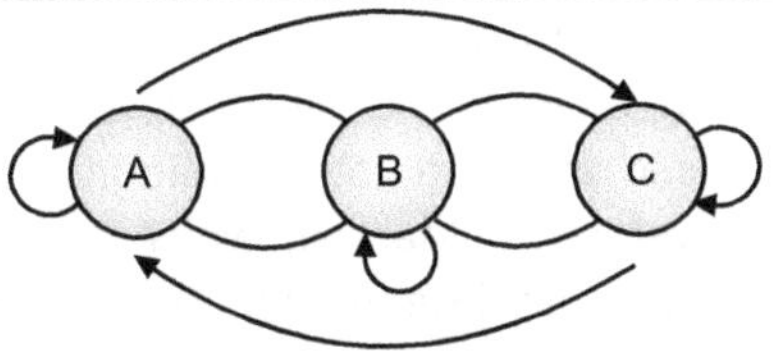

Fig. 3.17 : Diagram for markov chain : (A), (B) and (C) represent states and the arrows connecting the states represent transitions

3.5 TEXT MINING AND TOOLS

- For humanity to benefit from bioinformatics research, the sequence and structure of proteins and other molecules must be linked to functional data that links clinical medicine, pharmacology, sequence data, and structure data is in the form of biomedicine documents in online bibliographic databases such as PubMed.
- Mining these databases is expected to reveal the relationships between structure and function at the molecular level and their relationship to pharmacology and clinical medicine.
- Text mining automatically extracting from the documents, which is published in the form of unstructured free text, often in several languages is a non-trivial task.
- Although computer languages such as LIST Processing (LISP) have been developed expressly for handling free text, working with free text remains one of the most challenging areas of computer science.
- This is primarily because, unlike the analysis of the sequence of amino acids in a protein, natural language is ambiguous and often references data not contained in the document under study.
- Text mining is complicated because of the variability of how data are represented in atypical text document. Data on a particular topic may appear in the main body of text, in a footnote, in a table, or imbedded in a graphic illustration.

3.5.1 Natural Language Processing

The most promising approaches to text mining online documents rely on Natural Language Processing (NLP), a technology that encompasses a variety of computational methods ranging from simple keyword extraction to semantic analysis.

- The simples NLP systems use statistical methods to recognize not only relevant keywords, but their distribution within a document. In this way, it's possible to deduce context.
- The result of this more advanced analysis is document clusters, each of which represents data on a specific topic in a particular context.

- This capability of identifying documents or document clusters is used by the typical web search engines, such as Google or Yahoo, or the native PubMed interface.
- This approach is also used in commercial bibliographic database systems, such as EndNote, ProCite, and reference Manger, which create a local subset of PubMed data by capturing the native field definitions, such as author name, publication title, and MESH keywords.
- These products don't support the automatic integration of structure and sequence data with functional data.
- Their support for text mining of the data within a document is limited to simple user directed keyword search.

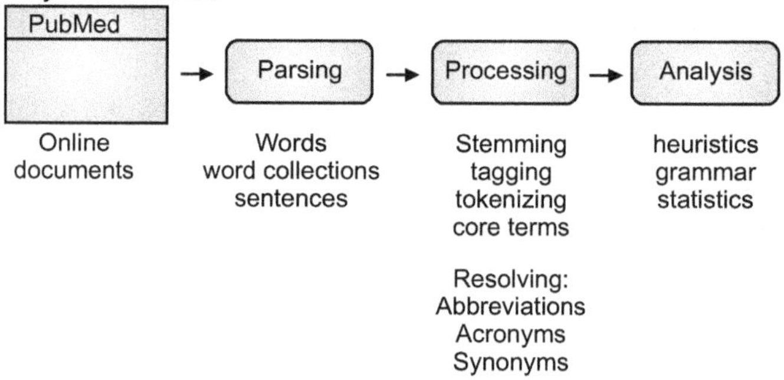

Fig. 3.18 : The NLP process

- The most advanced NLP systems work at the semantic level the analysis of how meaning is created by use and interrelationships of words, phrases, and sentences in sentence.
- These systems, which represent the leading edge of NLP R&D, are less reliable than systems based on keyword extraction and distribution technique in that they sometimes formulated incorrect rules and trends, resulting in erroneous search results.
- Regardless of the level of NLP, most systems follow the basic process illustrated in fig. Online document is first parsed into words, word collections, or sentences, depending on the NLP process used.
- The simplest systems simple look at individual words where as systems that support mining of document clusters focus on word collections to establish context. The most advanced NLP systems, which attempt to extract meaning from words and word order, parse the documents at the sentence level.
- The processing phase of NLP involves one or more of a variety of the following techniques-
  1. **Stemming :** Identifying the steam of each word.
     For example, "hybridized", "hybridizing" and "hybridization" would be stemmed to "hybrid".

As a result, the analysis phase of the NLP process has to deal with only the stem of each word, and not every possible permutation.

2. **Tagging :** identifying the part of speech represented by each word, such as noun, verb, or adjective.
3. **Tokenizing :** segmenting sentences into words and phrases. This process determines which word should be remained phrases, and which one should be segmented into individual words.

   For example, "Type II Rose" should be retained as a word phase, whereas "A girl having rose" would be segmented into four separate words.
4. **Core Terms :** Significant terms, such as protein names, are identified based on a directory of core terms. A related process is ignoring insignificant words, such as "the", "and", "a".
5. **Resolving Abbreviations, Acronyms, and Synonyms :** replacing abbreviations with the words they represent, and resolving acronyms and synonyms to a controlled vocabulary.

   For example, "DM" and "Diabetes Mellitus" could be resolved to "Type II Diabetes", depending on the controlled vocabulary.

- The analysis phase of NLP typically involves the use of heuristics, grammar, or statistical methods. Heuristic approaches rely on a knowledge base rules that are applied to the processed text.
- Grammar based methods use language models to extract information from the processed text. Statistical methods use mathematical models to derive context and meaning from words. Often these methods are combined in the same system.
- Heuristic or rule-based analysis uses IF-THEN rules on the processed words and sentences to infer associations or meaning.
- Consider the following rule-

  IF <protein name>
  AND <experimental method name> are in the same sentence
  THEN the <experimental method name> refers to the <protein name>

- This rule states that if a protein name, such as "hemoglobin", is in the same sentences as an experimental method, such as "microarray spotting". Then microarray spotting refers to hemoglobin. One obvious problem with heuristic methods is that there are exceptions to most rules.
- Grammar based methods use language models that serve as templates for the sentence and phrase level analysis. These templates tend to be domain-specific.
- Most statistical approach based on word frequency, a document is represented as a vector of word frequency, with the individual words or phrases forming the axes of the multi-dimensional space.

- This vector can be compared to a library of standard vectors, each of which represents a particular concept. In one statistical approach based on word frequency, a document represented as a vector of word frequency, with the individual words or phrases forming the axes of the multi-dimensional space.
- This vector can be compared to a library of standard vectors, each of which represents a particular concept. The closeness of two vectors represents similarity in concepts or at least content, this method can be used to automatically classify the contents of the document under analysis.

3.5.2 Text Summarization

In addition to NLP, the text mining is facilitated by text summarization, a process that takes a page or more of text as its input and generates a summary paragraph as the output.

- Each summary paragraph represents a sample of the source document. Text summarization utilities, such as the "AutoSummarize" feature within Microsoft Word, are useful in creating a rough abstract of a document when none has been provided by author.
- Text summarization is an imperfect, evolving technology that works well in niche areas, but not universally.

3.5.2.1 Tools

For most applications, data mining needn't involve writing neural networks or genetic algorithms in a traditional programming language. Instead, it can make use of variety of general-purpose and bioinformatics-specific tools, as well as several high-level languages.

- The most common languages used to perform data mining in bioinformatics are Perl, Python, and SQL. Perl and Python are scripting languages that are useful for implementing custom character and string-based data mining for textual and sequence data.
- The greatest limitation of Perl and Python is that they are interpreted language i.e. the scripts are not compiled, but instead execute at runtime in an interpreter. Data mining with Perl and Python is slower than using a well-written program using the same algorithms in c++.
- Time penalty associated with Python is less than that associated with Perl, because it is based primarily on modules written in c++. Python and Perl are open source free program. Script defined by the Perl and Python can be modified and executed within a few seconds without taking the time to compile source code.
- Examples of data mining tools

Tools	Examples
Languages	Perl, Python, SQL, XML
General-Purpose	Angoss, Clustran, Cross-Graph, Cross-z, Daisy, Data Distilleries, Database Marksman, DataMind, GVA, IBM Intelligent, Miner, Insightful Miner, Integral Solutions, KXEN, Magnify, MatLab, Neo Vista Solutions, Oracle Drawin, Quadstone, SAS, Spotfire, SPSS Clementine, StatPac, Syllogic, Think Analytics, Thinking Machines, Weka
Bioinformatics-Specific	MEME, PIMA, PrattWWW, SPEXS

- SQL is also an interpreted language. SQL lacks the flexibility of Perl or Python, in that its useful only for querying the relational database. SQL is not stand-alone application, but is normally a part of vendor-specific DBMS.
- Advantage of using SQL is that the language is portable from one relational database system to next. The SQL commands are identical, regardless of whether the database is manufactured by Oracle, Microsoft, or IBM.
- SQL are frequently embedded in another language so that they can perform operations on the returned data. XML is a data format that's the current heart of the online database development because of its extensibility and use of tags that provide contextual clues helpful in data mining.
- The disadvantage of XML is the lack of constraints on how it can be extended. Most of other bioinformatics-specific data-mining tools tend to optimized for a specific data-mining application, they tend to very efficient.
- The downside of using these specific tools is the need to learn several different packages if data-mining extend from nucleotide sequences to protein structure.

3.6 PATTERN MATCHING

Automated pattern matching is the ability of program to compare novel and known patterns and determine the degree of similarity.

Pattern Matching Applications in Bioinformatics

- Constructing controlled vocabulary
- Data mining
- Functional genomics
- Functional proteomics
- Genome sequencing
- Homologous gene identification
- Homologous protein identification
- Protein sequence alignment
- Protein structure prediction
- Rule based structure classifiers

3.6.1 Fundamentals

Sequence alignment is fundamental to inferring homology (common ancestry) and function.

- Another heuristic is that if the sequence of protein or other molecule significantly matches the sequence of protein with a known structure and function, then the molecules may share structure and function.
- The issue related to single pairwise sequence alignment, global versus local alignment, and multiple sequence alignment is introduced here.

Pairwise Sequence Alignment

Pairwise sequence alignment involves the matching of two sequences, one pair of elements at a time. The challenge in pairwise sequence alignment is to find the optimum alignment of two sequences with some degree of similarity.

- This optimum condition is typically based on a score that reflects the number of paired characters in the two sequences and the number and length of gaps required to adjust the sequences so that the maximum number of characters is in alignment.
- For example :
  Consider the ideal case of two identical nucleotide sequences, (A) and (B):
  a) ATTCGGCATTCAGTGCTAGA
  b) ATTCGGCATTCAGTGCTAGA

Assuming that the alignment-scoring algorithm counts one point per pair of aligned character (shown in bold type), then the score is one point for each of the 20 pairs. Now consider the case when several of the character pairs aren't aligned.

c) **ATTCGGCATT**CAGT**G**CTAGA

d) **ATTCGGCATT**GCTA**G**A

In this case, the score would be 11, because only 11 pairs of characters in sequences (C) and (D) are aligned. However, by examining the end of the sequences, it can be seen that the sequence of the last six characters are identical. By moving these last six characters ahead in sequence (D) by adding four spaces or gaps, the sequences become

e) **ATTCGGCATT**CAGT**GCTAGA**

f) **ATTCGGCATT - - - - GCTAGA**

- Now the score, based on the original algorithm of character pairings, is 16. However, because the score would have been 11 without the interested gaps, a penalty should be extracted for each gap interested into the sequence to favor alignments that can be made with as few gaps as possible.
- Assuming a gap penalty of -0.5 per gap, the alignment score becomes 10+6+ (4*-0.5) or 14. A more likely scenario is one in which the areas of similarity and difference are not obvious. Consider the sequences (G) and (H):
  g) **ATTCG**G**CATT**CAG**AG**C**G**AG**A**
  h) **ATTCG**A**CATT**GCT**AG**T**G**GT**A**
- Unlike the previous cases, there are no relatively long runs of character pairings, and the matching pairs are separated by unaligned characters.
- The alignment score is 1 point per aligned pair, or 13. One attempt is at visual alignment by adding four gaps into sequence (H) results in
  i) **ATTCG**G**CATT**CAGA**GCTAG**A
  j) **ATTCG**A**CATT - - - - GCTAG**TGGTA

- This alignment results in a score 12 or 14 alignments minus 2 points for the 4 gaps introduced into sequence (H), transforming it to sequence (I). In addition, a penalty of -0.5 per character pair is scored for an inexact match.
- In the case of sequences (G) and (I), there are 6 inexact matches, for a penalty of (6*-0.5=-3). Using this new alignment-scoring algorithm, and ignoring the length difference between the two sequences, the alignment score for the (G)-(I) alignment becomes

Alignment score= 14 alignments + 4 gaps+ 6 inexact matches
= 14 + (4*-0.5) + (6*-0.5)
= 14-2-3
= 9

- In this example, adding gaps result in a lower alignment score.
- Gap penalty is calculated as:

$$Penalty_{gap} = Cost_{opening} + Cost_{extension} \times Length_{gap}$$

Where

- Is the total gap penalty
- Cost of opening a gap in a sequence
- Is the cost of extending an existing gap by one character
- Is the length of the gap in characters

Local Versus Global Alignment

Sequence pair (E)-(F) is an example of a global alignment that is an attempt to line up the two sequences matching as many characters as possible, for the entire length of each segment.

- Global alignment considers all characters in a sequence, and bases alignment on the total score, even at the expense of stretches in the sequence that share obvious similarity.
- Global alignment is used to help determine whether two protein sequences are in the same family.

Multiple Sequence Alignment

In which three or more sequences must be aligned, is useful in finding conserved regulatory patterns in nucleotide sequences and for identifying structural functional domains in protein families.

- Multiple sequence alignment is much more challenging than single pairwise alignment.
- For nucleotide sequences, the problem appear as:

  j) TCAGAGCGAGA
  k) ATCCGGCCCGGCAGCGAGA
  l) CAAAATTCAGAGCGAGA
  m) ATCCGCAGAGCCCGGGGAGA

n) CCCGGCAGCGAGA
o) ATCCGTTTTTTTTTGAGA

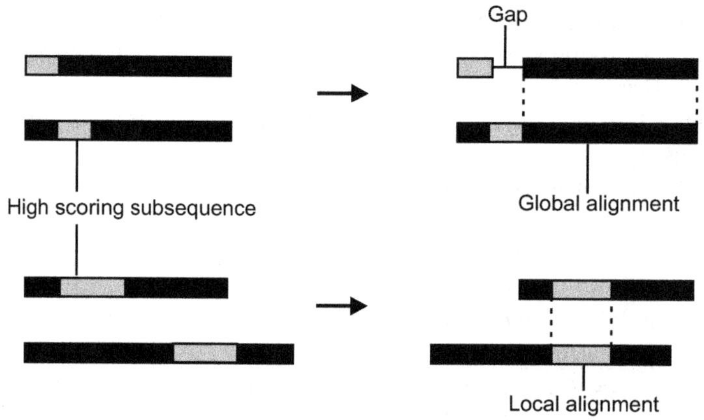

Fig. 3.19 : Diagram for local versus global alignment

- In an actual multiple sequence alignment, each sequence may consist of hundred characters, making manual gap insertions and other non-computational methods infeasible.

3.6.2 Computational Methods

A variety of computational method is available for sequence alignment, whether single, multiple, global or local. A sampling of major computational approaches to pattern matching and sequence alignment is listed in below table

Computational Methods of Sequence Alignment

Bayesian Methods
Dot Matrix
Dynamic Programing
Genetic Algorithm
Hidden Markov Models
Neural Networks
Scoring Matrices
Word –Based Techniques

(a) Dot Matrix Analysis

Because alignment by visual inspection of linear sequences hundreds characters or more in length was impractical, researchers developed is more visually intuitive method of pattern detection called the dot matrix method.

- In this method, one sequence along the top, and one along the side of the matrix, and a dot is placed at the intersection of matrix character pairs.
- Contiguous diagonal rows of dots indicate sequence of matching pairs, as in the dot matrix plot sequences (G) and (H).
- The dot matrix pattern for a pair of perfectly matching sequence would include a contiguous sequence of dots running down the center diagonal of the matrix.
- However, this pattern is rarely seen in practice. Most often, the diagonal patterns are difficult to discern without additional processing.
- The use of color and other methods of highlighting matching sequences, a variety of filters are often applied to the data.
- For example : A common filter is a combination of window and stringency. The window refers to the number of dot points examined at a time, while the stringency is the minimum number of matches required within each window.

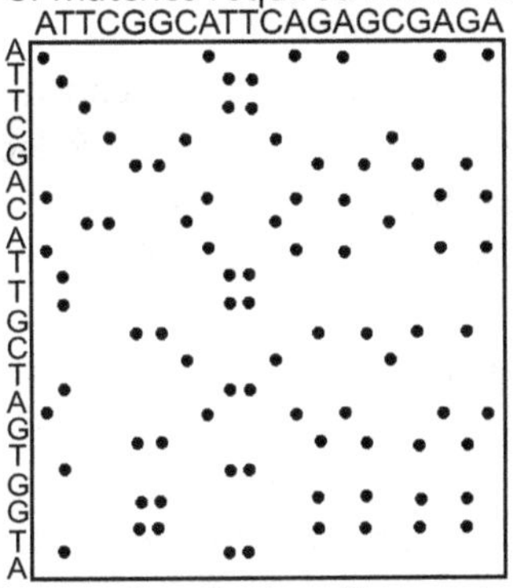

Fig. 3.20 : Diagram for dot matrix pairwise alignment of nucleotide sequences.

- Typical window stringency is combination of 15/10 for nucleotide sequences and much narrower combinations for polypeptide sequence, such as 1/1 or 3/2.
- It especially useful in identifying repeats repeating characters or short sequences within a sequence, as in mapping the repeated regions of whole chromosomes.
- Repeats of the same character, as in sequence (P), creates alignments with artificially high scores and make sequence alignment more difficult.
- These methods are most applicable to single pairwise alignment problems, especially those with relative high degrees of similarity.
- Sequences with lower degrees of similarity as well as multiple sequence alignment require methods that are more powerful.
- Diagram for dot matrix of pairwise alignment of sequences.
- Although window-stringency values are often established heuristically, they may also be based on dynamic averages, scores based on the occurrence of matches in aligned protein families, or on various methods of scoring the similarity of amino acids.

(b) Substitution Metrics

Protein structure and function surprisingly resistant to polypeptide substitution, to the degree that the substitutions don't alter the chemistry of the protein.

- Substitutions are common over large expanse of time and from one species to the next. In many cases, substitution of polypeptides to evaluation can be predicted.
- In this way, a matrix of likely polypeptides substitutions can be constructed. As in a dot matrix analysis, the amino acids are listed across the top and side of a matrix, typically using the amino acid code letters.
- An underlying assumption is that this association is symmetrically, in that either polypeptide can substituted for the other.
- Two popular substitution matrices are Percent Accepted Mutation (PAM) and Blocks Amino Acid Substitution Matrix (Blosum). Unlike dot matrix analysis, these matrices are static.
- These matrices aren't mere mathematically constructed design simply to facilitate computational sequence alignment, but they reflect the biology of the molecules represented by the sequences.
- For example : Each PAM matrix in the series is named after the level of change assumed by the matrix.
- A matrix value of "0" signifies that a substitution typically occurs at a random base rate, whereas
- For example :

  In the PAM-250 matrix, A and N substitute for each other at rate (0) that is expected by chance alone.

  Conversely, A and W substitute for each other at a rate (-6) much lower than expected for a random substitution.
- From the perspective of supporting sequence alignment, the main diagonal reveals the relative value of maintaining matches in the pairwise sequence alignment process.
- Although the values in the Blosum matrix means the same as in a PAM matrix, the Blosum matrices incorporate substitution scores that encompass a range of evolutionary periods and in some cases provide greater sensitivity over PAM matrices.
- Blosum takes its name from the blocks area of conserved amino acids used to define substitution patterns.
- Unlike PAM, which is based on a relatively small-scale set of closely related proteins, Blosum is based on a large-scale analysis of over 500 families of related proteins. Similarly Blosum doesn't explicitly consider evolutionary factors.

- Matrices aren't necessarily symmetric or based on the same alphabet. If the gap penalty figures are too high relative to the matrix scores, the gap penalty Fig. will override the matrix scores, and gaps will never appear in the sequence alignment.
- Conversely, if gap penalty figures are too low relative to the matrix scores, gaps will be used wherever possible in order to align the sequences. That is, simply because a substitution matrix is used doesn't guarantee biologically relevant results.

(c) Dynamic Programming

One way to be certain that the solution to a sequence alignment is the best alignment possible is to try every possible alignment, introducing one or more gaps at every position, and computing an alignment score based on aligned character pairs and inexact matches.

- Dynamic programing is a form of recursion in which intermediate results are saved in matrix where they can be referred to later by the program.
- The comparison can be linked to solving a series of complex mathematical equations, which the result of one equation feeding the input of another, with and without the benefit of pen and paper or other temporary storage and retrieval mechanism.
- Dynamic programming is processor and RAM intensive, but the technique of storing intermediate values in a matrix can transform an otherwise intractable problem requiring immense computational capabilities into one that is computationally feasible.
- For calculating the value of dynamic programing in sequence alignment consider the function: MaxValue = f (Ai, Bj)
- In this equation, MaxValue is some function of variables Ai and Bj.
- Where i and j are indices to the variables defined in the tree structure.
- Consider the following possible definition of MaxValue:

  MaxValue = (Ai x Bj)

Dynamic Programming Problem

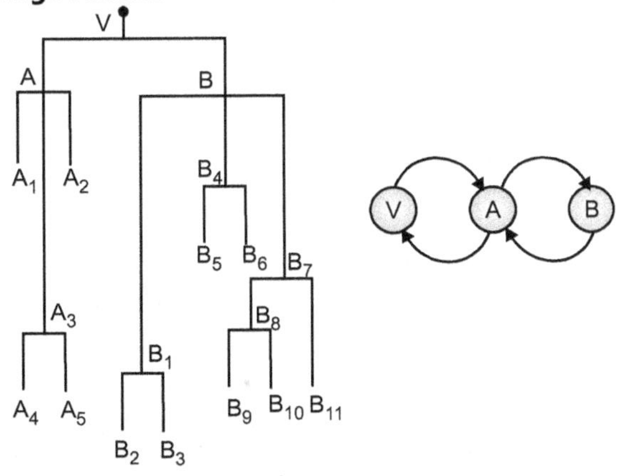

Fig. 3.21

- In this example, the solution is simply the largest value of A and the largest value of B. however, consider the following definition of MaxValue:

$$\text{Max Value} = \sqrt[3]{14 \times A^2/\log(A^2 + B^2)}$$

- In this example, the solution to MaxValue is less obvious and much more computationally intensive.

$$A = \begin{bmatrix} 2 \\ 3 \\ 8 \\ 4 \\ 1 \end{bmatrix} ; B = \begin{bmatrix} 9 \\ 11 \\ 1 \\ 0 \\ 3 \\ 8 \\ 1 \\ 7 \\ 5 \\ 3 \\ 2 \end{bmatrix}$$

- Solving for the first value of Ai (A1 = 2) and ignoring the specific equation for MaxValue for clarity
  MaxValue1, 1 = f (A1, B1) = f (2, 9) = 5
  MaxValue1, 2 = f (A1, B2) = f (2, 11) = 3
  MaxValue1, 3 = f (A1, B3) = f (2, 1) = 0
  MaxValue1, 4 = f (A1, B4) = f (2, 0) = 2
  MaxValue1, 5 = f (A1, B5) = f (2, 3) = 8
  MaxValue1, 6 = f (A1, B6) = f (2, 8) = 0
  MaxValue1, 7 = f (A1, B7) = f (2, 1) = -2
  MaxValue1, 8 = f (A1, B8) = f (2, 7) = 1
  MaxValue1, 9 = f (A1, B9) = f (2, 5) = 2
  MaxValue1, 10 = f (A1, B10) = f (2, 3) = 8
  MaxValue1, 11 = f (A1, B11) = f (2, 2) = 4
- The brute force methods of solving for MaxValue is to recursively walk down each of the tree and try the various combinations of A and B in the MaxValue equation.
- If the branches of A and B have hundreds of sub-branches, representing hundreds of values, then the problem is likely computationally infeasible.
- This is especially true if the MaxValue function, which must be evaluated for each combination of variables, is also computationally intensive.

- Instead of solving complex CPU and RAM intensive problem, the task is decomposed into hundreds or even thousands of easily and quickly solved problems.
- The solution set of MaxValue computed earlier for A1 appears in the first row of the matrix. Examining only this first row, it can be seen that there are two solutions to MaxValue, B5 and B10, each of which results in value of 8.
- With the completed solution matrix available for examination, it's a trivial matter to locate the best values for I and j, second-best, and so on. The same approach can be extended to any number of dimensions. Consider adding third variable the equation for MaxValue now takes the form:

  MaxValue = f (Ai, Bj, Ck)
- In this new equation, MaxValue is some function of variable Ai, Bj, Ck, where i, j, k are indices to the variables defined in the tree structure. However, the matrix of solutions is now much larger, and is better presented as a3D structure.
- To bring the power of dynamic programming into the realm of pairwise sequence alignment, consider MaxValue to be the aligned score for pairwise alignment of two sequences.
- MaxValue takes into account gap penalties, correct alignments, and imperfect alignments. After the matrix is filled in using the alignment score to determine MaxValue, the highest scoring path is followed back to the beginning of the alignment to define the best alignment of elements in the sequence, including gaps.
- For example :

  q) ATCGAGCA-GCATG...

  r) - - - - - GCATGCT...
- In this example, sequence q appears across the top and sequence r is listed across the side. The characters involved in the local alignment appear in bold.
- The three special provisions of this algorithm that favors local alignments are-
  1. Negative numbers are not allowed in the scoring matrix.
  2. Inexact matches are penalized.
  3. The best score is sought anywhere in the matrix, and not simply in the last column or row.
- Even though dynamic programming guarantees to find the best local or global alignment because the technique considers all possible alignments, the technique is computationally intensive.

(d) Word Methods

- BLAST and FASTA is called as word method of sequence alignment because these algorithm work at the level of words multiple polypeptides or nucleic acids instead of with individual polypeptides or nucleic acids.
- Both methods of sequence alignment are fast enough to support searching for alignments of query sequences against entire nucleotide or protein databases.

- The first step in the FASTA algorithm is to create a hash table of words from the query sequence. Hashing is a function that maps words to integers to get smaller set of values so that the search space is minimized.
- For Protein, word length is typically one or two amino acids long. For nucleic acid sequences, the word length is usually from four to six characters. In either case, the longer the word length, the more rapid and the less through the search.
- The characters are compared to those in the database, which has previously been processed into words of the same length. FASTA uses the Blosum50 substitution matrix to score the top-10 alignments that contains the most similar words. Producing an "optimized score" FASTA produces an expectation score, E, which represents the expected number of random alignments with z-scores greater than or equal to the value observed, thereby providing an estimate of the statistical significance of the results.

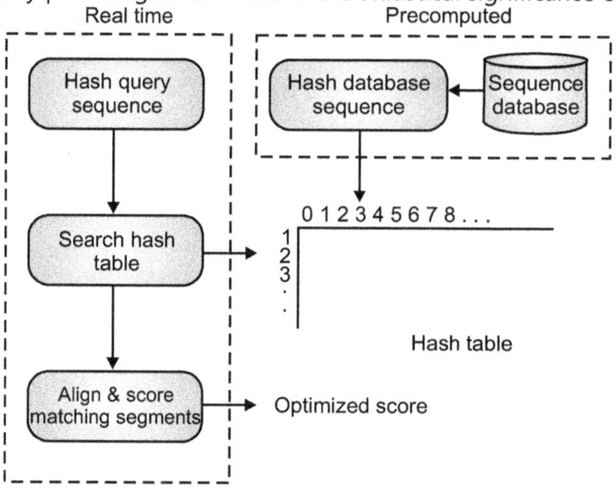

Fig. 3.22 : Diagram for FASTA algorithm flowchart.

- Although FASTA was the fire widely used program for sequence alignment against genome length sequences. BLAST is the more popular of the word-based algorithm for sequence alignment. Like FASTA, BLAST is a heuristic approach to sequence alignment that provides speed through a hashing technique. BLAST also differs from FASTA in that words are typically 3characters long for proteins and 11 characters in length for nucleotide sequences.
- Like FASTA BLAST also searches a pre-computed hash table of sequences in the protein or database. However, where BLAST excels that the matching words are then extended to the maximum length possible, as indicated by an alignment score. The latest version of BLAST can attempt gapped alignment. One of the major issues of both BLAST and FASTA results is how to interpret the significance of results. An individual score depend on a

number of variables, including the lengths of the sequences being aligned, the gap penalties, and the alignment scoring system used.

(e) Bayesian Methods

- Bayesian statistical methods can be used to determine pairwise sequence alignment and to estimate the evolutionary distance between DNA sequences.
- Bayesian methods involve examining the probabilities of all possible alignment, gap scores and substitution matrix values to access the probability of an alignment.
- Bayesian based tools such as the Bayesian block aligner, a workstation based tool available from the center for bioinformatics at Rensselaer and Wadsworth Center of New york Department of Health, performance better than dynamic programming in some cases, and not in all cases. The Block Aligner manipulates two sequences to find the highest-scoring contiguous regions (blocks), which are then joined in various combinations to form alignments.
- The Bayesian Block Aligner, which works with both DNA and protein sequences, doesn't require the user to specify a particular substitution matrix or gap scoring system.
- A web based Bayesian analysis tool, the Bayesian algorithm for Local Sequence Alignment (BALSA) is also available from the center.

3.6.2.1 Multiple Dequence Slignment

- Applications of multiple sequence alignment : aligning three or more sequences range from suggesting homologous relationships between several proteins to predicting probes for other members of the same family of similar sequences in a proteome.
- Although multiple sequence alignment can be performed on nucleotide sequences, its more often performed on polypeptide sequences, and draws upon many of the techniques used for single pairwise sequence alignment.

(a) Dynamic Programming

- This method is used for pairwise sequence alignment are easily extended to encompass multiple sequences.
- Algorithmically, there is little difference between a two or three dimensional alignment problem. Three or four sequence alignment is limit for workstation class hardware.
- For desktop work in multiple sequence alignment, several heuristic methods have been developed that provide results in reasonable time, even though it's usually impossible to prove that the results achieved through these methods are the best attainable.

(b) Progressive Strategies

- It takes the salami-slice approach to multiple sequence alignment. Instead of addressing the multi-dimensional problem head-on, this method breaks the multiple sequence alignment challenge into a series of pairwise alignment problem.

- The first pair of sequences is aligned, and then that result is aligned with the third sequence, and so on. Aligning each subsequent search with the previous alignment.
- Alternatively, the first pair of sequences can serve as the basis for aligning all subsequent sequences, which are then combined at the end of the process. Other alignment schemes are possible as well.
- The problem with progressive method is that the validity of the result varies greatly as a function of the order in which pairs of sequences are aligned.

(c) Iterative Strategy

- To overcome the limitation of progressive strategy iterative methods have been developed that correct the problem by repeatedly realigning subgroup of sequences. This method includes the use of genetic algorithm and HMMs.
- Approaches based on genetic algorithm generally start with a random definition of gap insertions and deletions and use the alignment score as the fitness function.
- Multiple alignment methods based on HMMs have been incorporated into a variety of tools. "Data Mining" a HMM is a statistical method for an ordered sequence of symbols, acting as a stochastic state machine that generate a symbol each time a transition is made from one state to next.
- A limitation of a HMM approach is that the model must be trained before it can be used. As such, HMMs tend to be problem-specific, albeit powerful.

(d) Other Strategies

- There are dozens of approaches to multiple sequence alignment, some relegated to specific laboratories, and other vying for use as a standard in the bioinformatics field. Many of these methods are highly specialized at solving specific types of multiple sequence alignment problems.

For example :

- eMOTIF method is optimized for identifying motifs in protein sequence.
- BLOCK analysis is used for working with conserved regions in multiple sequence alignment.

Tools for Pattern Matching

- Pattern-matching tools can be used in search engines and data-mining application, nucleotide and peptide sequence alignment applications generally dictate the use of bioinformatics-specific tools.
- Sequence alignment tools designed for nucleotide and polypeptide pattern alignment, there are support utility for format conversion, sequence editors, and protein and nucleotide database.

Tools	Examples
Nucleotide Pattern Alignment	BLASTN, BLASTX, TBLASTX, DotLet, BALSA
Polypeptide Pattern Alignment	BLASTP, PHI-BLAST, PSI-BLAST, Smith-Waterman, ScanPROSITE, ExPASy, DotLet, BALSA
Utilities	READSEQ, Text Editors
Protein Sequence Database	SWISS-PROT, TrEMBL, PROSITE, BLOCKS
Nucleotide Sequence Database	GenBank, Entrez Nucleotide database
Sequence Editor	CINEMA, GeneDoc, MACAW

(1) Nucleotide Pattern Matching

(a) BLAST

- The best known and most used nucleotide pattern-matching programs are the original Nucleotide-Nucleotide BLAST sometimes referred to as BLASTN and its derivative.
- In additional to the most resent version of BLAST, two popular derivatives are BLASTX (Nucleotide Query Blast) and TBLASTX (Nucleotide Query Translated Database).
- Executing a BLAST search for a pattern match involves simply filling out the template. The search string representing the nucleotide sequence data to be searched for is entered, in FASTA format, in the search field. The entire string can be used in the search, or only a subset location in the "From" and "To" fields of the "Set sequence" area.

(b) BALSA

- The BALSA tool, from the Center for Bioinformatics at Rensselaer and Wadsworth Center of the New York Department of Health, provides Web-based access to Bayesian-based sequence alignment.
- A virtually identical tool, BALSA Database Query, is available for database queries using either the PDB or the Structural Classification of Proteins (SCOP) databases.
- BALSA determines the probability that a given pair of sequences should be aligned by sampling alignments in proportion to their joint posterior probability.
- Output, which consists of the posterior probability for each scoring matrix/gap penalty/gap extension combination, is sent to the e-mail address entered on the form.
- A separate output is provided for each matrix-gap entry specified.

(2) Polypeptide Pattern Matching

(a) BLASTP

- Protein-protein BLAST (BLASTP) shares many of the features and options of BLASTN, with a focus on polypeptide Sequences instead of nucleotide sequences.
- The BLASTP interface is similar to the interface used with BLASTN. A feature in the basic BLASTP search is the "Do CD-Search" option, which is checked to compare protein sequences to the conserved domain (CD) database maintained by NCBI.
- The "DO CD-Search" option may be used to identify the conserved domains (module with distinct evolutionary origin and function) present in a protein sequence.

- Advanced options include the ability to specify a substitution matrix and gap costs. The PSSM field holds the matrix automatically computed by PSI-BLAST (Position Specific Iterative BLAST). A position specific scoring matrix (PSSM) is a matrix of scores representing a locally conversed region of a sequence of motif. PSI-BLAST, which is based on the BLAST algorithm, is enhanced to be more sensitive than BLASTP. A feature recently added to BLASTP is the ability to specify a PHI pattern, which is used by PHI-BLAST (Pattern Hit Initiated BLAST) to search for similarities that are presumably also homologues.

(b) Smith-Waterman

- The Smith-Waterman dynamic programming algorithm is available on the UCSC Kestrel Server, which is an experimental, high-performance, 512-processor system.
- Compared to the BLASTP interface with its array of options, the interface presented by the Kestrel Server appears somewhat limited.
- The Kestrel implementation of Smith-Waterman supports the use of PAM-10 through PAM-500 and BLOSUM30 through BLOSUM100 substitution matrices against the SWISS-PROT or NR protein databases, or a nucleotide search against the dbEST part 1 database.

(c) DotLet

- The DotLet dot matrix analysis program, available on the Expert Protein Analysis System (ExPASy) server, is one of the most popular of the Web-based dot matrix analysis programs.
- The program a Java applet supports the pairwise analysis of nucleotide or polypeptide sequences that are pasted into the pop-up input fields accessed by the "input" button. DotLet also supports a variety of matrices, sliding window size (1 to 15), and zoom (1:1 to 1:8) through pull-down menus along the top of the screen.

(3) Utilities

- Most pattern matching data accepts data in the FASTA format. Format conversion can be performed manually with a text editor or sequence editing utility such as READSQE. A web-based version of READSQE is available through the Bioinformatics & Molecular Analysis Section of the National Institute of Health.

(4) Sequence Databases

- The key protein databases used for sequence alignment are SWISS-PROT, TrEMBL, and PROSITE. These and other databases and tools are available through the ExPASY server of the Swiss Institute of Bioinformatics.
- SWISS-PROT is a highly annotated protein sequence database that is highly integrated with other databases in the ExPASy system. The TrEMBL database is a supplement of SWISS-PROT.
- PROSITE is a database of protein families and domains that contains high-level profiles such as categories of toxins, inhibitors, chaperone proteins, and hormones.

SUMMARY

- Data mining isn't an endpoint, but is one stage in an overall knowledge discovery process. It is an iterative process in which preceding are modified to support new hypothesis suggested by the data.
- Data mining is the process of identifying patterns and relationship in data that often are not obvious in large, complex data sets. As such data mining involves pattern recognition and, by extension, pattern discovery.
- In bioinformatics, pattern recognition is most often concerned with the automatic classification of character sequence representative of the nucleotide bases or molecular structures, and of 3D protein structures
- The pattern matching and pattern discovery components of data mining are often performed by machine learning techniques. Machine learning isn't a single technology or approach, but encompass a variety of methods that represent the convergence of several disciplines, including statistics, biological modeling, adaptive control theory, psychology, and artificial intelligence (AI).
- **Inductive Logic Programming :** It uses a set of rules of heuristics to categorize data. A common heuristics to use change an attribute of the data that will subset the data according to the attribute.
- **Genetic Algorithm :** Genetic algorithm are based on evolutionary principles wherein a particular function or definition that best fits the constraints an environment survives to the next generation, and the other functions are eliminated.
- **Neural Networks :** Neural networks are simulations loosely patterned after biological neurons. In molecular biology, they learn to associate input patterns with output patterns in a way that allows them to categorize new patterns and to extrapolate trends from data.
- **Statistical Methods :** The statistical methods used to support data mining are generally some form of feature extraction, classifications or clustering. Statistical feature extraction is concerned with recovering the defining data attributes that may be obscured by imperfect measurement, improper data processing, or noise in the data.
- **Decision Tree :** Decision trees are hierarchically arranged question and answers that lead to classification. As shown figure decision trees are formed by input nodes and tests on input data whose leaf nodes are categorize of those data.
- **Hidden Markov Model :** A powerful statistical approach to constructing classifiers that deserves a separate discussion is the use of Hidden Markov Modeling. Hidden Markov Model (HMM) is a statistical model for an ordered sequence of symbols, acting as a stochastic state machine that generate a symbol each time a transition made from one state to the next. Transitions between states are defined by transition probability.
- **Text Mining and Tools :** For humanity to benefit from bioinformatics research, the sequence and structure of proteins and other molecules must be linked to functional

data that links clinical medicine, pharmacology, sequence data, and structure data is in the form of biomedicine documents in online bibliographic databases such as PubMed.

- **Natural Language Processing :** The most promising approaches to text mining online documents rely on Natural Language Processing (NLP), a technology that encompasses a variety of computational methods ranging from simple keyword extraction to semantic analysis.
- **Text Summarization :** In addition to NLP, the text mining is facilitated by text summarization, a process that takes a page or more of text as its input and generates a summary paragraph as the output.
- **Pattern Matching :** Automated pattern matching is the ability of program to compare novel and known patterns and determine the degree of similarity.
- **Pairwise Sequence Alignment :** Pairwise sequence alignment involves the matching of two sequences, one pair of elements at a time.
- **Local Versus Global Alignment :** Sequence pair (E)-(F) is an example of a global alignment that is an attempt to line up the two sequences matching as many characters as possible, for the entire length of each segment.
- **Multiple Sequence Alignment :** In which three or more sequences must be aligned, is useful in finding conserved regulatory patterns in nucleotide sequences and for identifying structural functional domains in protein families.
- **Dot Matrix Analysis :** Because alignment by visual inspection of linear sequences hundreds characters or more in length was impractical, researchers developed is more visually intuitive method of pattern detection called the dot matrix method.
- **Substitution Metrics :** Protein structure and function surprisingly resistant to polypeptide substitution, to the degree that the substitutions don't alter the chemistry of the protein.
- **Dynamic Programming :** One way to be certain that the solution to a sequence alignment is the best alignment possible is to try every possible alignment, introducing one or more gaps at every position, and computing an alignment score based on aligned character pairs and inexact matches.
- **Word Methods :** BLAST and FASTA is called as word method of sequence alignment because these algorithm work at the level of words multiple polypeptides or nucleic acids instead of with individual polypeptides or nucleic acids.
- **Bayesian Methods :** Bayesian statistical methods can be used to determine pairwise sequence alignment and to estimate the evolutionary distance between DNA sequences.
- **Multiple Sequence Alignment :** Applications of multiple sequence alignment- aligning three or more sequences range from suggesting homologous relationships between several proteins to predicting probes for other members of the same family of similar sequences in a proteome.

- **Progressive Strategies :** It takes the salami-slice approach to multiple sequence alignment. Instead of addressing the multi-dimensional problem head-on, this method breaks the multiple sequence alignment challenge into a series of pairwise alignment problem.
- **Iterative Strategy :** To overcome the limitation of progressive strategy iterative methods have been developed that correct the problem by repeatedly realigning subgroup of sequences. This method includes the use of genetic algorithm and HMMs.
- **Other Strategies :** There are dozens of approaches to multiple sequence alignment, some relegated to specific laboratories, and other vying for use as a standard in the bioinformatics field. Many of these methods are highly specialized at solving specific types of multiple sequence alignment problems.
- **Tools for Pattern Matching :** Pattern-matching tools can be used in search engines and data-mining application, nucleotide and peptide sequence alignment applications generally dictate the use of bioinformatics-specific tools
- **Nucleotide Pattern Matching :**

  BLAST: The best known and most used nucleotide pattern-matching programs are the original Nucleotide-Nucleotide BLAST sometimes referred to as BLASTN and its derivative.

  BALSA: The BALSA tool, from the Center for Bioinformatics at Rensselaer and Wadsworth Center of the New York Department of Health, provides Web-based access to Bayesian-based sequence alignment.

Polypeptide Pattern Matching

- **BLASTP:** Protein-protein BLAST (BLASTP) shares many of the features and options of BLASTN, with a focus on polypeptide Sequences instead of nucleotide sequences.
- **Smith-Waterman:** The Smith-Waterman dynamic programming algorithm is available on the UCSC Kestrel Server, which is an experimental, high-performance, 512-processor system.
- **DotLet:** The DotLet dot matrix analysis program, available on the Expert Protein Analysis System (ExPASy) server, is one of the most popular of the Web-based dot matrix analysis programs.
- **Utilities:** Most pattern matching data accepts data in the FASTA format. Format conversion can be performed manually with a text editor or sequence editing utility such as READSQE. A web-based version of READSQE is available through the Bioinformatics & Molecular Analysis Section of the National Institute of Health.
- **Sequence Databases:** The key protein databases used for sequence alignment are SWISS-PROT, TrEMBL, and PROSITE. These and other databases and tools are available through the ExPASy server of the Swiss Institute of Bioinformatics.

QUESTIONS

MAY 2012

1. Explain in detail the various methods of data mining for extracting patterns from data. **[8]**

Ans. : Please refer Section No. 3.1.1.

MAY 2013

2. A What are the types of machine processes? Explain any two machines learning processes. **[8]**

Ans. : Please refer Section No. 3.4.

3. Write short notes on:
   (i) Pairwise Sequence Alignment (PSA)
   (ii) Multiple Sequence Alignment (MSA) **[8]**

Ans. : Please refer Section No. 3.6.1. **OR**

4. (a) Explain the text mining with NLP Process. **[8]**

Ans. : Please refer Section No. 3.5.1.

(b) Explain computational methods of Sequence alignment.

Ans. : Please refer Section No. 3.6.2.

(c) Dynamic programming

Ans. : Please refer Section No. 3.6.2.

(d) Word method

Ans. : Please refer Section No. 3.6.2.

MAY 2014

5. (a) Explain text mining with NLP process. **[8]**

Ans. : Please refer Section No. 3.5.1.

(b) Write short notes on:
(i) Pairwise Sequence Alignment (PSA)

Ans. : Please refer Section No. 3.6.1.

6. Multiple Sequence Alignment (MSA)

Ans. : Please refer Section No. 3.6.1. **OR**

7. (a) What are the various computational methods of sequence alignment ? Explain any Two methods in detail. **[8]**

Ans. : Please refer Section No. 3.6.2.

(b) How the machine learning techniques are used in bioinformatics ? Discuss any two machine learning methods with BI applications. **[8]**

Ans. : Please refer Section No. 3.4.

❍ ❍ ❍

UNIT IV

MODELING, SIMULATION AND COLLABORATION

4.1 MODEL

"A model is an abstraction of a real world system."

In other words, it is

- A representation of the objects or quantities within the system.
- The rules that govern the interaction between them
- Systems that are best suited to being simulated are dynamic, interactive and complicated.

4.2 SIMULATION

"Simulation is RUNNING a model to PREDICT the result of experimental CHANGES in the system."

- Simulation is nothing but doing "What If" analysis. What happens if I change this? What happens if I don't?

4.3 INTRODUCTION

Experimental molecular biology research is often a painstakingly slow process that typically involves a long sequence of carefully performed experiments, using a variety of equipment and laboratory specialists.

- For example: Positively identifying a protein by structure may takes years of work.
- The protein must be isolated, purified, crystallized and then imaged.
- Because each step may involve dozens of failed attempts. many scientist. Not primarily interested in the experimental methods.
- In determining protein structure, the primary alternative to experimental or web-lab techniques is bioinformatics.
- Although computational methods may be able to deliver solution to a molecular biology problem such as structure determination in days or weeks instead of month or years. The solution is only as good as the formulation of the problem.
- In case of protein structure determination or prediction, formulating the problem entails creating a model of the molecule and the major environmental factors that may influence its structure.
- With a valid model definition, arriving at a solution that is, using the model to drive a simulation of the molecules behavior and structure is simply a matter of executing a program and then evaluating the result. The example of modeling and simulation in

bioinformatics is the "Killer app" on the desktop microcomputer –the one application that raised the status of the technology from a hobbyist's plaything to a "must have" in business and in the laboratory-was the now –defunct electronic spreadsheet, VisiCalc:

- This spreadsheet enabled accountants, engineers and physicists to interactively run a variety of what it scenarios or implicit attempts at problem formulation to predict the outcomes of virtually any activity that they could express mathematically.
- VisiCalc's initial success was due largely to its easy- to- understand user interface of rows and columns of cells interrelated by position and formulas and a powerful back-end that interpreted the formulas and graphed the output.

4.4 APPLICATIONS OF MODELING AND SIMULATION IN BIOINFORMATICS

- Clinical What If analysis
- Drug Discovery and Development
- Exploring Toxicology
- Exploring Genetic Drift
- Exploring Molecular Mechanisms of Action
- Personal Health Prediction
- Drug Efficacy Prediction
- Drug Side-Effects Prediction
- Gene Expression Prediction
- Protein folding Prediction
- Protein Function Prediction
- Protein Structure Prediction
- Metabolic pathway visualization
- Pharmacokinetic Visualization

4.5 DRUG DISCOVERY

Pharma, the primary backer of bioinformatics R and D worldwide, is keenly interested in automating and speeding the drug discovery and development process.

- The typical drug discovery and development process show in figure. an involves an often arduous series of events that starts with perhaps 5,000 candidate drug molecules and ends with a single product that can be brought to market .
- Because any technology that can shorten the discovery and development process has the potential to save the industry billions of dollars, there is considerable Rand D involved in replacing or supple minting the drug discovery process with modeling and simulation.

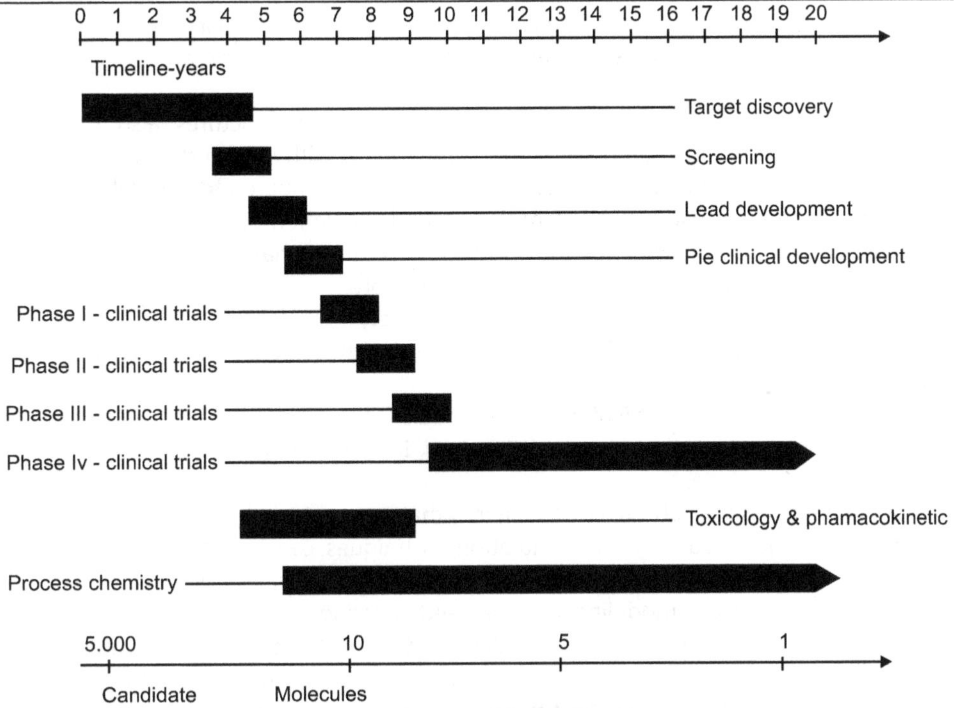

Fig. 4.1 (a) : Drug discovery & development process

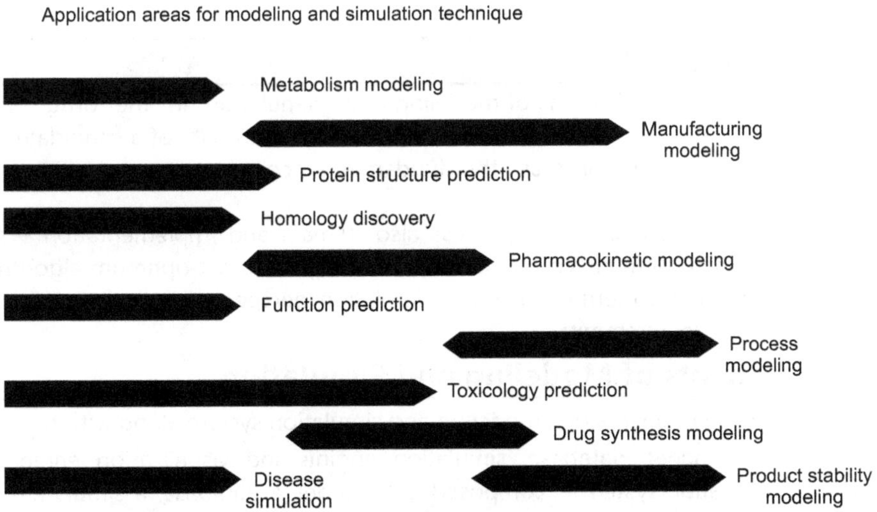

Fig. 4.1 (b) : Application areas for modeling and simulation technique

- A better understanding of the underlying metabolism of particular disease or condition can suggest which molecules will be most effective for treatment, and which ones may cause toxic reaction in a patient.
- Similarly, assuming that protein molecules with similar structures also have similar function, modeling protein structure and comparing it with known drugs can potentially serve as a more effective screener for candidate drugs, compared to wet- lab techniques.
- Later in the drug discovery process, modeling and simulation of pharmacokinetics and of drug absorption can potentially be used to shorten clinical trials.

Currently, each phase of clinical trials takes a year or more.

Phase 1 : Involving about 100 subject , deals with safety

Phase 2 : This involves about 200 subjects, deals with evidence for efficacy at various dosages.

Phase 3 : Involving up to about 5,000 subjects , deals with assessing the

Phase 4 : This begins with the release of the drug. Involves monitoring patients for adverse reactions.

- The FDA approves only about 1molecule in 5 that makes it to phase 1 clinical trial.
- As shown in Fig. modeling and simulation techniques can also be applied to various aspects of the drug development process.
- For example : process modeling can be used, starting around year nine of the drug discovery and development process, to develop the most effective development process.
- Similarly the manufacturing process can be modeled to determine the best use of materials product stability and best method of product synthesis – all without modifying the actual process.

4.6 FUNDAMENTALS

The numerous potential applications of modeling and simulation in the drug discovery process illustrate that whether the intent is to predict the toxicity of a candidate drug or to streamline the screening process, the fundamental components and processes are identical.

- However. The drug discovery process also domain and implementation – specific issues, including numeric considerations, selecting the most optimum algorithms for a given problem. Determining which simulation perspective best fits the problem, and hardware requirements.

4.6.1 Components of Modeling and Simulation

Discuss in brief the components of a modeling and simulation system along with the process.

System includes a model, database, simulation engine and visualization engine. Every modeling and simulation system is composed of a model, a database, a simulation engine and a visualization engine.

- The user and some form of feedback device such as computer monitor are normally considered key elements as well.
- These components aren't necessarily separate entities as shown in [Fig. 4.2] but may be combined and integrated in various ways.
- For example : the model and data may be combined within the simulation engine, or the simulation engine and visualization engine may be combined.
- Regardless of how they are represented in a system, each component is necessary for operation of the simulation.
- The components of a simulation system typically vary in form. Complexity, and completeness, as a function of what is being modeled and the required fidelity of the simulation.
- For example : the model which can be a mathematical equation, a logical description encoded as rules, or a group of algorithms that describes objects and their interrelationship in the real world, defines the underlying nature of the simulation.

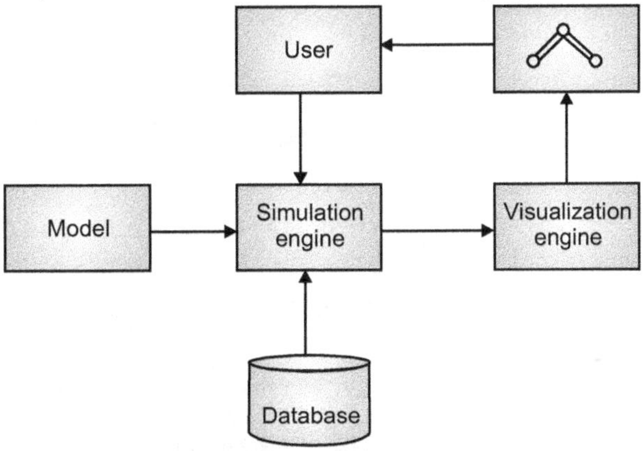

Fig. 4.2 : Components of modeling and simulation

The database may take the form of a few lines of data embedded as statements within the model code, or consist of separate text file that describes variables and constants that can be used with the underlying model.

- However in most bioinformatics applications, the database consists of a large, complex system that contains libraries of data that can be applied to the underlying model.
- The contents of the database typically range from physical constants. Such as the band lengths of covalently bound atoms, to user : defined input such as heuristics regarding situation in which the underlying model can be applied.
- The simulation engine consists of functions that are evaluated over time, and triggered by time, events, or the value of intermediate simulation results.

- The simulation engine takes the model, data from the database, and direction from the user to create on output that corresponds to a condition in the real world, such as a description of the folding of a protein molecule in an aqueous solution. The visualization engine takes the output of the simulation engine and formats it into a more user friendly form.
- For example: a string of digits can be formatted into a 30 rendition of a protein structure. The visualization engine may be little more than a text- formatting utility or it can take the form of a high – performance, real – time, high – resolution 30 rendering engine.

4.6.2 Modeling and Simulation Process

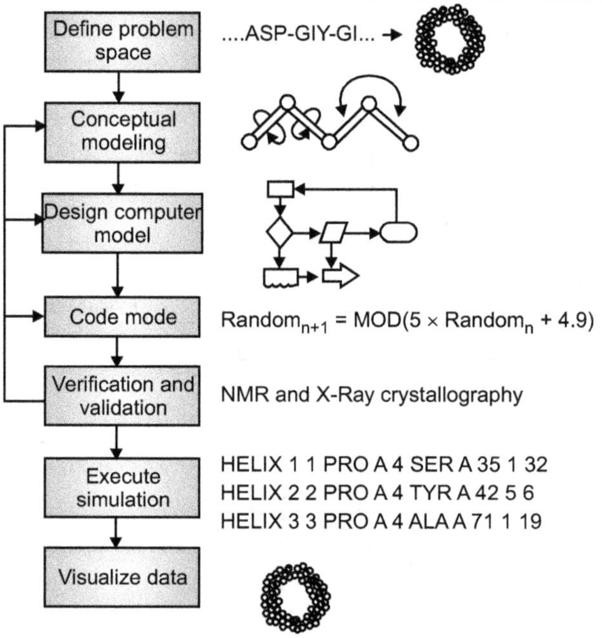

Fig. 4.3 : Process of modeling and simulation

The basic modeling and simulation process outlined in [Fig. 4.3] is application to most problems in bioinformatics.

1. The first step is to define the problem space such as protein structure from amino acid Sequence data : one application of modeling among the many depicted by [Fig. 4.3].

- Defining the problem space involves specifying the objectives and requirements of the simulation, including the required accuracy of results.

- This phase of the process can also involve establishing how an observer in some experimental frame observes or interacts with some part of reality.
- An experimental frame defines the set of conditions under which a system will be observed, including initial states, terminal conditions, specification for data collations and observable variables and their magnitudes.
- The system represents a collection of objects, their relationship and the behaviors that characterize them as some part of reality.
- The underlying assumption in defining the problem space is that the phenomenon or problem to be modeled can be positively identified and measured.

2. Once the problem space has been defined, the next place in the modeling and simulation process is conceptual modeling which involves mapping the system objects, relationships, processes and behaviors to some sort of organized structure.

- For example **:** in predicting protein structure from sequence data **,** the conceptual modeling might entail using ab initio methods i.e. working from first principles **,** such as bond length and angles to construct the secondary and tertiary structures **.**
- Activities at this phase of the process include documenting assumptions about the system so that the appropriate simulation methods can be selected**.**
- For example : it ab initio methods are going to be used to predict protein structure from sequence data then an underlying assumption is that the data on amino acid sequence , bond length , bond angles and related atomic – level data are not only available , but the data are accurate to some verifiable level **.**

3. The next phase of modeling and simulation process is translating the conceptual model into data structures and high level descriptions of computational procedures. Designing the computer model involves extracting from the conceptual model only those characteristics of the original system that are deemed essential, as determined by the model's ultimate purpose.

- For example :

  The purpose of predicting protein structure from sequence data may be to allow the end-user to visualize the protein structure.

  So that a high degree of accuracy isn't that essential.

4. Designing the computer model, like defining the problem space and conceptual modeling, is largely an art.

- Designing a simple model that adequately mimics the behavior of the system or process under study is creative process that incorporates certain assumptions.
- The art of making good assumptions may well be the most challenging component of modeling. Considering success depends as much on the domain experience of the modeler as it does on the nature of the system to be modeled.

5. Coding of the computer model involves transferring the symbolic representations of the system into executable computer code.

- Model coding marks the transition of the modeling process from an artistic endeavor to a predominantly scientific one, defined by software engineering principles.
- Model level coding may involve working with a low level computer language such as c++ or a high-level shell designed especially for modeling and simulation.

6. Once the model is in the form of executable code. It should be subject to verification and validation.

- Verification is the process of demining that the model coded in software accurately reflects the conceptual model by testing the internal logic of a model to confirm that it is functioning as intended.
- The simulation system and its underlying model are consistent with the real world usually through comparison with data from the system being simulated.
- For example :

  In a system designed to predict protein structure, the validation process would include comparing model data with protein structure data from NRM and X-ray crystallography.

7. Executing the simulation ideally generates the output data that can illustrate or answer the problem initially identified in the problem space.

- Depending on the methods used, the amount of process and time required to generate the needed data may be extensive.

8. Visualizing the output data opens the simulator output to human inspection, especially if the output is in the form of 3D graphics that can be accessed qualitatively instead of in tables of textual data.

- Documentation, although not represented as a formal step is key to model validation, reuse and communication with others.
- For example :

  The data format used by many molecular modeling systems follows the PDB format which includes extensive documentation with each molecule described in the database.

4.7 PROTEIN STRUCTURE

Knowledge of protein structure is generally considered a prerequisite to understanding protein function and by extension, a cornerstone of proteomics research.

- Because months and sometime years are involved in verifying protein structure through experimental methods. Computational methods of modeling and predicting protein structure are currently viewed as the only viable means of quickly determining the structure of a newly discovered protein.

- Proteins, like gens, don't exit as linear sequences of molecules but assume complex compact 3D shapes. Protein shapes are characterized as secondary, tertiary or quaternary.
- The primary protein configuration : the simple linear sequence of covalently bound amino acid is functionally uninteresting. The secondary structure is the local geometry along the sequence, typically in the form of sheets, coils, loops and helices.
- Most proteins are composed of a combination of secondary structures. A protein tertiary structure describes how the molecules folds in 3D space. Quaternary structure describes the complex configuration of a protein that is interacting with other molecules in 3D space.
- There are two main computational alternatives to experimental methods of determining or predicting secondary and tertiary protein structure from sequence data.
- The first approach is based on ab initio methods which involve reasoning from first principles. The second approach often termed heuristic methods is based on some form of pattern matching using knowledge of existing protein structures.
- The ab initio method relies on molecular physics and ignores any relationship of the molecule with other proteins. Heuristic methods in contrast use information contained in known protein structure. [Fig. A] shows flowchart of the methods available for determining or predating protein structure from protein structure data.
- The difference between the two approaches can be appreciated with parallel approaches in archaeology. When a fossilized skeleton of a small animals discovered .one approach to reconstructing the physical structure of the animal.

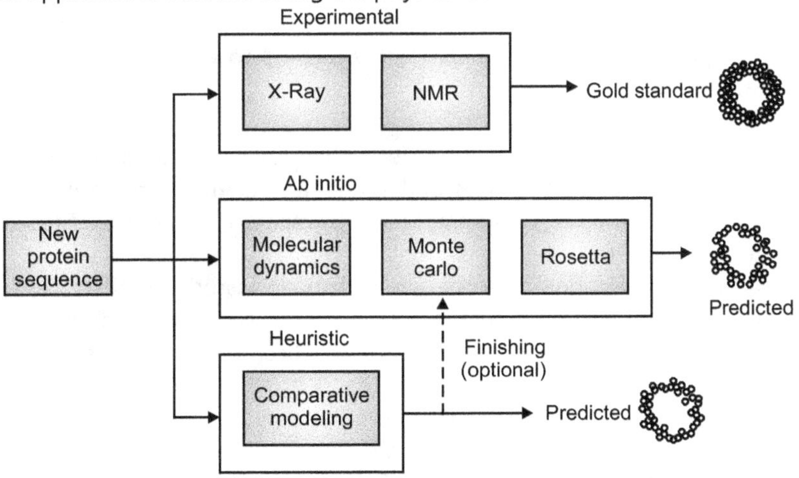

Fig. 4.4 : Computational methods of protein structure prediction versus experimental protein structure determination methods

- Ab initio and heuristic methods promise to provide less accurate but more timely results compare to experimental methods that can require a year or more of research per molecule and its lifecycle is to reason from first principles, using the size, arrangement, thickness of the various bones, the size of the brain case and other physical indicators, such as the bowing of the long bones (which indicate the amount of musculature present).
- Wear patterns on the teeth might suggest a diet rich in grains and the presence of cannies may suggest the animal was omnivorous. The second approach to assessing the fossil of the extinct animal is to compare the skeleton with those of known animals.
- The leg and arm bones may approximate those of small modern monkey. For example : The teeth may approximate those of a modern primate with large, flat molars and prominent cannies.
- Comparing fossilized skeleton of animals with those of modern animals is frequently practiced because it's easy, rapid and to the best of our knowledge, fairly accurate.
- Reasoning from first principles is usually reserved for those cases where there is nothing resembling the newly discovered fossil in the current fossil record. For example : First principles may be used to reconstruct the general body shape and stature of the extinct animal, but given no indication of the extinct animal, but given no indication of the skin or hair coloring.
- Similarly, in bioinformatics, ab initio and heuristic methods of determining protein structure are commonly used in parallel or sequentially because of the accuracy limitations of either approach when used alone.
- For example : Hand editing is commonly applied to ab initio data to improve the accuracy of the results.

Protein Classification

- Proteins may be classified according to both structural and sequence similarity. For structural classification, the sizes and spatial arrangements of secondary structures described in the above paragraph are compared in known three-dimensional structures.
- Classification based on sequence similarity was historically the first to be used. Initially, similarity based on alignments of whole sequences was performed. Later, proteins were classified on the basis of the occurrence of conserved amino acid patterns.
- Databases that classify proteins by one or more of these schemes are available. In considering protein classification schemes, it is important to keep several observations in mind. First, two entirely different protein sequences from different evolutionary origins may fold into a similar structure.

- Conversely, the sequence of an ancient gene for a given structure may have diverged considerably in different species while at the same time maintaining the same basic structural features.
- Recognizing any remaining sequence similarity in such cases may be a very difficult task. Second, two proteins that share a significant degree of sequence similarity either with each other or with a third sequence also share an evolutionary origin and should share some structural features also. However, gene duplication and genetic rearrangements during evolution may give rise to new gene copies, which can then evolve into proteins with new function and structure.
- **Terms Used for Classifying Protein Structures and Sequences :** The more commonly used terms for evolutionary and structural relationships among proteins are listed below. Many additional terms are used for various kinds of structural features found in proteins.
- Descriptions of such terms may be found at the CATH Web site the Structural Classification of Proteins (SCOP) Web site and a Glaxo-Wellcome tutorial on the Swiss bioinformatics Expasy Web site.
- **Active Site :** A localized combination of amino acid side groups within the tertiary (three-dimensional) or quaternary (protein subunit) structure that can interact with a chemically specific substrate and that provides the protein with biological activity. Proteins of very different amino acid sequences may fold into a structure that produces the same active site.
- **Architecture :** the relative orientations of secondary structures in a three-dimensional structure without regard to whether or not they share a similar loop structure.
- **Fold :** A type of architecture that also has a conserved loop structure.
- **Blocks :** A conserved amino acid sequence pattern in a family of proteins. The pattern includes a series of possible matches at each position in the represented sequences, but there are not any inserted or deleted positions in the pattern or in the sequences. By way of contrast, sequence profiles are a type of scoring matrix that represents a similar set of patterns that includes insertions and deletions.
- **Class :** A term used to classify protein domains according to their secondary structural content and organization. Four classes were originally recognized by Levitt and Chothia (1976), and several others have been added in the SCOP database. Three classes are given in the CATH database: mainly-α, mainly-β, and α–β, with the α–β class including alternating α /B and α+β structures.
- **Core :** The portion of a folded protein molecule that comprises the hydrophobic interior of α-helices and β-sheets. The compact structure brings together side groups of amino acids into close enough proximity so that they can interact. When comparing protein structures, as in the SCOP database, core is the region common to

most of the structures that share a common fold or that are in the same superfamily. In structure prediction, core is sometimes defined as the arrangement of secondary structures that is likely to be conserved during evolutionary change.

- **Domain (Sequence Context) :** A segment of a polypeptide chain that can fold into a three-dimensional structure irrespective of the presence of other segments of the chain. The separate domains of a given protein may interact extensively or may be joined only by a length of polypeptide chain. A protein with several domains may use these domains for functional interactions with different molecules.
- **Family (Sequence Context) :** A group of proteins of similar biochemical function that are more than 50% identical when aligned. This same cutoff is still used by the Protein Information Resource (PIR). A protein family comprises proteins with the same function in different organisms (orthologous sequences) but may also include proteins in the same organism (paralogous sequences) derived from gene duplication and rearrangements
- **Family (Structural Context) :** As used in the FSSP database (Families of structurally similar proteins) and the DALI/FSSP Web site, two structures that have a significant level of structural similarity but not necessarily significant sequence similarity.
- **Fold :** Similar to structural motif, includes a larger combination of secondary structural units in the same configuration. Thus, proteins sharing the same fold have the same combination of secondary structures that are connected by similar loops. An example is the Rossman fold comprising several alternating α helices and parallel β strands. In the SCOP, CATH, and FSSP databases, the known protein structures have been classified into hierarchical levels of structural complexity with the fold as a basic level of classification.
- **Homologous Domain (Sequence Context) :** An extended sequence pattern, generally found by sequence alignment methods, that indicates a common evolutionary origin among the aligned sequences. A homology domain is generally longer than motifs.
- **Module :** A region of conserved amino acid patterns comprising one or more motifs and considered to be a fundamental unit of structure or function. The presence of a module has also been used to classify proteins into families.
- **Motif (sequence context) :** A conserved pattern of amino acids that is found in two or more proteins. In the Prosite catalog, a motif is an amino acid pattern that is found in a group of proteins that have a similar biochemical activity, and that often is near the active site of the protein.
- **Motif (Structural Context) :** A combination of several secondary structural elements produced by the folding of adjacent sections of the polypeptide chain into a specific three-dimensional configuration.

- **Primary Structure :** the linear amino acid sequence of a protein, which chemically is a polypeptide chain, composed of amino acids joined by peptide bonds.
- **Profile (Sequence Context) :** a scoring matrix that represents a multiple sequence alignment of a protein family. The profile is usually obtained from a well-conserved region in a multiple sequence alignment. The profile is in the form of a matrix with each column representing a position in the alignment and each row one of the amino acids. Matrix values give the likelihood of each amino acid at the corresponding position in the alignment. The profile is moved along the target sequence to locate the best scoring regions by a dynamic programming algorithm. Gaps are allowed during matching and a gap penalty is included in this case as a negative score when no amino acid is matched
- **Profile (Structural Context) :** A scoring matrix that represents which amino acids should fit well and which should fit poorly at sequential positions in a known protein structure. Profile columns represent sequential positions in the structure, and profile rows represent the 20 amino acids. As with a sequence profile, the structural profile is moved along a target sequence to find the highest possible alignment score by a dynamic programming algorithm. Gaps may be included and receive a penalty. The resulting score provides an indication as to whether or not the target protein might adopt such a structure.
- **Quaternary Structure :** The three-dimensional configuration of a protein molecule comprising several independent polypeptide chains.
- **Secondary Structure :** The interactions that occur between the C, O, and NH groups on amino acids in a polypeptide chain to form α-helices, β-sheets, turns, loops, and other forms, and that facilitate the folding into a three-dimensional structure.
- **Superfamily :** A group of protein families of the same or different lengths that are related by distant yet detectable sequence similarity. Members of a given superfamily thus have a common evolutionary origin.
- **Supersecondary Structure :** A term with similar meaning to a structural motif. Tertiary structure is the three-dimensional or globular structure formed by the packing together or folding of secondary structures of a polypeptide chain.

Secondary Structure

Secondary Structure Prediction : A set of techniques in bioinformatics that aim to predict the local secondary structures of proteins and RNA sequences based only on knowledge of their primary structure amino acid or nucleotide sequence, respectively.

- For proteins, a prediction consists of assigning regions of the amino acid sequence as likely alpha helices, beta strands (often noted as "extended" conformations), or turns. The success of a prediction is determined by comparing it to the results of the DSSP algorithm applied to the crystal structure of the protein; for nucleic acids, it may be determined from the hydrogen bonding pattern.

- Specialized algorithms have been developed for the detection of specific well-defined patterns such as transmembrane helices and coiled coils in proteins, or canonical microRNA structures in RNA.
- The best modern methods of secondary structure prediction in proteins reach about 80% accuracy; this high accuracy allows the use of the predictions in fold recognition and ab initio protein structure prediction, classification of structural motifs, and refinement of sequence alignments.
- The accuracy of current protein secondary structure prediction methods is assessed in weekly benchmarks such as LiveBench and EVA.

Tertiary Structure

The practical role of protein structure prediction is now more important than ever. Massive amounts of protein sequence data are produced by modern large-scale DNA sequencing efforts such as the Human Genome Project.

- Despite community wide efforts in structural genomics, the output of experimentally determined protein structures typically by time-consuming and relatively expensive X-ray crystallography or NMR spectroscopy is lagging far behind the output of protein sequences.
- The protein structure prediction remains an extremely difficult and unresolved undertaking. The two main problems are calculation of protein free energy and finding the global minimum of this energy.
- A protein structure prediction method must explore the space of possible protein structures which is astronomically large. These problems can be partially bypassed in "comparative" or homology modeling and fold recognition methods, in which the search space is pruned by the assumption that the protein in question adopts a structure that is close to the experimentally determined structure of another homologous protein.
- On the other hand, the de novo or ab initio protein structure prediction methods must explicitly resolve these problems.

Quaternary Structure

In the case of complexes of two or more proteins, where the structures of the proteins are known or can be predicted with high accuracy, protein–protein docking methods can be used to predict the structure of the complex.

- Information of the effect of mutations at specific sites on the affinity of the complex helps to understand the complex structure and to guide docking methods.

4.7.1 Ab Initio Methods

Pure ab initio methods of determining protein structure are based on sequence data and the physics of molecular physics.

- Reasoning from first principles assumes that the shape of a protein can be defined as a function of the amino acid sequence, the temperature, pressure, PH and other local conditions without knowledge of the biology associated with the molecule.
- For example :
  The fact that protein unfolds or becomes denatured at elevated temperatures and reverts to its normal, active, folded state can be modeled irrespective of the structure or function of the structure or function of the protein.
- However, unlike our knowledge of physics or other hard science, our understanding of the first principles of molecular biology is largely incomplete.
- As a result, attempts thus far at using first principles as the basis for determining protein structure have been successful primarily as a means of defining limited areas (finishing) of the global protein architecture.
- For example : With the overall protein structure approximately known reasoning from first principles can be used to define a particular bond in the structure.
- Because of the computational demands associated with ab initio methods. Assumptions and simplifications are required for all but the smallest proteins.
- Additional assumptions are that bond lengths are constant and that bond length is a function of the two atoms involved in the bond.
- Bond angles, which are a function of the relative position of three atoms, are also assumed to be constant.
- Bond angles, which are limited to the range of about 100 to 180 degrees, are a function of the type of atoms involved and the number of free electrons available for bonding.

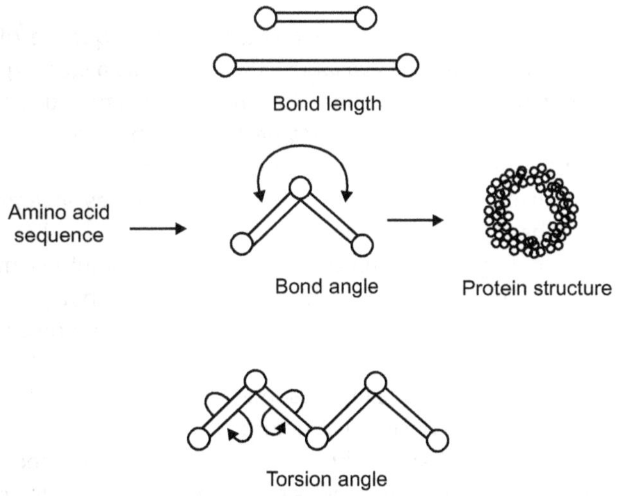

Fig. 4.5 : Ab initio protein structure determination.

- Based on the proteins amino acid sequence (primary structure). Secondary and tertiary structures are computed.
- A tertiary structure typically takes the form of XYZ coordinates for each atom in the protein molecule.
- Many ab initio methods assume that protein secondary and tertiary structures are a function of bond lengths, bond angles and torsion angles.

4.7.2 Heuristic Methods

While ab initio methods of protein structure prediction can be used to identify novel structures from sequence data alone, they're too computationally intensive to work with all but smallest proteins.

- For most proteins of unknown structure, short of x-ray crystallography and nuclear magnetic resonance (MNR) studies, heuristic methods offer the fastest, most accurate means of delivering structure from amino acid sequence data.
- Heuristic methods use a database of protein structures to make predictions about the structure of newly sequence proteins.
- A basic premise of heuristic methods is that most newly sequenced proteins share structural similarities with proteins whose structures and sequences are known, and that these structures can serve as templates for new sequences.
- It's also assumed that because relatively substantial changes in amino acid sequence may not significantly alter protein structure, similarly in sequences implies similarity in structure.
- The primary limitation of a heuristic approach to protein structure prediction is that it can't model a novel structure.
- There must be a suitable template meaning that the sequence of the template and the new protein can be aligned available to work with as a starting point.
- For this reason, heuristic approaches often have difficulty with novel mutations that include structural changes in the new (target) protein molecule.
- The main heuristic method of predicting protein structure from amino acid sequence data is comparative modeling that is, finding similarities in amino acid sequence, independent of the molecules lineage.
- Comparative modeling is sometimes confused with homology modeling. However, homology implies ancestral relationships, and assumes that protein from the same families share folding motifs even if they don't share folding motifs even if they don't share the same sequence.
- In contrast, comparative modeling assumes that protein with similar amino acid sequences share the same basic 3D structure.
- Comparative modeling is an, multi-phase process. As outlined in [Fig. 4.6] given protein sequence data, the main phases of process are template selection, alignment, model building and evaluation.

- 3D visualization is often performed as part of the evaluation phase. The key activities in each phase of the comparative modeling process are outlined here.

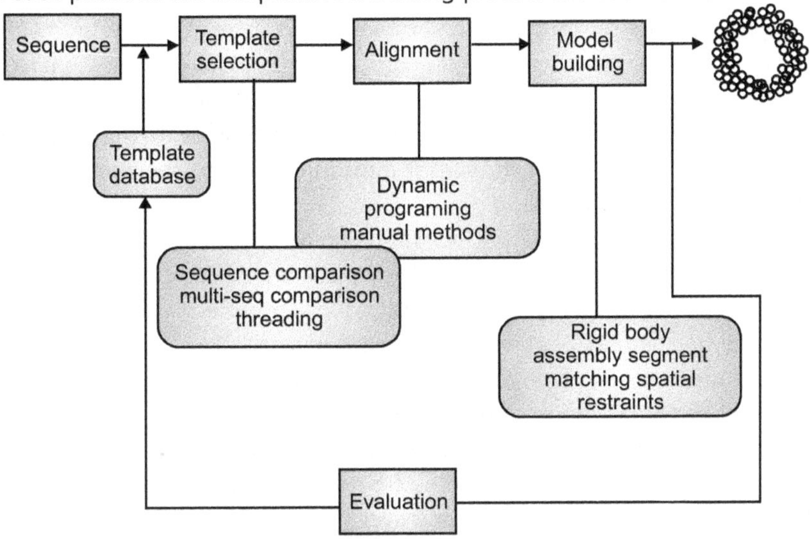

Fig. 4.6 : Comparative modeling process

- Not illustrated is the optional use of ab initio methods at the end of the model building phase to reduce errors in the computed structure.
- **The First :** Phase of the comparative modeling process, template selection, involves searching a template database for the closest match or matches to the new (target) molecule, based on the targets amino acid sequence.
- The goal of template selection is to discover a link between target protein and a known protein structure.
- **The Second :** Phase is alignment the goal of this phase is to align the sequence of polypeptides in the target sequence with that of the template structure in order to position the target and template in the same 3D orientation.
- Once the libraries of templates that match the target protein have been identified, the actual model building or assembly can begin.
- In evaluation process, visualization is key as a first pass screening tool used to validate gross measures, such as whether the model has the correct fold.

4.8 SYSTEM BIOLOGY

Just as genomics research, which focuses on sequencing of human and other genomes, is being supplanted by proteomic research as the work of sequencing has become commonplace, proteomic research has a limited lifespan as well.

- The focuses of bioinformatics will eventually coverage with clinical medicines at the cellular and the organ system level so called system biology.
- A major challenge in modeling and simulating systems biology is interesting high and low-level methods so that a more accurate picture of the entire biological process can be obtained.
- Integrating models of protein structure and function with those of biochemical pathways promises to provide insight into disease processes and by extension, the most efficacious designer drugs.
- Although some researchers are working with systems biology today, for the most part they are limited by both data and computational methods and power.
- A single cell might contain tens of thousands of molecules, each integrating with each other in complex ways not yet understood.
- Furthermore, not only must researchers understand the function of normal cells, but they must be able to model and simulate cells involved in cancer or HIV.
- For example : Today, the focus is on what can be practically accomplished with current technology and data, such as creating physiologically complete models and simulations of the heart, pancreas and liver.
- Although very broad clinical simulations of these and other organs have been developed for teaching purposes, the kinds of models applicable to drug research are at much greater level of in real time.
- With time, these requirements will be more easily met, as affordable desktop computing power continues in performance.
- What remains is for researchers to discover how to best apply this hardware towards solving the next generation of bioinformatics challenges.
- Systems biology (also known as Systeomics) is an emerging approach applied to biomedical and biological scientific research. Systems biology is a biology based interdisciplinary field of study that focuses on complex interactions within biological systems, using a holistic approach (holism instead of the more traditional reductionism) to biological and biomedical research.
- Particularly from year 2000 onwards, the concept has been used widely in the biosciences in a variety of contexts. One of the outreaching aims of systems biology is to model and discover emergent properties, properties of cells, tissues and organisms functioning as a system whose theoretical description is only possible using techniques which fall under the remit of systems biology.
- These typically involve metabolic networks or cell signaling networks. Systems biology makes heavy use of mathematical and computational models.
- Systems biology can be considered from a number of different aspects.

- As a field of study, particularly, the study of the interactions between the components of biological systems, and how these interactions give rise to the function and behavior of that system (for example : the enzymes and metabolites in a metabolic pathway).
- As a paradigm, usually defined in antithesis to the so-called reductionist paradigm (biological organization), although fully consistent with the scientific method. The distinction between the two paradigms is referred to in these quotations:
- "The reductionist approach has successfully identified most of the components and many of the interactions but, unfortunately, offers no convincing concepts or methods to understand how system properties emerge...the pluralism of causes and effects in biological networks is better addressed by observing, through quantitative measures, multiple components simultaneously and by rigorous data integration with mathematical models".
- "Systems biology is about putting together rather than taking apart, integration rather than reduction. It requires that we develop ways of thinking about integration that are as rigorous as our reductionist programmes, but different. It means changing our philosophy, in the full sense of the term".
- As a series of operational protocols used for performing research, namely a cycle composed of theory, analytic or computational modeling to propose specific testable hypotheses about a biological system, experimental validation, and then using the newly acquired quantitative description of cells or cell processes to refine the computational model or theory.
- Since the objective is a model of the interactions in a system, the experimental techniques that most suit systems biology are those that are system wide and attempt to be as complete as possible. Therefore, transcriptomics, metabolomics, proteomics and high throughput techniques are used to collect quantitative data for the construction and validation of models.
- As the application of dynamical systems theory to molecular biology. Indeed, the focus on the dynamics of the studied systems is the main conceptual difference between systems biology and bioinformatics.
- As a socioscientific phenomenon defined by the strategy of pursuing integration of complex data about the interactions in biological systems from diverse experimental sources using interdisciplinary tools and personnel.
- This variety of viewpoints is illustrative of the fact that systems biology refers to a cluster of peripherally overlapping concepts rather than a single well delineated field. However the term has widespread currency and popularity as of 2007, with chairs and institutes of systems biology proliferating worldwide.

4.8.1 Tools

Modeling and simulation are complex operations that tax even the most advanced hardware.

- Developing modeling and simulation systems de novo requires knowledge of advanced computing techniques, from markov modeling to network computing and numerical calculus.
- Fortunately, a wide variety of modeling simulation tool is available on the web and from commercial vendors.
- For example :
  A tool such as prospect (protein structure prediction and evaluation computer tool kit) a threading based protein structure prediction program, can be used as part of a comparative modeling process.
- A commercial system, such as extend, can be used to determine the most cost-effective means of staffing the research lab, based on a model of individual researcher output and the overall protein structure modeling process.

Table 4.1 : Modeling and simulation tools

Tool	Examples
1. Database	CATH, GenBank, GenCensus, ModBase, PDB, Presage, SWISS-PROT+TrEMBL
2. Template search	123D, BLAST, DALI, FastA, Matchmaker, PHD, PROFIT, Threader, UALA-DOE FRSVR
3. Sequence Alignment	BCM server, BLAST, Block maker, CLUSTAL, FASTA III, MULtalin
4. Modeling	Coposer, Congen, CPH Models, Dragon, ICM Insight II, Modeller, Look, Quanta, Sybyl, Scwrl, Seiss-Mod, What If.
5. Verification	Anolea, Aqua, Biotech, Errat, Procheck, Proceryon, Prosall, PROVE, SQUID, VERIFY3DWHATCHECK
6. Visualization	CHIMERA, SWISS-PDBViewer, RasMol, Pymol
7. Academic	SLAM III
8. Commercial	Extend, Crystal Ball, MedModel, ProModel simul8, Micro Saint, ACSL, Arna, GPSS/H iThink, MAST, MODSIM III simprocess, Taylor II

Draw and explain Collaboration Communication model with appropriate examples.

4.9 COLLABORATION AND COMMUNICATION

When the human genome project started in 1990. Web browsers hadn't been invented cell phones were lunch kit-sized luxury items the volume of e-mail was a distant fourth behind telephone, fax and surface mail communications and academic journal publisher expected printed manuscripts for submissions.

- Today e-mail competes head on with surface mail and the telephone as a means of communications in business and academia.
- Networks support real-time collaboration between researchers distributed around the globe and academic publishing revolves around timely e-mail submissions.
- As another indicator of the shift in perception of the increased worth of electronic communications, the national library of congress changed its policy on electronic documents and accepted the first copyright application for an electronic book this authors the Hitchhikers Guide to the wireless web in July of 2001.

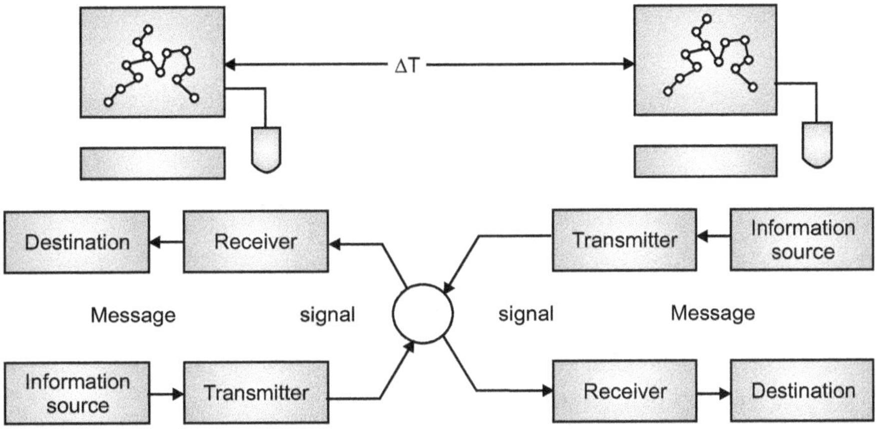

Fig. 4.7 : Collaboration and communication model

- The time delay (delta T) which is a function of the system design and bandwidth, defines the level of communications and collaboration possible.
- Engineers commonly characterize electronic communication as either asynchronous or synchronous fax, e-mail, streaming video, online journals, bulletin boards, newsgroups, and voicemail are forms of asynchronous communications.
- Synchronous or real time communications includes the use of the telephone, instant messaging, chat rooms and video conferencing.
- Electronic communication is essential to most R & D activities in bioinformatics. However, collaboration is even more valuable.
- Collaboration the act of working in a group to achieve a common goal follows basic model define [Fig. 4.7].
- In order to achieve common goal there is a real or virtual place for collaborations to work and share perspectives to view common work and to interactively evaluate and critique each other's contributions to achieving the goal.
- Communication and collaboration rely on a variety of technology for the creation, modification, use and transfer of data activities that taken together constitute knowledge management.

- As described in following sections, the technology requirements increase as a function of the collaboration communication hierarchy.

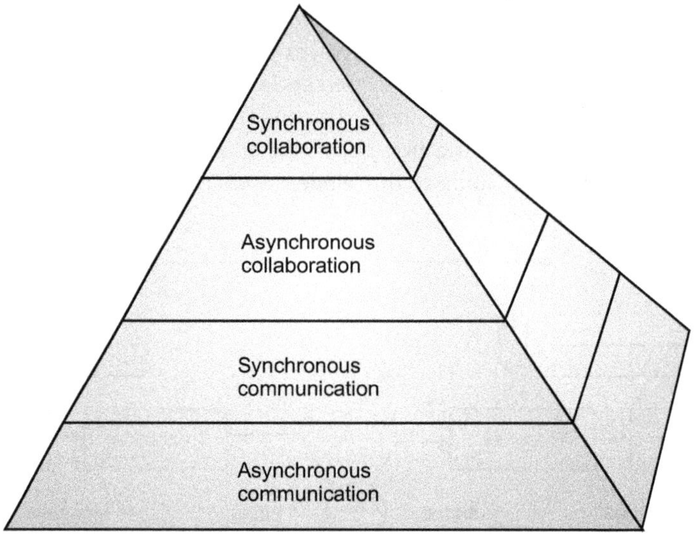

Fig. 4.8 : Collaboration and communication hierarchy

4.9.1 Asynchronous Communication

The most common form of asynchronous electronic communications in bioinformatics is e-mail and its derivatives, including bulletin boards and news-groups, web posting, online publications, streaming (pre-recorded) video, and fax.

- The real benefits of asynchronous communications minimal disruption of workflow is also its main limitation.

4.9.2 Synchronous Communication

Synchronous communication generally requires a more robust technology infrastructure than dose asynchronous communication, especially in terms of bandwidth to support a higher level of interactively.

- Video conferencing, instant messaging, and chat rooms are example of synchronous communications that are useful in bioinformatics R & D.

4.9.3 Asynchronous Collaboration

Asynchronous collaboration can be supported by e-mail and voicemail communications exchanged according to prearranged schedule or on an as needed basis.

- Collaboration can be viewed as a layer of management or process control over a basic communication infrastructure.

4.9.4 Synchronous Collaboration

The key technological issues in synchronous collaboration are time, reliability and bandwidth, this type of collaboration requires a more robust synchronous communication infrastructure.

- Synchronous collaboration necessarily incorporates technologies that provide a virtual common workplace, such as an electronic whiteboard and a means of working with applications and data interactively.
- The popular synchronous collaboration technologies are peer to peer screen sharing, commercial online conferencing services and application-specific integrated collaborators.

4.10 STANDARDS

Communications and collaboration are based on standards that span low-level life formats and hardware signal protocols to high-level application program interface (APIs) and user interface designs.

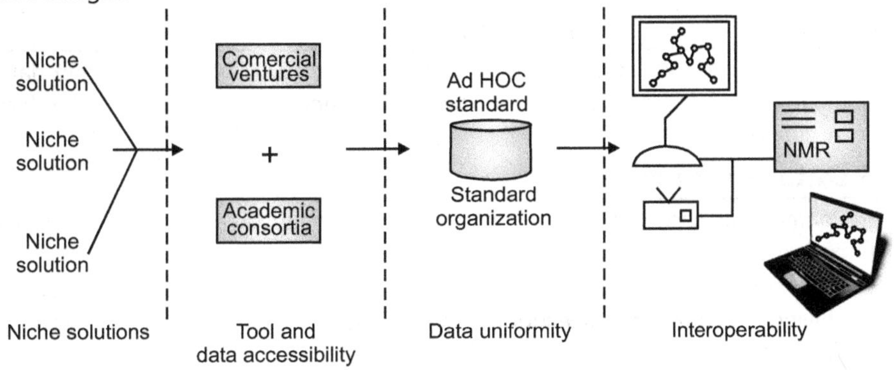

Fig. 4.9 : Evolution of standards

- The data uniformity stage represents the first real installation of standards.

4.10.1 Niche Solution

The path to standards typically starts as a body of niche solutions that are designed to satisfy specific needs, without regard(or time to regard) for connectivity with other systems in order to solve other problem.

- Example of early niche solutions in bioinformatics include stand-alone dot matrix alignment programs that require sequence data to be either typed or pasted into the program, and whose output had to be manually copied and pasted into other applications.

4.10.2 Tool and Data Accessibility

Tool and data accessibility phase of standards evolution involves restricted sharing of the niche solutions among the members of bioinformatics R & D community.

- Applications that have the greatest general appeal to other researchers are typically either distributed through academic and government sponsored consortia or transformed into commercial ventures.

Table 4.2 : Major bioinformatics file formats

ASN. 1	MSF	Plain/Raw
DNAstrider	NBRF	Pretty
EMBL	Olsen	ZUker
Fitch	PAUP/NEXUS	
GCG	PDB	
GenBank/GBFF	Pearson/FASTA	
IG/Standford	Phylip/phylip3.2	
MmCIF	PIR/CODATA	

- The number and variation of file formats used for nucleotide and protein data is an indicator of the amount of variability in the applications used in bioinformatics computing.

4.10.3 Data Uniformity

There are numerous reasons for developing data uniformity or a common file format for popular applications.

- A common file format for applications reduces that cost of maintenance and data archiving minimizes the likelihood of data loss and results in more efficient use of software tools.
- Another motivation for establishing data uniformity through standards is to improve the reliability of searching the online bioinformatics databases.

4.10.4 Interoperability

The final stage of standards evolution interoperability is the ability of a device or application to work seamlessly with tools and devices from multiple industries.

- True interoperability isn't limited to bioinformatics, but extends to general purpose tools, such as databases and spreadsheets, and to other specialized areas, such as NMR equipment.
- Interoperability makes it possible for a Universal Serial Bus(USB) printer to work with Dell workstation running Linux or a Macintosh computer running OS X or for an NMR machine to output files directly to a format compatible with the PDB.

Table 4.3 : Standards Organizations

In addition to this sampling of standards organizations that affect bioinformatics, there are hundreds of additional standards working committees that informally influence standards.

ACR/NEMA	American College Of Radiology/National Electronic Manufactures Association
ANSI	American National Standards Institute
ASTM	American Society For Testing And Material
CEN	European Committee For Standardization
EDIFACT	Electronic Data Interchange For Administration Commerce And Transport
EUCLIDES	European Clinical Data Exchange Standard
FCC	Federal Communications Commission
HCFA	Health Care Financing Administration
HHCC	Georgetown Home Health Classification
HIPAA	Health Insurance Portability And Accountability Act
HISP	Healthcare Informatics Standards Board
IEC	International Electro technical Commission
IEEE	Institute Of Electrical And Electronics Engineers
ISO	International Standards Organization
JPEG	Joint Photographic Expert Group
NANDA	North American Nursing Diagnosis Association
NIST	National Institute Of Standard And Technology
OSI	Open System Interconnection
UCC	Uniform Code Council

4.11 ISSUES

Many issues are external to the bioinformatics field and are tied to the internal pharmaceutical companies.

- In addition, there are several internal issues associated with establishing and maintaining collaborations. As described in the following paragraphs, these include platform dependence, intellectual property, and economics.

4.11.1 Platform Dependence

There's something to be said for a world which everyone is limited to single make and model of desktop computer.

• For example :

If the bioinformatics community standardized on vanilla 1 GHz pentium4 computers running Linux, managing networks, creating applications and sharing files and applications would be non-issues.

- However, computationally intensive applications, such as sequence alignment, might require weeks or months of processing time.

4.11.2 Security

Collaboration implies trust and requires a degree of connectivity between workstations and other devices.

- Whenever this connectivity takes the form of a wired or wireless connection to the internet, internets, or an intranet, it represents a security risk.
- The greatest threats to the typical bioinformatics lab are computer viruses, worms or Trojan horses.

4.11.3 Intellectual Property

When it comes to collaboration, there are two major camps: academic and business.

- At the individual researcher level, the motivation for collaboration are typically the same in each camp the thrill and challenge of pushing the envelope of scientific discovery while achieving personal career advancement.
- At higher levels in business and academia, the dimension of economics is usually added to mix. Lab administrators are necessarily concerned with continuing funding from corporate, government or other sources.

4.11.4 Economics

In every commercial or academic endeavor, progress is a function of operating costs and the availability of funding.

- For example :
  Overhead, payroll, hardware, software and infrastructure costs represent the main expenditures for atypical bioinformatics laboratory.
- Web servers, workstations and network cables, routers firewalls and related hardware are fortunately, commodity items that tend to follow a trend of decreasing price to performance ratio.
- One of the largest variables in the economics of establishing and maintaining a bioinformatics laboratory capable of collaborating with the larger bioinformatics community is obtaining software servers, workstations, and high-performance clusters.

SUMMARY

- **Model:** "A model is an abstraction of a real world system."
- **Simulation:** "Simulation is RUNNING a model to PREDICT the result of experimental CHANGES in the system."
- The example of modeling and simulation in bioinformatics is the "Killer app " on the desktop microcomputer the one application that raised the status of the technology from a hobbyist's plaything to a "must have" in business and in the laboratory was the now defunct electronic spreadsheet, VisiCalc.
- Application of modeling and simulation: Clinical What –If analysis, Drug Discovery and Development, Exploring Toxicology, Exploring Genetic Drift, Exploring Molecular Mechanisms of Action, Personal Health Prediction, Drug Efficacy Prediction, Drug Side Effects Prediction, Gene Expression Prediction, Protein folding Prediction, Protein Function Prediction, Protein Structure Prediction, Metabolic pathway visualization, Pharmacokinetic Visualization.
- Drug Discovery : Pharma, the primary backer of bioinformatics R and D worldwide, is keenly interested in automating and speeding the drug discovery and development process.
- The typical drug discovery and development process show in Fig. an involves an often arduous series of events that starts with perhaps 5,000 candidate drug molecules and ends with a single product that can be brought to market .
- Protein structure: Knowledge of protein structure is generally considered a prerequisite to understanding protein function and by extension, a cornerstone of proteomics research.
- The primary protein configuration – the simple linear sequence of covalently bound amino acid is functionally uninteresting. The secondary structure is the local geometry along the sequence, typically in the form of sheets, coils, loops and helices.
- A protein tertiary structure describes how the molecules folds in 3D space. Quaternary structure describes the complex configuration of a protein that is interacting with other molecules in 3D space.
- Pure ab initio methods of determining protein structure are based on sequence data and the physics of molecular physics.
- Systems biology is a biology-based inter-disciplinary field of study that focuses on complex interactions within biological systems, using a holistic approach (holism instead of the more traditional reductionism) to biological and biomedical research.
- Communication and collaboration rely on a variety of technology for the creation, modification, use and transfer of data activities that taken together constitute knowledge management.

- Communications and collaboration are based on standards that span low-level life formats and hardware signal protocols to high-level application program interface (APIs) and user interface designs.
- Many issues are external to the bioinformatics field and are tied to the internal pharmaceutical companies.
- In addition, there are several internal issues associated with establishing and maintaining collaborations. As described in the following paragraphs, these include platform dependence, intellectual property, and economics.

QUESTIONS

MAY 2013

1. (a) Explain in detail Primary, Secondary, Tertiary and Quaternary structures of Proteins. **[10]**

Ans. : Please refer Section 4.8.

(b) Explain the process of Drug discovery. What high-throughput screening methods are employed in screening drugs? **[8]**

Ans. : Please refer Section 4.5. **OR**

2. (a) Discuss in brief the components of a modeling and simulation system along with the process. **[8]**

Ans. : Please refer Section 4.6.1 and 4.6.2.

(b) Draw and explain Collaboration-Communication model with appropriate examples. **[10]**

Ans. : Please refer Section 4.9.

MAY 2014

3. (a) Draw and explain Collaboration-Communication model with appropriate examples. **[10]**

Ans. : Please refer Section 4.9.

(b) Explain with neat block diagram the components of modeling and simulation Systems. **[8]**

Ans. : Please refer Section 4.6.1.

4. (a) What is the importance of protein structure in protein function ? Discuss the method to predict the protein structures from sequence data ? **[10]**

Ans. : Please refer Section 4.7.

(b) Explain the process of Drug discovery. What high-throughput screening methods are employed in screening drugs? **[8]**

Ans. : Please refer Section 4.5.

UNIT V

BIOINFORMATICS TOOLS

5.1 INTRODUCTION

5.1.1 Bioinformatics Tools

Bioinformatics tools are software programs that are designed for extracting the meaningful information from the mass of molecular biology/biological databases and to carry out sequence or structural analysis.

- Factors that must be taken into consideration when designing bioinformatics tools, software and programs are:
  (a) The end user (the biologist) may not be a frequent user of computer technology.
  (b) These software tools must be made available over the internet given the globe distribution of the scientific research community.

5.1.2 Major Categories of Bioinformatics Tools

There are both standard and customized products to meet the requirements of particular projects. There are datamining software that retrieves data from genomic sequence databases and visualization tools to analyze and retrieve information from proteomic databases.

- These can be classified as homology and similarity tools, protein functional analysis tools, sequence analysis tools and miscellaneous tools.
- Here is a brief description of a few of these, everyday bioinformatics is done with sequence analysis programs, like the EMBOSS and staden packages, structure prediction programs like THREADER or PHD or molecular imaging/modeling programs like RasMol and WHATIF.

5.1.3 Homology And Similarity Tools

Homologies sequences are sequences that are related by divergence from a common ancestor.

Thus the degree of similarity between two sequences can be measured while their homology is a case of being either true or false. This set of tools can be used to identify similarities between novel query sequences of unknown structure and function and database sequences whose structure and function have been elucidated.

5.1.4 Protein Function Analysis

This group of program allows you to compare your protein sequence to the secondary (or derived) protein database that contain information of motifs, signature and protein domains.

Highly significant hits against this different pattern databases allow you to approximate the biochemical function of your query protein.

5.1.5 Structure Analysis

This set of tools allows you to compare structure with the known structure databases. The function of a protein is more directly a consequence of its structure rather than its sequence with structural homologies tending to share functions. The determination of a protein 2D/3D structural is crucial in the study of its function.

5.1.6 Sequence Analysis

This set of tools allows you to carry out further more detailed analysis, identification of mutations, hydropathy regions, CPG islands and compositional biases. The identification of these and other biological properties are all clues that aid the search to elucidate the specific function of your sequence.

5.1.7 Examples Of Bioinformatics Tools

(1) BLAST (Basic Local Alignment Search Tool)

- It comes under the category of homology and similarity tools. It is a set of search program designed for the windows platform and is used to perform fast similarity searches regardless of whether the query is for protein DNA.
- Comparison of nucleotide sequences in a database can be performed. Also a protein database can be searched to find a match against the queried protein sequence.
- NCBI has also introduced the new queuing system to BLAST (QBLAST) that allows user to retrieve results at their convenience and format their results multiple times with different formatting options.

Depending on the type of sequence to compare, there are different programs:

  - blastp compares an amino acid query sequence against a protein sequence database.
  - blastn compares a nucleotide query sequence against a nucleotide sequence database.
  - blastx compares a nucleotide query sequence translated in all reading frames against a protein sequence databases.
  - tblastn compares a protein query sequence against a nucleotide sequence database dynamically translated in all reading frames.
  - tblastx compares the six-frames translations of a nucleotide sequence against the six-frame translations of a nucleotide sequence database.

(2) FASTA

- Fast homology search A11 sequences. An alignment program for protein sequences created by Pearsin and Lipman in 1998. The program is one of the many heuristic algorithm proposed to speed up sequence comparision.
- The basic idea is to add a fast prescreen step to locate the highly matching segments between two sequences, and then extend these matching segments to local alignment using more rigorous algorithms such as Smith Waterman.

(3) EMBOSS

EMBOSS (European Molecular Biology Open Software Suite) is a software analysis package. It can work with data in arrange of formats and also retrieve sequence data transparently from the web. Extensive libraries are also provided with this package, allowing other scientists to release their software as open source. It provides a set of sequence analysis programs and also supports all UNIX platforms.

(4) Clustalw

It is a fully automated sequence alignment tool for DNA and protein sequences. It returns the best match over a total length of input sequences, be it a protein or a nucleic acid.

(5) RasMol

It is a powerful search tool to display the structure of DNA, protein and smaller molecules. Protein explorer, a derivative of rasmol, is an easier to use program.

(6) PROSPECT

PROSPECT (Protein Structure Prediction and Evaluation Computer Toolkit) is a protein threading to construct a proteins 3D model.

(7) PatternHunter

PatternHunter, based on Java, can identify all approximate repeats in a short time using little memory on a desktop computer.

Its features are its advanced patented algorithm and data structures, and the java language used to create it. The java language version of pattern hunter is just 40 KB only 1% the size of Blast while offering a large protein of its functionality.

(8) COPIA

COPIA (Consensus Pattern Identification and Analysis) is a protein structure analysis tool for discovering motifs (Conserver regions) in a family of protein sequences. Such motifs can be then used to determine membership to the family for new protein sequences, predict secondary and tertiary structure and function of proteins and study evolution history of the sequences.

5.1.8 Applications of Programs In Bioinformatics

(1) Java in Bioinformatics

Since research centers are scattered all around the globe ranging from private to academic settings and a range of hardware and OS's are being used, Java is emerging as a key player in bioinformatics. Physiome sciences computer based biological solution technologies and bioinformatics solutions patternhunter are two examples of the growing adoption of Java in bioinformatics.

(2) Perl in Bioinformatics

String manipulations, regular expression matching, file processing, data format inter-conversion, etc. are the common text processing tasks performed in bioinformatics.

5.1.9 Bioinformatics Projects

(1) Biojava

The BioJava project is dedicated to providing Java tools for processing biological data which includes objects for manipulating sequences, dynamic programming, file parsers, simple statistical routins etc.

(2) Bioperl

The BioPerl project is an international association of developers of perl tools for bioinformatics and provides an online resource for modules, scripts and web links for developers of perl-based software.

(3) Bioxml

A part of the bioperl project, this is a resource to gather XML documentation, DTD's and XML aware tools for biology in one location.

5.2 WORKING WITH FASTS

FASTA (Fast homology search A11 sequences) it uses the Pearson and Lipman algorithm to search for similarity between one sequence (the query) and any group of sequences of the same type (nucleic acid or protein) as the query sequence. FASTA is generally best to make protein-protein comparisons, but it can also compare DNA sequence to DNA databases. The related program TFASTA allows a protein query sequence to be compared to DNA databank.

- The original FASTA program was designed for protein sequence similarity searching. FASTA added the ability to do DNA: DNA searches, translated protein: DNA searches, and also provided a more sophisticated shuffling program for evaluating statistical significance.
- There are several programs in this package that allow the alignment of protein sequences and DNA sequences.

Input

- FASTA takes a given nucleotide or amino acid sequence and searches a corresponding sequence database by using local sequence alignment to find matches of similar database sequences. The FASTA program follows a largely heuristic method which contributes to the high speed of its execution. It initially observes the pattern of word hits, word-to-word matches of a given length, and marks potential matches before performing a more time-consuming optimized search using a Smith-Waterman type of algorithm.
- The size taken for a word, given by the parameter ktup, controls the sensitivity and speed of the program. Increasing the ktup value decreases number of background hits that are found. From the word hits that are returned the program looks for segments that contain a cluster of nearby hits. It then investigates these segments for a possible match.

5.2.1 FASTA Algorithm

- FASTA starts by making a generalization from the concepts of dot plots. In dot plot, regions of similarity between two sequences show up as diagonals.
- FASTA goes a step forward and calculates the sum of the dots along each diagonal. FASTA is a "word" based method. It looks for matching "word" or the sequence patterns called the k-tuples. It then builds a local alignment based upon these word matches.
- FASTA makes a list of all words (sequence patterns of 1 or 2 amino acids, or 5 or 6 nucleotides) in each sequence. It matches identical words from each list and then creates diagonals by joining adjacent matches.
- FASTA then rescores the highest scoring regions using a replacement matrix (e.g. scoring matrices like PAM and Blosum).
- FASTA joins together the high scoring diagonals allowing for gaps. The best score from that is called initn.
- FASTA finally uses Smith-Waterman algorithm to identify an optimal local alignment around the regions it has discovered. This last alignment step is a local alignment step and is only applied to a small number of sequences that had high initn values after the database search.

The four step is FASTA used to calculate similarity scores between a pair of sequences are as follows :

(a) Find Runs Of Identical Words

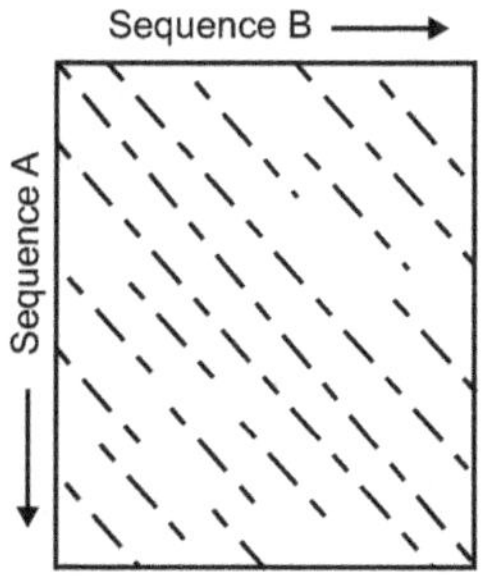

Fig. 5.1 : Find runs of identical words

(b) Rescore Using PAM Matrix

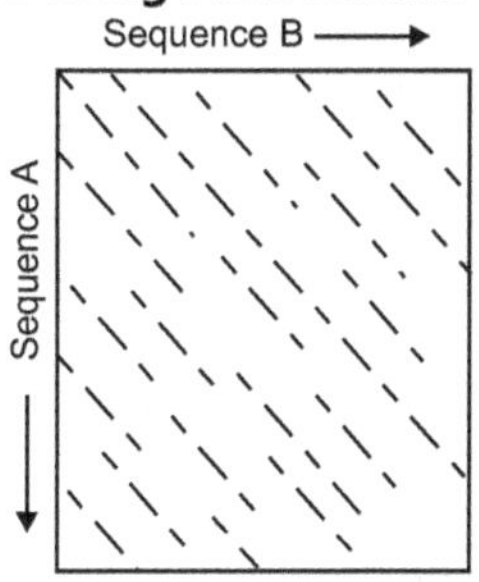

Fig. 5.2 : Rescore using PAM matrix

- Identify regions shared by two sequences that have the highest density of single residue identity (ktup=1) or two consecutive identities (ktup=2).
- Keep the best score rescan the best regions identified in 1st step using the PAM-250 matrix. The single best score is stored as init1 for reporting later.

(c) Join Segments Using Gaps and Eliminate Other Segments

Determine if gaps can be used to join the regions identified in 2nd step. If so, determine a similarity score for the gapped alignment, which is reported as initin.

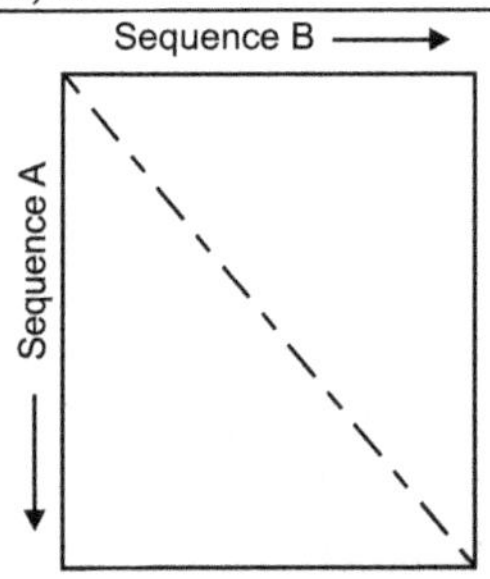

Fig. 5.3 : Join Segments using gaps and eliminate other segments

(d) Use DP To Create The Optimal Alignment

Construct an optimal alignment of the query sequence and the library sequence (smith-waterman algorithm). This score is reported as the optimized score. FASTA uses hash coding method in the initial search for regions of similarity. In hash coding a lookup table showing the position of each sequence word of length K (a k-tuple), is constructed for each sequence. The k-tuple length is user defined and is usually 1 or 2 for protein sequences i.e. either the position of each of the individual 20 amino acids or the positions of each the 400 possible dipeptides are located.

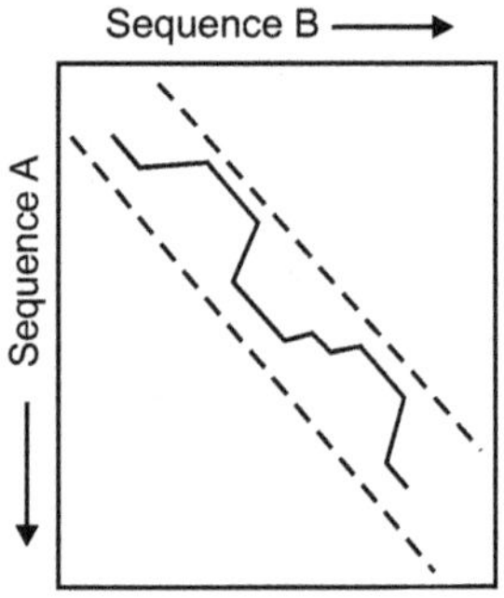

Fig. 5.4 : Use DP to create the optimal alignment

For nucleic acid sequences, the k-tuple is in the range of 5 to 20. It is much more than the proteins case because short k-tuples are much more common due to the 4 letter alphabet of nucleic acids. The larger the k-tuple chosen, the more rapid but less through is the database search.

5.2.2 FASTA Implementation

- FASTA at the EBI is one of the most popular FASTA implementation. Proteomes and genomes FASTA provides sequence similarity and homology searching against complete proteome or genome databases using the FASTA programs.
- SNP (Single Nucleotide Polymorphism) sequences can be searched with the FASTA server at the EBI.

5.2.3 The Histogram

The first part of the FASTA output is the histogram (if you have enabled the option). The histogram compares the predicted extreme value distribution of local similarity scores, represented by asterisk with the actual numbers obtained, represented by equal signs. The histogram can be used to determine whether or not the statistical theory for the distribution of local alignment is valid for this particular search.

5.2.4 The Sequence Listing

The first column identifies the database sequences reported by database, database accession number and database identifier. The next column reports the total length of the database sequence. The final score are reported in the opt column and the E() value for that particular database sequence is reported in the last column.

5.2.5 Significance of The E-values

- FASTA calculates an E-value (expectation of significance). E() values represent the number of sequences having a given Z-opt score (or better) totally at random. The smaller the number, the less likely that a given alignment occurred by chance and more likely the alignment represents some true relationship between query and database sequences.
- The steps for calculation of extreme value distribution to calculate the significance of similarity scores found in database search are follows :
- The average score for sequences in the same length range is determined.
- The average score is plotted against logarithm of average sequence. The points are fitted to a straight line by linear regression.
- A z score, the number of standard deviations from the fitted line, is calculated for each score. High scoring presumably related or low complexity sequences and also of very low scoring alignments that do not fit the straight line are removed from consideration.

Step 1 : Through 5 are repeated one or more times.

Z scores are used to calculate the probability that a score greater than z would be found between unrelated sequences, using the extreme value distribution equation-

P(Z>z)=1-exp^(-e-1.2825z-0.5772</sup)

- The expected value of a database for similar sequences is this score times the number of sequences in the database: E(Z>z)=oxp(Z>z)

5.2.6 Recommended Steps For A FASTA Search

The following strategy is recommended for searches with fasta for finding the most homologous sequences in a database search while avoiding false negative matches:

- Comparison should be done using protein sequences by even translating DNA sequences if possible.
- Search non redundant protein database like PIR or swiss port with ktup= 2.
- Look for agreement between the real and the theoretical distribution of sources. For a match to be significant E() should be<0.05.
- If the search has correctly identified homologous sequences, then the corresponding E() values should be much less than 0.02, while scores between unrelated sequences should be much greater than this value.
- If there are no E() less than 0.1 then the search has not found any sequences with significant similarity to probe sequences.

- If there are no matches with E() less than 0.1 then repeat the search with FASTA with ktup=1, or else use the search. If FASTA now finds matches with E() less than 0.02 then the sequences may be homologous, if there is not a low complexity region in the probe sequence. Sequences with score of 0.2 to 10 may also be homologous but have marginal sequence similarity.
- For further study of this possibility select some of these marginal sequences and use them as probe sequences for additional database searches with significant similarity may then be found.
- Confirm homology of marginal matches by using database sequence many times to calculate the significance of the real alignment.
- The program press (http://Fasta.bioch.virginia.edu/Fasta/press.htm) performs the task of sequence shuffling.
- Protein sequence alignments with 50% identity in a short 20-40 amino acid region are common in unrelated proteins. To be truly significant, the alignment should extend over a longer region.

5.2.7 Other Implementations And Extensions Of FASTA

There are several implementations of the FASTA algorithm are as follows.

FASTA	Compares a protein sequence to another protein sequence or a protein library or a DNA sequence to a DNA sequence library.
TFASTA	Compares a protein sequence to a DNA sequence library by translating each DNA sequence into all 6 possible reading frames and then comparing each frame to the protein sequence.
LFASTA	Identifies one or more regions of similarity between two sequences.
PLFASTA	Present dot matrix plot of regions of sequence similarity between two sequences.

- There are versions of FASTA that are designed to align a DNA sequence allowing gaps and frame shifts. If a DNA sequence has a high possibility of errors such as EST sequences, then the translated sequence may be inaccurate due to amino acid changes or frame shifts. These programs are designed to go around such errors by matching substituted amino acids and incorrect reading frames.

5.2.8 FASTA Programs

Program	Description
FASTAX and FASTAY	To translate a probe DNA sequence in three reading frames and compares all three frames to a protein sequence database. FASTAX and TFASTX allow only frame shifts between codons.
TFASTAX and TFASTAY	To compare a probe probe sequence to a DNA sequence database, calculating similarities with frame shifts to the forward and reverse orientations. FASTAY and TFASTY allow substitutions and frame shifts within a codon.

- The FASTA algorithm has been adapted for searching through apattern database instead of sequence database. The FASTA algorithm normally identifies sequence similarity very rapidly by a method for finding common patterns or k-tuples in the same order in two sequences. In Fasta-pat & Fasta-swap, the same rapid method is used to find common patterns.
- Fasta-pat performs a faster method of comparing sequences to pattern by means of a lookup table as described. Fasta-swap performs a more rigorous search for the most significant matches of sequence to patterns. This combination of program and pattern database has been found to be useful for finding distant relatives of the probe sequence that may be missed in a search for sequence similarity.

5.2.9 FASTA Programs From University of Virginia

Lalign	Provide a specified number of best set alignments of a pair of sequences using the Smith-Waterman dynamic programming algorithm with subsequent improvements.
Plalign	Version of Lalign that provides a dot matrix type plot of the best alignments between two sequences.
Lfasta	Provides a specified number of best alignments of a pair of sequences using the FASTA algorithm.
Plfasta	Version of Lfasta that provides a dot matrix type plot of the best alignments between two sequences.
Prss	As discussed earlier, prss creats a library of a specified number of shuffled sequences of the same length and amino acid composition as the library sequence.
Prdf	Prdf perform the same task as prss except that fasta algorithm is used to align the sequences. The program runs much faster than prss.

5.2.10 The Databases Available For FASTA Searching (at the RCR) Are

Peptide (protein) sequence databases :

sp:*	Swissprot Amos Bairoch's protein sequence databases
gp:*	Genpept Translation of all GenBank DNA seqs (according to exons in features tables)
pir:*	Protein Information Resource
pir1:*	Annotated PIR entries
pir2:*	New PIR entries
pir3:*	Unverified PIR entries
pir4:*	Unencoded or Untranslated
Nrl-3-D:*	Sequences from 3-dimensional Structure Brookhaven protein Data Bank
Prosite	Consensus seqs of conserved protein Data Bank
TFD	Transcription Factor Database

5.2.11 Nucleotide Sequence Databases VECTOR-Vector Sequence

MALARIA : Malaria genomic sequences : gb* : All GenBank (includes EMBL, DDBJ, PDB) updated daily.

5.2.12 GenBank SubDivisions

gb-ba:*	Bacterial
gb-in:*	Invertebrate
gb-om:*	Other Mammalian (Non-rodent, non-primate)
gb-ov:*	Other vertebrate (Non-mammalian vertebrates)
gb-or:*	Organelle
gb-pat:*	Patents
gb-ph:*	Phage
gb-pl:*	Plant
gb-pr:*	Primate
gb-ro:*	Rodent
gb-st:*	Structural RNA
gb-sy:*	Synthetic Sequences (Recombinant Construct etc)
gb-un:*	Unannotated
gb-vi:*	Viral
gb-est:*	Expressed Sequence Tags (short cDNAS) now has sections est1 to est9 with more added each quater
gb-sts:*	Sequence Tagged Sites
gb-gss:*	Genomic Survey Sequences (Large Genomic Contigs)
gb-htg:*	High throughput Genomic Sequences (single Pass Sequences Churned out by the genome projects, unannotated and filled with errors)
gb-tag:*	ESTs+ STS+GSS+HTG

5.2.13 Uses

FASTA is pronounced "fast A", and stands for "FAST-All", because it works with any alphabet, an extension of "FAST-P" (protein) and "FAST-N" (nucleotide) alignment.

- The current FASTA package contains programs for protein: protein, DNA:DNA, protein: translated DNA (with frame shifts), and ordered or unordered peptide searches. Recent versions of the FASTA package include special translated search algorithms that correctly handle frame shift errors (which six-frame-translated searches do not handle very well) when comparing nucleotide to protein sequence data.
- In addition to rapid heuristic search methods, the FASTA package provides SSEARCH, an implementation of the optimal Smith-Waterman algorithm. A major focus of the package is the calculation of accurate similarity statistics, so that biologists can judge whether an alignment is likely to have occurred by chance, or whether it can be used to infer homology.
- The web-interface to submit sequences for running a search of the European Bioinformatics Institute (EBI)'s online databases is also available using the FASTA programs.

- The FASTA file format used as input for this software is now largely used by other sequence database search tools (such as BLAST) and sequence alignment programs (Clustal, T-Coffee, etc.).

5.3 BLAST

BLAST is an algorithm for comparing primary biological sequence information, such as the amino acid sequences of different proteins or the nucleotide of DNA sequences.

- BLAST search enables a researcher to compare a query sequence with library or database of sequences that resemble the query sequence about a certain threshold. Different types of a BLAST available according to a query sequence.
- For example :

  Following the discovery of a previously unknown gene in the mouse, the scientist will typically perform a BLAST search of the human gene; BLAST will identify sequences in the human genome that resemble the mouse gene based on similarity of sequence. BLAST is a similarity search program developed at NCBI (National Center For Biotechnology Information).
- It is available as free service over the internet that provides very fast, accurate and sensitive database searching.
- BLAST uses a heuristic algorithm that seeks local as opposed to global alignments and is therefore able to detect relationships among sequences that share only isolated regions of similarity.

5.4 WORKING WITH BLAST

BLAST like FASTA is a word based method. However, one major difference is that BLAST requires a preformatted search database.

Input

Input sequences are in FASTA or GenBank format and weight matrix.

Output

BLAST output can be delivered a variety of formats. These formats include HTML, plain text and XML formatting.

- For NCBIs web-pages, the default format for output is HTML. When performing a BLAST on NCBI, the results are given in a graphical format showing the hits found, a table showing sequence identifiers for hits with scoring related data as well as alignments for the sequence of interest and the hits with corresponding BLAST scores for these.
- If one is attempting to search for a proprietary sequence or simply one that is unavailable in databases available to the general public through sources such as NCBI, there is a BLAST program available for download to any computer at no cost.

BLAST goes through the three steps that are summarized here:

(1) Find the list of high scoring words (W). BLAST takes each word from the query sequence (typically w is 3 for amino acids and 11 for nucleotides), and locates all similar words in the current test sequence.

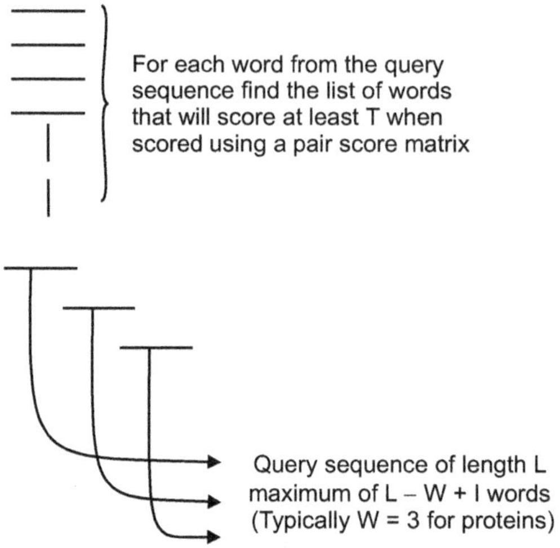

Fig. 5.5

(2) Diagram for find the list of high scoring words. Compare the word list to the database and identify the exact matches, if similar words are found, BLAST tries to expand the alignment to the adjacent words, without allowing for gaps.

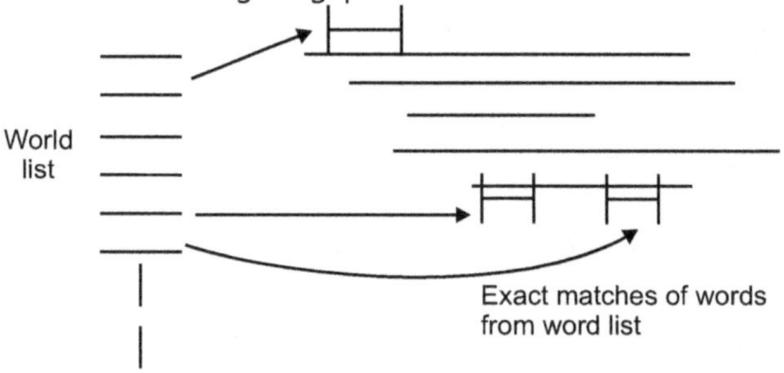

Fig. 5.6

(3) After all words are tested, a set of maximal segments pair (MSPs) is chosen for that database sequence. Several short, non-overlapping MSPs may be combined in a statistical test to create a larger, more significant match.

BLAST Algorithm

To run, BLAST requires a query sequence to search for, and a sequence to search against (also called the target sequence) or a sequence database containing multiple such sequences.

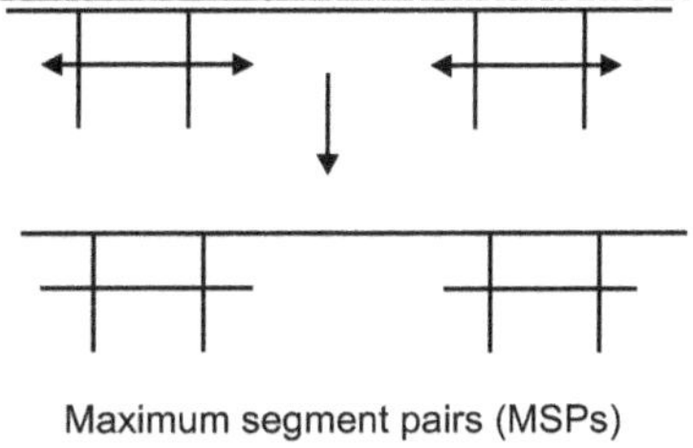

Fig. 5.7 : Chosen the MSPs

- BLAST will find sub-sequences in the database which are similar to subsequences in the query. In typical usage, the query sequence is much smaller than the database, example, the query may be one thousand nucleotides while the database is several billion nucleotides. The main idea of BLAST is that there are often high-scoring segment pairs (HSP) contained in a statistically significant alignment. BLAST searches for high scoring sequence alignments between the query sequence and sequences in the database using a heuristic approach that approximates the Smith-Waterman algorithm.
- The exhaustive Smith-Waterman approach is too slow for searching large genomic databases such as GenBank.

  Therefore, the BLAST algorithm uses a heuristic approach that is less accurate than the Smith-Waterman algorithm but over 50 times faster. The speed and relatively good accuracy of BLAST are among the key technical innovations of the BLAST programs.

An overview of the BLASTP algorithm (a protein to protein search) is as follows:

(1) Remove low-complexity region or sequence repeats in the query sequence

"Low-complexity region" means a region of a sequence composed of few kinds of elements. These regions might give high scores that confuse the program to find the actual significant sequences in the database, so they should be filtered out. The regions will be marked with an X (protein sequences) or N (nucleic acid sequences) and then be ignored by the BLAST program. To filter out the low-complexity regions, the SEG program is used for protein sequences and the program DUST is used for DNA sequences. On the other hand, the program XNU is used to mask off the tandem repeats in protein sequences.

(2) Make a *k*-letter word list of the query sequence

Take $k=3$ for example, we list the words of length 3 in the query protein sequence (k is usually 11 for a DNA sequence) "sequentially", until the last letter of the query sequence is included.

The method is illustrated in Fig. 5.8.

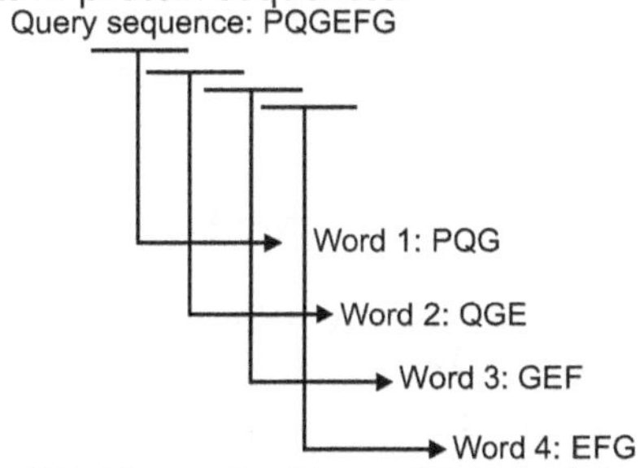

Fig. 5.8 : The method to establish the *k*-letter query word list

(3) List the possible matching words :

This step is one of the main differences between BLAST and FASTA. FASTA cares about all of the common words in the database and query sequences that are listed in step 2; however, BLAST only cares about the high-scoring words. The scores are created by comparing the word in the list in step 2 with all the 3-letter words. By using the scoring matrix (substitution matrix) to score the comparison of each residue pair, there are 20^3 possible match scores for a 3-letter word. For example the score obtained by comparing PQG with PEG and PQA is 15 and 12, respectively. For DNA words, a match is scored as +5 and a mismatch as -4, or as +2 and -3. After that, a neighborhood word score threshold *T* is used to reduce the number of possible matching words. The words whose scores are greater than the threshold *T* will remain in the possible matching words list, while those with lower scores will be discarded. For example : PEG is kept, but PQA is abandoned when T is 13.

(4) Organize the remaining high-scoring words into an efficient search tree.

This allows the program to rapidly compare the high-scoring words to the database sequences.

(5) Repeat step 3 to 4 for each *k*-letter word in the query sequence.

(6) Scan the database sequences for exact matches with the remaining high-scoring words. The BLAST program scans the database sequences for the remaining high-scoring word, such as PEG, of each position. If an exact match is found, this match is used to seed a possible ungapped alignment between the query and database sequences.

(7) Extend the exact matches to high-scoring segment pair (HSP).

The original version of BLAST stretches a longer alignment between the query and the database sequence in the left and right directions, from the position where the exact match occurred. The extension does not stop until the accumulated total score of the HSP begins to decrease. A simplified example is presented in Fig. 5.9.

Query sequence : R P P Q G L F

Database sequence: D P **P E G** V V

→ Exact match is scanned

Score: -2 7 7 2 6 1 -1

→ HSP

Optimal accumulated score = 7+7+2+6+1=23

Fig. 5.9 : The process to extend the exact match

To save more time, a newer version of BLAST, called BLAST2 or gapped BLAST, has been developed. BLAST2 adopts a lower neighborhood word score threshold to maintain the same level of sensitivity for detecting sequence similarity. Therefore, the possible matching words list in step 3 becomes longer. Next, the exact matched regions, within distance A from each other on the same diagonal in Fig. 5.10 will be joined as a longer new region.

Finally, the new regions are then extended by the same method as in the original version of BLAST, and the HSPs' (High-scoring segment pair) scores of the extended regions are then created by using a substitution matrix as before.

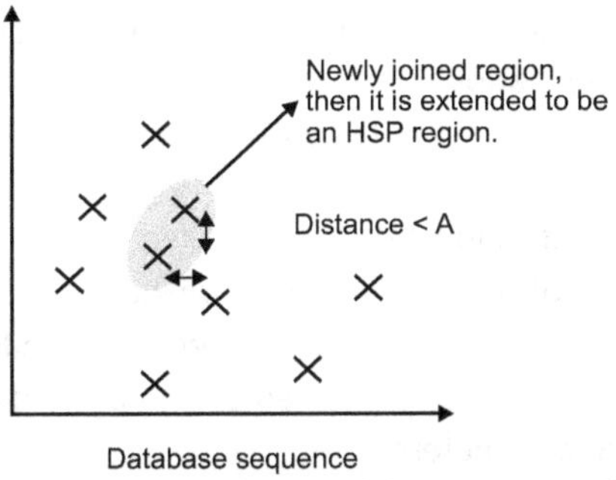

Fig. 5.10 : The positions of the exact matches

(8) List all of the HSPs in the database whose score is high enough to be considered :

We list the HSPs whose scores are greater than the empirically determined cutoff score *S*. By examining the distribution of the alignment scores modeled by comparing random sequences, a cutoff score *S* can be determined such that its value is large enough to guarantee the significance of the remaining HSPs.

(9) Evaluate the significance of the HSP score :

- BLAST next assesses the statistical significance of each HSP score by exploiting the Gumbel extreme value distribution (EVD). (It is proved that the distribution of Smith-Waterman local alignment scores between two random sequences follows the Gumbel EVD. For local alignments containing gaps it is not proved.). In accordance with the Gumbel EVD, the probability *p* of observing a score *S* equal to or greater than x is given by the equation.

$$P(S \geq x) = 1 - \exp(-e^{-\lambda(x-\mu)})$$

Where, $\mu = [\log(Km'n')]/\lambda$

- The statistical parameters λ and K are estimated by fitting the distribution of the un-gapped local alignment scores, of the query sequence and a lot of shuffled versions (Global or local shuffling) of a database sequence, to the Gumbel extreme value distribution. Note that λ and K depend upon the substitution matrix, gap penalties, and sequence composition (the letter frequencies). m′ and n′ are the effective lengths of the query and database sequences, respectively.
- The original sequence length is shortened to the effective length to compensate for the edge effect (an alignment start near the end of one of the query or database sequence is likely not to have enough sequence to build an optimal alignment). They can be calculated as : $m' \approx m - (\ln k_{mn})/H$ and $n' \approx n - (\ln k_{mn})/H$.
- Where H is the average expected score per aligned pair of residues in an alignment of two random sequences. Altschul and Gish gave the typical values, λ = 0.318 λ = 0.318,

λ = 0.318, K = 0.13 and H = 0.40, for un-gapped local alignment using BLOSUM62 as the substitution matrix. Using the typical values for assessing the significance is called the lookup table method; it is not accurate. The expect score *E* of a database match is the number of times that an unrelated database sequence would obtain a score *S* higher than *x* by chance. The expectation *E* obtained in a search for a database of *D* sequences is given by, $E \approx 1 - e^{-p\,(s\,>\,x)\,D}$. Furthermore, when $p < 0.1$, E could be approximated by the Poisson distribution as, $E \approx pD$

- This expectation or expect value "E" (often called an *E* score or *E*-value or *e*-value) assessing the significance of the HSP score for un-gapped local alignment is reported in the BLAST results. The calculation shown here is modified if individual HSPs are combined, such as when producing gapped alignments (described below), due to the variation of the statistical parameters.

(10) Make Two or More HSP Regions into a Longer Alignment

Sometimes, we find two or more HSP regions in one database sequence that can be made into a longer alignment. This provides additional evidence of the relation between the query and database sequence. There are two methods, the Poisson method and the sum-of-scores method, to compare the significance of the newly combined HSP regions. Suppose that there are two combined HSP regions with the pairs of scores (65, 40) and (52, 45), respectively. The Poisson method gives more significance to the set with the maximal lower score (45>40). However, the sum-of-scores method prefers the first set, because 65+40 (105) is greater than 52+45(97). The original BLAST uses the Poisson method; gapped BLAST and the WU-BLAST uses the sum-of scores method.

(11) Show the Gapped Smith-Waterman Local Alignments of the Query and each of the Matched Database Sequences

The original BLAST only generates un-gapped alignments including the initially found HSPs individually, even when there is more than one HSP found in one database sequence.

BLAST2 produces a single alignment with gaps that can include all of the initially-found HSP regions. Note that the computation of the score and its corresponding *E*-value involves use of adequate gap penalties.

(12) Report every match whose expect score is lower than a threshold parameter *E*.

5.4.1 BLAST Implementations

The major BLAST implementations available on the WWW

Name of the program	Address (URL)
BLAST network service on Expasy	http://us.expasy.org/tools/blast/
BLAST at EMBnet-CH/SIB (switzerland)	http://www.ch.embnet.org/software/BottomBLAST.html?
BLAST at NCBI	http://www.ncbi.nlm.nih.gov/BLAST/
WU-BLAST at the EBI	http://www.ebi.ac.uk/blast2/
BLAST at PBIL (Lyon)	http://npsa.-pbil.ibcp.fr/cgibin/npsa-automat.pl?page=npsa-blast.html

5.4.2 BLAST Services (From NCBI)

There are number of services available from NCBI related to BLAST.

(1) Nucleotide BLAST

It searches allow one to input nucleotide sequences and compare these against other nucleotides.

(2) Standard Nucleotide – Nucleotide BLAST

It takes nucleotides sequences in FASTA format. GenBank accession number or GI numbers and compares them against the NCBI nucleotide databases.

(3) MEGABLAST

This program uses a "greedy algorithm" for nucleotide sequence alignment searches and concatenates many queries to save time spent scanning the database.

- It is optimized for aligning sequences that differ slightly and is up to 10 times faster than more common sequence similarity programs.
- It can be used to compare two large sets of sequences against each other and gives the results very quickly.

(4) Protein BLAST

Protein BLAST allows one to input protein sequences and compare these against other protein sequences.

(5) Standard Protein – Protein BLAST

This takes protein sequences in FASTA format, GenBank Accession numbers or GI numbers and compares them against the NCBI protein databases.

(6) Pattern Hit Initiated BLAST (PHI-BLAST)

PHI-BLAST combines matching of regular expression pattern with a position specific iterative protein search. PHI-BLAST can locate other protein sequences that both contain the regular expression pattern and are homologous to a query protein sequence.

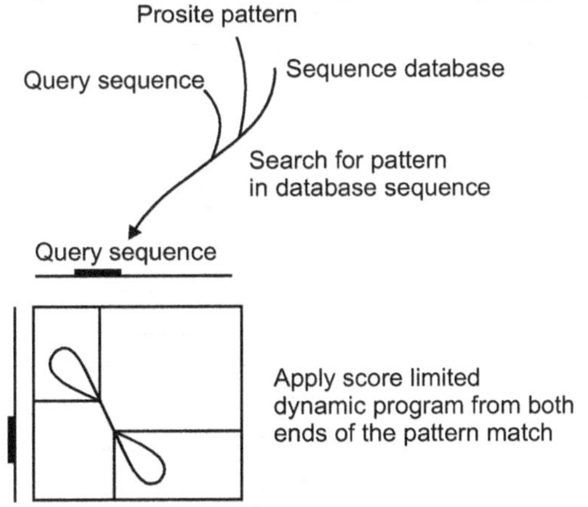

Fig. 5.11

5.4.3 Search For Short, Nearly Exact Sequence

- This search is similar to the standard protein-protein BLAST with parameters set automatically to optimize for searching with short sequence. A short query is more likely to occur by chance in the database.
- Therefore increasing the expected value threshold and also lowering word size is often necessary before results can be returned.
- "Low complexity" has also been removed since this filters out larger percentage of a short sequence, resulting in little or no query sequence remaining. Also for short sequence searches the matrix is changed to PAM-30 that is better suited to finding short regions of high similarity.
- **Translating Blast**

  Translating BLAST searches translate either query sequences or databases from nucleotides to proteins so that protein-nucleotide sequences can be performed.
- **Translated Query-Protein DB (blastx)**

  Converts a nucleotide query sequence into a protein sequences in all 6 reading frames. The translated protein products are then compared against NCBI protein database.
- **Protein Query- Translated DB (tblastn)**

  Takes a protein query sequences and compares it against NCBI nucleotide database that has been translated in all six reading frames.
- **Translated Query- Translated DB (tblastx)**

  Converts a nucleotide query sequence database which has been translated in all six reading frames.
- **Pair-Wise BLAST**

  Pair-wise BLAST performs a comparison between two sequences using the BLAST algorithm. Note that the program considers a "sequence1" to the query sequence and "sequence2" to be the subject sequence.

5.4.4 BLAST Program Option

Program	Query Sequence	Database	Type of alignment
Blastp	Protein	Protein	Gapped
Blastn	Nucleic acid	Nclecleic acid	Gapped
Blastx	Translated nucleic acid	Protein	Each frame gapped
Tblastn	Protein	Translated Nucleotide acid	Each frame gapped
Tblastx	Translated Nucleotide acid2	Translated Nucleotide acid1	Ungapped

5.4.5 Databases

Some of the databases available for BLAST searching (at NCBI) are :

(1) Peptide (Protein) Sequence Databases

nr	All non-redundant GenBank CDS translation+ PDB+ Swissprot+ PIR
month	All new or revised GenBank CDS translation+ PDB+ Swissprot+ PIR released in the last 30 days.
swissprot	The SWISS-PROT Sequence database
yeast	Yeast (saccharomyces Cerevisiae) protein sequences
pdb	Sequences derived from the 3D structure Brookhaven Protein Data Bank.
kabat	Kabats database of sequences of immunological interest.
alu	Translations of select Alu repeats

(2) Nucleotide Sequence Databases

nr	All non-redundant GenBank+EMBL+DDBJ+PDB Sequences (but no EST's or STS's)
month	All new or revised GenBank+EMBL+DDBJ+PDB Sequences released in the last 30 days.
dbest	Expressed Sequence Tags dbsts=Sequence Tagged Sites
yeast	Yeast (saccharomyces Cerevisiae) genomic nucleotide sequences
pdb	Nucleotide sequences derived from 3D protein structures in the Brookhaven Protein DataBank.
kabat	Kabats database of sequences of immunological interest
vector	Vector subset of GenBank
mito	Database of mitochondrial Sequences
alu	Select Alu repeats
epd	Eukaryotic Promoter Database
gss	Genome survey sequence, include singlepass genomic data, exon-trapped sequences and Alu PCR Sequences.

5.4.6 Filtering and Gapped BLAST

Filtering is the process of removing the undesired sequences from the query sequence prior to the search.

- BLAST filters regions of low-complexity. If your sequence contains large region of "low complexity" it may not significant hits to the database.
- You can turn off filtering by setting the "Filter" option to "None" using the pull down tab.

5.4.6.1 Summary of Filter Programs

Sequence Type	Description	Relevant Programs
Repeats	Low complexity DNA sequences, highly repetitive sequences, VNTRs (variable number of tandem repeats), and the like.	Dust for nucleic acid, XNU for amino acid RepeatMasker to screen against known human genomic repeat sequences.
Low information content sequences	Runs of single amino acid or few amino acids; runs of pyrimidines or purines in DNA.	Dust for nucleic acids, SEG for amino acids.
Vector	Due to experimental procedures, fragments of vector sequence can often be found in sample sequences usually at the beginning or end, but occasionally with a sequence.	Cross match
Structural Nucleic Acid Sequences	DNA sequences that encode structural RNAs (rRNA, rRNA, snRNA etc) that do not encode proteins.	

5.4.7 Gapped Blast

- Gapped-BLAST is also known as BLAST 2.0. It represents BLAST plus a new heuristic for gapped alignments. Version 2.0 of BLAST allows the introduction of gaps (detection and interactions) into alignment.
- With a gapped alignment tool, homologous domains do not have to be broken into several segments. Also, the scoring of gapped tends to be more biologically meaningful than ungapped results.
- The programs, blastn and blastp, offer fully gapped alignments, blastx and tblastn have 'in-frame' gapped alignments and use sum statistics to link alignments from different frames. The program tblastx provides only ungapped alignments.

5.4.7.1 Blast 2.0 Parameters

Parameter	Description
DATALIB	Database, or group of databases, chosen
MATRIX	Distance Matrix used : BL062 (default), PAM40, PAM20, PAM250
CUTOFF	Score Sg, chosen to limit Gapped Extensions to about 2% of the database entries.
EXPECT	Number of random Hits expected to be found (default=10) E-value.
FILTER	Option to use one of the two filters.

Output of the BLAST 2.0 is as follows

- Information on query sequence and databases used.
- Histogram, like the FASTA histogram.

- Descriptions (default=100) of Hits found in the databases.
- Scores in bits E-values: number of hits expected to be reported by chance.
- Alignments found (default=50).
- Parameters used in the BLAST search.

5.4.7.2 Three Major Refinements Have Been Included In BLAST 2.0 Are

(1) Two-hit Method

The original "extension of word pairs" procedure in BLAST is the main time consuming step. The "two hit" method has the following characteristics :

1. It requires two non-overlapping word pairs on same diagonal (no gaps) within distance A of each other based on the observation that HSPs are much longer than word pairs identify best HSP in nearly all cases has at least two word pairs.
2. Decrease T (T is the threshold parameter; as T increases the speed increases and the probability of missing weak similarity also increases) to achieve comparable sensitivity.

(2) Do non-gapped Extension

1. Do this only for the cases where two diagonal "word pairs" are within distance A of each other.
2. Find only the best non-gapped extension. This local region consists of "Two Word Pair+ non-gapped (ungapped) extensions".
3. Proceed with step3 (the gapped alignment), only if the score S of the ungapped extension is above some cutoff score Sg.

(3) Generate Gapped Alignment

Original BLAST calculates combined P(N) probability for all local regions found. Here, we have non-gapped extensions. If this best non-gapped extension has a score S than the cutoff Sg, then :

1. Apply dynamic programming to extend the non-gapped extension in both directions.
2. In this dynamic programming alignment, consider only alignments that drop the score more than an amount Xg below the best score seen. This limits the region of the two sequences over which the dynamic programming alignment is done.
3. Choose the score Sg so as to limit gapped extensions to about 2% of the database entries.

5.4.8 PSI-BLAST

PSI-BLAST (Position Specific Iterated-BLAST) is an implementation of BLAST for finding protein families. Instead of using a single amino acid at a given position in the query sequence, it is better to use a combination of amino acids known to be present at the same position in that protein and related ones. The search of sequence databases will thereby be expanded to include additional related sequences that might otherwise be missed. The major difficulty with such an expanded search is that an alignment of related sequences must already be available in order to know variations at each position in the query sequence.

PSI-BLAST has been designed to provide information on this variation starting with a BLAST search by a single query sequence.

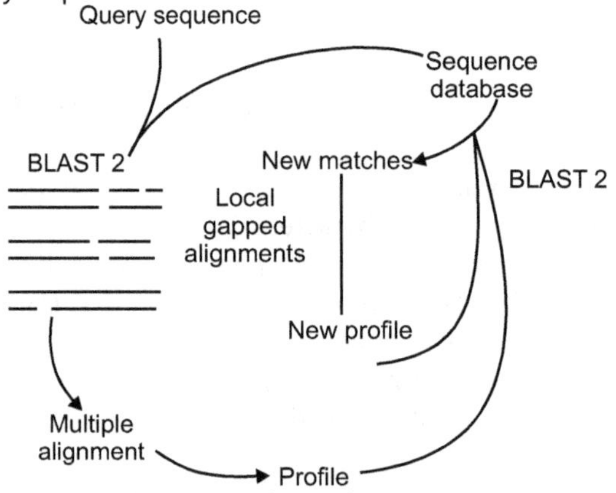

Fig. 5.12 : Schematic BLAST 2.0

5.4.8.1 Applications

- Distant homology detection.
- Fold assignment.
- Domain /identification.
- Evolutionary analysis.
- Sequence annotation/ function assignment.
- Profile export to other programs.
- Sequence clustering.
- Structural genomics target selection.

The method used by PSI-BLAST involves a series of repeated steps or iterations as follows :

1. A database search of a protein sequence database is performed using a query sequence.
2. The result of search are presented and can be accessed visually to see if any database sequences that are significantly related to the query sequence are present.
3. If such is the case, user decides to go through another iteration of the search.
4. The high scoring sequence matches found in the first step are aligned and from the alignment a sequence motif that indicates variations at each aligned position is produced.

   The database is then searched with this motif. The search has thus been expanded to include sequences that match the variations found in the motif at each sequence position.
5. The results are again displayed, indicating any newly discovered sequences that are significantly related to the motif sequences in addition to those found in the previous iteration.

6. Again, an opportunity is given to go through another iteration of the program, but this time including any newly recruited sequences to refine the motif. In this fashion, a new family of sequences that are significantly similar to the original query sequence can be found. It simple and easy to use program and is very useful for exploring protein family relationships.

5.4.8.2 Searching Motifs With PSI-BLAST

Psi-Blast is used to search a protein sequence database with a query sequence motifs, a matrix with rows representing sequence positions and columns representing variations in that position.

The motif represents the observed variations in the alignment of a related protein. PSI-BLAST can be used to find database matches almost as rapidly as Blastp finds matches to aquery sequence.

There are some differences between the motifs found by Psi-Blast:

1. The motif covers the entire sequence length whereas motifs usually cover only a short stretch of the sequences.
2. The same gap penalties are used as throughout the procedure and there is no position specific penalty as is other programs.
3. Each subsequent motif is based on using the query sequence as a master template for producing a multiple sequence alignment of the same length as the query sequence.
4. Columns in the alignment involve varying number of sequences depending on the extent of the local alignment of each sequence with the query, and columns with gaps in the query sequence are ignored.

Sequences > 98% similar to the query are not included in order to avoid biasing the motif.

Thus, the alignment is a compilation of the pair-wise alignments of each matching database sequence with the query sequence and is not a true multiple sequence alignment.

5.4.8.3 Problems With PSI-BLAST Approach

The main difficulty with searching for subtle sequence relationships based on similarities is determining the significance of the motifs that are found.

Such similarities may be evidence of structural of evolutionary relationships but they could also be due to matching of random variations that have no common origin or function. Protein structures are in general comprised of a tightly packed core and outside loops. Amino acid substitutions within the core are common but only certain substitutions will work at a given amino acid position in a given structure.

Another difficulty is that the procedure follows a "greedy algorithm".

With this, once additional sequences which match the query are found, then these newly found sequences influences the finding of more sequences like themselves and so on.

5.4.8.4 Position Specific Scoring Matrices

Once the motifs has been found, the frequencies of amino acids in each column are adjusted :

- Weighing the sequence to reduce the influence of the more alike sequences.
- Adding more counts (pseudocuments) representing other amino acid substitutions found among the observed types is to increase the statistical power of the matrix.
- These procedures are called Position Specific Scoring Matrices (PSSM).
  The resulting score in each column of the scoring matrix are scaled using the same scaling factor 1 as the BLOSUM62 scoring matrix in order that a threshold value T for HSPs and other statistical parameters used by Blastp may also be used by Psi-Blast.
- At each iteration, previously matched sequences with an E values less than 0.001 are used to produce the next motifs, but this value may aloes be changed.

5.4.8.5 Related Programs

Blastp	The first round of Psi-Blast is the same of Blastp. If one isn't looking for distant homologues, then Blastp will suffice.
Psi-Tblastn	This is a strategy to make a PSSM by Psi-Blast in the normal way, and then use it to search a DNA sequence in all 6 frames.
RPS-Blast	The key sequence is searched versus a library of premade PSSMs representing known protein families.
HMMER	HMMER searches are similar strategy to RPABLAST. HMMER uses HMM rather than a PSSM to represent the known protein families. HMMs are more efficient at dealing with gaps in comparison between distant homologous.
SAM	For matching sequences to greatest range of super family members, use SAM. A sequence can be extensively analyzed to the level of fold recognition at the SAM site.
PsiPred	PsiPred is a secondary structure prediction system that first aligns homologous using Psi-Blast and then issues a consensus secondary structure prediction.

5.5 FASTA & BLAST ALGORITHEM COMPARISON

FASTA	BLAST
FASTA searches for all matching words of length k.	BLAST searches for the most unusual or high scoring words (protein of length 3, nucleic acids of length11).
FASTA3 calculates statistical parameters from unrelated sequences during databases search.	BLAST2 calculates parameters for the scoring matrix and penalty combination and uses in database search. Other versions of BLAST calculate significance of matching regions rather than of a local alignment with gaps.

(Contd.)

FASTA	BLAST
Low complexity regions can give high scoring matches with sequences that are not related to the query sequence. FASTA3 does not remove low complexity regions. FASTA3 provides the programs prss3 to shuffle one sequence by individual amino acids or by window of amino acids.	BLAST2 provides facility to remove low complexity regions.

SUMMARY

- Bioinformatics tools are software programs that are designed for extracting the meaningful information from the mass of molecular biology/biological databases and to carry out sequence or structural analysis.
- **Examples of Bioinformatics Tools**
- **BLAST (Basic Local Alignment Search Tool)**
  BLAST is an algorithm for comparing primary biological sequence information, such as the amino acid sequences of different proteins or the nucleotide of DNA sequences.
- **FASTA**
  The program is one of the many heuristic algorithm proposed to speed up sequence comparison. The basic idea is to add a fast prescreen step to locate the highly matching segments between two sequences, and then extend these matching segments to local alignment using more rigorous algorithms such as Smith Waterman.
- **EMBOSS**
  EMBOSS (European Molecular Biology Open Software Suite) is a software analysis package. It can work with data in arrange of formats and also retrieve sequence data transparently from the web.
- **Clustalw**
  It is a fully automated sequence alignment tool for DNA and protein sequences. It returns the best match over a total length of input sequences, be it a protein or a nucleic acid.
- **RasMol**
  It is a powerful search tool to display the structure of DNA, protein and smaller molecules. Protein explorer, a derivative of rasmol, is an easier to use program.
- **PROSPECT**
  PROSPECT (Protein Structure Prediction and Evaluation Computer Toolkit) is a protein threading to construct a proteins 3D model.
- **PatternHunter**
  PatternHunter, based on Java, can identify all approximate repeats in a short time using little memory on a desktop computer. Its features are its advanced patented algorithm and data structures, and the java language used to create it.

- **COPIA**

  COPIA (Consensus Pattern Identification and Analysis) is a protein structure analysis tool for discovering motifs (Conserver regions) in a family of protein sequences.

QUESTIONS

MAY 2013

1. A Explain in detail FASTA algorithm and the recommended steps for a FASTA search.

Ans. : Please refer Section 5.2.1.

2. Explain BLAST algorithm. Discuss Gapped BLAST with its major refinements.

Ans. : Please refer Section 5.4 and 5.4.7.

OR

3. A Discuss Similarities and Differences of FASTA and BLAST tools for sequence alignment.

Ans. : Please refer Section 5.5.

4. Discuss the applications of PSI-BLAST program which explores protein family relationships.

Ans. : Please refer Section 5.4.8.

MAY 2014

1. Define PSI BLAST. Explain its importance in Bioinformatics application.

Ans. : Please refer Section 5.4.8 and 5.1.8.

2. Differentiate between FASTA and BLAST algorithms. **[8]**

Ans. : Please refer Section 5.5.

3. Explain in detail FASTA algorithm and the recommended steps for FASTA Search.

Ans. : Please refer Section 5.2.1.

4. List several implementations of FASTA algorithm. Explain any two in detail.

Ans. : Please refer Section 5.2.2.

❍ ❍ ❍

UNIT VI

FURHTER SCOPE

6.1 INTRODUCTION

6.1.1 Introduction to Environmental Bio-technology

- Environmental biotechnology is rapidly developing, increasingly important branch of science that has implications for both the prevention and cleans up of pollution in domestic and industrial waste streams.
- Environmental biotechnology is the used in waste treatment and pollution prevention. Environmental biotechnology can more efficiently clean up many wastes than conventional methods and greatly reduce our dependence on methods for land-based disposal.
- Every organism ingests nutrients to live and produces by products as a result. Different organisms need different types of nutrients. Some bacteria thrive on the chemical components of waste products.
- Environmental engineers use bioremediation, the broadest application of environmental biotechnology, in two basic ways. They introduce nutrients to stimulate the activity of bacteria already present in the soil at a waste site, or add new bacteria to the soil. The bacteria digest the waste at the site and turn it into harmless by products. After the bacteria consume the waste materials, they die off or return to their normal population levels in the environment. Bioremediation is an area of increasing interest. Through application of biotechnical methods, enzyme bioreactors are being developed that will pretreat some industrial waste and food waste components and allow their removal through the sewage system rather than through solid waste disposal mechanisms.
- Waste can also be converted to biofuel to run generators. Microbes can be induced to produce enzymes needed to convert plant and vegetable materials into building blocks for biodegradable plastics.
- In some cases, the byproducts of the pollution-fighting microorganisms are themselves useful. For example : methane can be derived from a form of bacteria that degrades sulfur liquor, a waste product of paper manufacturing. This methane can then be used as a fuel or in other industrial processes.
- Environmental biotechnology involves application of biotechnology i.e. use of living organism to the management of environmental problems and understanding of the specific application of metabolic capability and molecular biology of microorganisms for exploitation of many areas of biotechnology to reverse and prevent environmental problems.

- Environmental Biotechnology utilizes the biochemical potential of microorganisms and plants for the preservation and restoration of the environment. It promotes sustainable and efficient use of natural resources like fungi, plants, algae, and bacteria in the industrial processes. Our biological systems have the capability to absorb and control pollutants like free carbon sources from our environment and keep our surroundings clean and green.
- Integrated with the industrial processes, it helps in forming a balanced industrial framework that has better efficiency, makes better use of natural resources, and also keeps environment green.
- Green manufacturing technologies and sustainable development are the key issues that environmental biotechnology addresses.

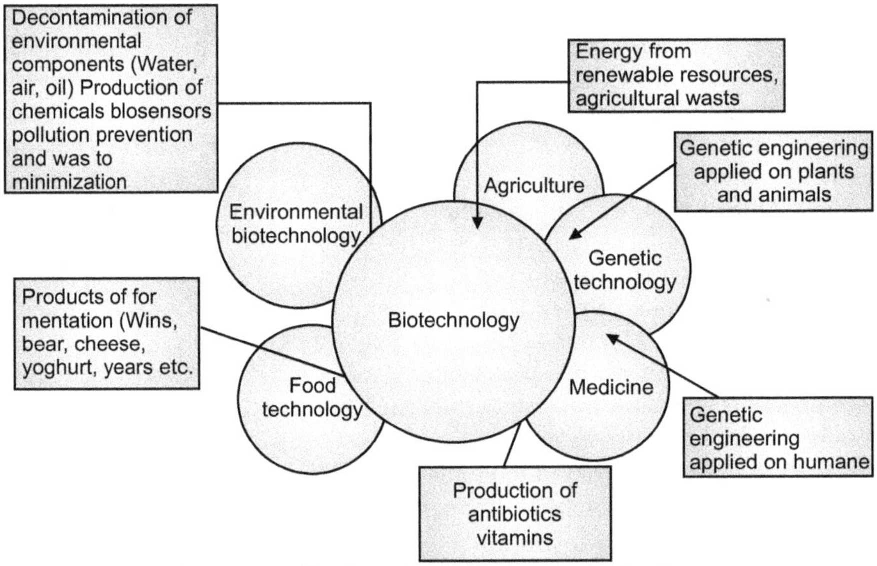

Fig. 6.1 : Application of environment biotechnology

6.1.2 Advantages

The uses and methods of environmental biotechnology applications have many diverse implications and benefits. Biotechnology is constantly being used to :

- Help adapt organisms and engineer useful ways to help clean up the environment and keep it green for the future generations.
- As well as eliminating the pollutants and wastes that affect our environment, there is a need to be able to promote and sustain the development of our society with the lowest possible impact on the environment.

- All biological processes have role in the removal of pollutants. Using biotechnology is enabling researchers and scientists take advantage this new versatility of organisms to convert and degrade certain compounds.
- New breakthroughs in methods of biotechnology applications including genomics, proteomics, bioinformatics, sequencing and imaging are all producing vast amounts of information.
- When it comes to the field of environmental microbiology, new studies are beginning to open up to an era of new possibilities and discoveries in the world of biodegradation.
- Both changes to the functional and metagenomic approaches are adding to our understanding and knowledge about the importance of having different pathways and types of networks to use in particular environments.
- Those compounds and will only continue to speed up the biomediation processes. This process is essential to the improving and preservation efforts to conserve resources and help the environment, as well as protect it from further damage.
- It seems as through marine types of environment are especially prone to this kind of occurrence because of the kinds of activities on coastlines such as oil spills.
- Not only are pollutants from humans a constant source of trouble, but also adding to that are the tons of gallons of petroleum that is entering the marine environment every year and coming from natural sources.
- Even though this has a high level of toxicity, a large portion of the petroleum that enters the marine system is being eliminated by the degrading activities caused by microbial sources.
- Biotechnology applications will continue to have a large impact on the environmental activities and help lessen the concern of degradation that is currently a large problem facing the environment. By using techniques and methods of biotechnology applications, scientists are able to help improve and slow down the degradation process as well as work to preserve the environment and work towards more suitable conservation methods.

6.1.3 Applications

Environmental biotechnology finds use in various fields and industries. In this section we have listed certain most popular and commonly practiced applications of environmental biotechnology around us.

Bio-Compositing

It involves combining organic materials under certain controlled conditions that decomposes them at a faster rate than they would decompose under natural conditions in free surroundings.

Bioenergy

We hear about fuels like biogas, biomass, and hydrogen being used for industrial, domestic, and space exploration purposes. All these fuels belong to the category of Bioenergy. Of late, need of the hour has been become finding alternate resources of energy that are clean and equally efficient. Energy generation from organic waste or biomass is the finest example of green energy. Biomass energy supply demand balances have become a component of energy sector analysis and planning and assumed greater importance in countries.

Bioremediation

Bioremediation is a clean up technology that uses naturally occurring microorganisms to degrade hazardous substances into less toxic or nontoxic compounds.

Bio-Transformation

Bio-Transformation is a process of Biological changes of complex compound to simpler toxic to non-toxic or vice-versa. It is used in manufacturing industries where toxic substances are released as bi-products.

E-Biomarker

E-Biomarker is a biological response to a chemical that gives a measure of exposure and, of toxic effect. Biological markers can provide molecular evidence of the correlation among oils and their sources.

6.1.4 Microbial World in Relation to Environmental Biotechnology

Environmental biotechnology can simply be described as "the optimal use of nature, in the form of plants, animals, bacteria, fungi and algae, to produce renewable energy, food and nutrients in a synergistic integrated cycle of profit making processes where the waste of each process becomes the feedstock for another process". Microorganisms are unicellular (capable of existence as single cells), too small to be seen with naked eye.

Among all forms of life on the earth, microorganisms predominate in numbers of species and in biomass, but their occurrence is generally underappreciated because of their small size and the need for a microscope to individual cells. Although a light microscope is generally required to visualize a single microbial cell, microbial colonies and communities can readily be observed in nature.

1. Archaea are a group of unicellular prokaryotic cells that sometimes produce methane (CH4) during their metabolism, and which often live in extreme environments such as high temperature, low pH or high salt concentrations. They are specially adapted to these conditions by means of special types of membranes and metabolism.

2. Bacteria are also unicellular prokaryotic organisms. They have a unique type of cell wall and cell membrane that distinguishes them from archaea. Bacteria live everywhere that life exists on earth except the most extreme environments, including in associations with animals and plants. Most are beneficial or harmless, but some cause diseases.

3. Algae are plant-like, photosynthetic, eukaryotic organisms that live wherever there is light and moisture. They convert carbon dioxide (CO_2) to organic material and produce oxygen (O_2) during photosynthesis, the same as plants. Protozoa are animal like, nonphotosynthetic eucaryotes common in moist environments, including the intestinal tracts of animals.

4. Most protozoans are motile because they are predatory on other microbes and have to catch and ingest their food. Daphnia are small, planktonic crustaceans, between 0.2 and 5 mm in length. Daphnia are members of order Cladocera, and are one of the several small aquatic crustaceans commonly used in environmental biotechnology research.

5. Fungi are nonphotosynthetic eucaryotes, generally non-motile, that absorb their nutrients directly from the environment. The kingdom includes mushrooms, molds and yeast. Yeast is truly unicellular, while molds and mushrooms, although they have a vegetative multicellular stage, produce unicellular spores. Molds live mainly in the soil and are responsible for the decomposition (biodegradation) of organic material.

Molds grow by filament formation and form reproductive structures (spores) that are spread by wind and water. Yeast reproduces by budding and lives in environments high in sugar. They metabolize sugars to reproduce ethanol and carbon dioxide.

6. Viruses are made up of nucleic acid (DNA or RNA) and protein and have some of the characteristics of life. But they lack ribosomes (for protein synthesis), membranes, and means to generate energy, which are properties of cells. The study of viruses developed within the field of bacteriology, and virology has developed into a major branch of microbiology.

- Viruses should considered microbes, but they are not microorganisms since they are noncellular.
- Viruses are considered obligate intracellular parasites because they can only replicate in association with a host cell which they infect. All kinds of cells include plant; animal and microbial are susceptible to virus infections. Since cell damage results from most viral infections, viruses are agents of disease. Although viruses are too small to be seen by conventional light microscopy, they can be visualized and photographed by means of electron microscopy.

6.2 INTRODUCTION TO GENETIC ENGINEERING

Genetic engineering, also called genetic modification, is the direct manipulation of an organism's genome using biotechnology. New DNA may be inserted in the host genome by first isolating and copying the genetic material of interest using molecular cloning methods to generate a DNA sequence, or by synthesizing the DNA, and then inserting this construct into the host organism.

- Genes may be removed, or "knocked out", using a nuclease. Gene targeting is a different technique that uses homologous recombination to change an endogenous gene, and can be used to delete a gene, remove exons, add a gene, or introduce point mutations. Genetic engineering alters the genetic make-up of an organism using techniques that remove heritable material or that introduces DNA prepared outside the organism either directly into the host or into a cell that is then fused or hybridized with the host.

- This involves using recombinant nucleic acid (DNA or RNA) techniques to form new combinations of heritable genetic material followed by the incorporation of that material either indirectly through a vector system or directly through micro-injection, macro injection and micro-encapsulation techniques.
- Genetic engineering does not normally include traditional animal and plant breeding, in vitro fertilization, induction of polyploidy, mutagenesis and cell fusion techniques that do not use recombinant nucleic acids or a genetically modified organism in the process.
- However the European Commission has also defined genetic engineering broadly as including selective breeding and other means of artificial selection. Cloning and stem cell research, although not considered genetic engineering, are closely related and genetic engineering can be used within them.
- Synthetic biology is an emerging discipline that takes genetic engineering a step further by introducing artificially synthesized genetic material from raw materials into an organism.
- If genetic material from another species is added to the host, the resulting organism is called transgenic. If genetic material from the same species or a species that can naturally breed with the host is used the resulting organism is called cisgenic. Genetic engineering can also be used to remove genetic material from the target organism, creating a gene knockout organism.
- In Europe genetic modification is synonymous with genetic engineering while within the United States of America it can also refer to conventional breeding methods. The Canadian regulatory system is based on whether a product has novel features regardless of method of origin.
- In other words, a product is regulated as genetically modified if it carries some trait not previously found in the species whether it was generated using traditional breeding methods (e.g., selective breeding, cell fusion, mutation breeding) or genetic engineering. Within the scientific community, the term genetic engineering is not commonly used; more specific terms such as transgenic are preferred.
- Plants, animals or microorganisms that have changed through genetic engineering are termed genetically modified organisms or GMOs. Bacteria were the first organisms to be genetically modified.
- Plasmid DNA containing new genes can be inserted into the bacterial cell and the bacteria will then express those genes.

- These genes can code for medicines or enzymes that process food and other substrates. Plants have been modified for insect protection, herbicide resistance, virus resistance, enhanced nutrition, tolerance to environmental pressures and the production of edible vaccines. Most commercialized GMO's are insect resistant and/or herbicide tolerant crop plants.
- Genetically modified animals have been used for research, model animals and the production of agricultural or pharmaceutical products. They include animals with genes knocked out, increased susceptibility to disease, hormones for extra growth and the ability to express proteins in their milk.

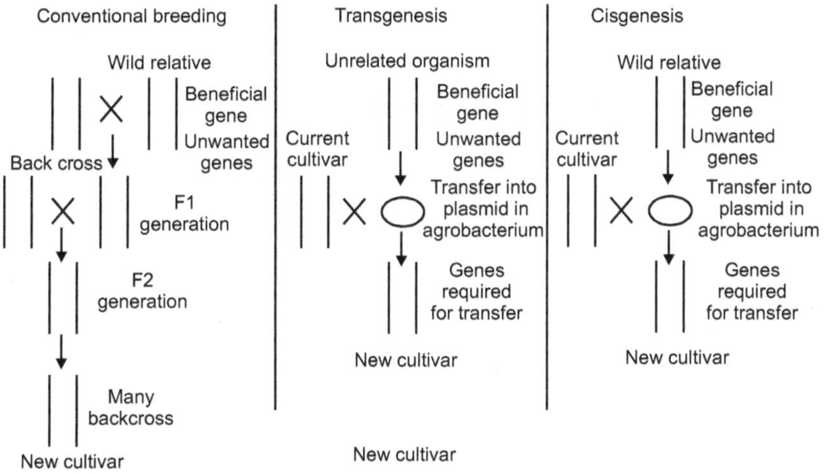

Fig. 6.2 : Comparison of conventional plant breeding with transgenic and cisgenic genetic modification

6.2.1 Applications

Genetic engineering has applications in medicine, research, industry and agriculture and can be used on a wide range of plants, animals and microorganisms.

Medicine

- In medicine, genetic engineering has been used to mass-produce insulin, human growth hormones, follistim (for treating infertility), human albumin, monoclonal antibodies, antihemophilic factors, vaccines and many other drugs.
- Vaccination generally involves injecting weak, live, killed or inactivated forms of viruses or their toxins into the person being immunized. Genetically engineered viruses are being developed that can still confer immunity, but lack the infectious sequences.
- Mouse hybridomas, cells fused together to create monoclonal antibodies; have been humanized through genetic engineering to create human monoclonal antibodies. Genetic engineering has shown promise for treating certain forms of cancer.

- Genetic engineering is used to create animal models of human diseases. Genetically modified mice are the most common genetically engineered animal model.
- They have been used to study and model cancer (the oncomouse), obesity, heart disease, diabetes, arthritis, substance abuse, anxiety, aging and Parkinson disease.
- Gene therapy is the genetic engineering of humans by replacing defective human genes with functional copies. This can occur in somatic tissue or germline tissue. If the gene is inserted into the germline tissue it can be passed down to that person's descendants.
- Gene therapy has been successfully used to treat multiple diseases, including X-linked SCID, chronic lymphocytic leukemia (CLL), and Parkinson's disease. In 2012, Glybera became the first gene therapy treatment to be approved for clinical use in either Europe or the United States after its endorsement by the European Commission.
- There are also ethical concerns should the technology be used not just for treatment, but for enhancement, modification or alteration of a human beings' appearance, adaptability, intelligence, character or behavior.
- The distinction between cure and enhancement can also be difficult to establish. Transhumanists consider the enhancement of humans desirable.

Industrial

- Using genetic engineering techniques one can transform microorganisms such as bacteria or yeast, or transform cells from multicellular organisms such as insects or mammals, with a gene coding for a useful protein, such as an enzyme, so that the transformed organism will over express the desired protein.
- One can manufacture mass quantities of the protein by growing the transformed organism in bioreactor equipment using techniques of industrial fermentation, and then purifying the protein.
- Some genes do not work well in bacteria, so yeast, insect cells, or mammalians cells, each a eukaryote, can also be used.
- These techniques are used to produce medicines such as insulin, human growth hormone, and vaccines, supplements such as tryptophan, aid in the production of food (chymosin in cheese making) and fuels.
- Other applications involving genetically engineered bacteria being investigated involve making the bacteria perform tasks outside their natural cycle, such as making biofuels, cleaning up oil spills, carbon and other toxic waste and detecting arsenic in drinking water.

Agriculture

- The genetic engineering of agricultural crops can increase the growth rates and resistance to different diseases caused by pathogens and parasites. This is beneficial as it can greatly increase the production of food sources with the usage of fewer resources that would be required to host the world's growing populations.

- These modified crops would also reduce the usage of chemicals, such as fertilizers and pesticides, and therefore decrease the severity and frequency of the damages produced by this chemical pollution. Ethical and safety concerns have been raised around the use of genetically modified food. A major safety concern relates to the human health implications of eating genetically modified food, in particular whether toxic or allergic reactions could occur. Gene flow into related non-transgenic crops, off target effects on beneficial organisms and the impact on biodiversity are important environmental issues. Ethical concerns involve religious issues, corporate control of the food supply, intellectual property rights and the level of labeling needed on genetically modified products.

Bio-Art and Entertainment

- Genetic engineering is also being used to create BioArt. Some bacteria have been genetically engineered to create black and white photographs. Genetic engineering has also been used to create novelty items such as lavender-colored carnations, blue roses, and glowing fish.

6.2.2 Current Developments in Genetic Engineering

- In the mid-1990s the international guidelines established by the Declaration of Helsinki were modified to allow certain forms of cell manipulation in order to develop germ cells for therapeutic purposes. Scientists are also exploring genetic engineering as a means of combating the HIV virus.
- In 1997 the cloning of an adult sheep by Scottish scientist Ian Wilmut brought new urgency to the cloning issue. Prior to this development, cloning had been successful only with immature cells, not those from an adult animal. The breakthrough raised the prospect of human cloning and prompted an international debate regarding the ethical and legal implications of cloning.
- In November 2001, scientists first successfully inserted the DNA from one human cell into another human egg. Although the eggs began to replicate, they died shortly after the procedure. Human cloning has caused the most intense debate on the issue, with the debate focusing upon scientific, moral, and religious concerns over this possibility. Scientists do not expect that human cloning will be possible for several years.
- Dolly lived for six years before dying in February 2003, which is about half of the normal life expectancy of a sheep. Proponents of the cloning experiments suggest that cloning opens a number of possibilities in scientific research, including the nature of certain diseases and the development of genetically enhanced medications. Scientists have also successfully cloned endangered animals.

6.3 BIOTECHNOLOGY

- Contrary to its name, biotechnology is not a single technology. Rather it is a group of technologies that share two (common) characteristics working with living cells and their molecules and having a wide range of practice uses that can improve our lives.

- Biotechnology can be broadly defined as "using organisms or their products for commercial purposes." As such, (traditional) biotechnology has been practices since the beginning of records history. (It has been used to :) bake bread, brew alcoholic beverages, and breed food crops or domestic animals.
- But recent developments in molecular biology have given biotechnology new meaning, new prominence, and new potential. It is (modern) biotechnology that has captured the attention of the public. Modern biotechnology can have a dramatic effect on the world economy and society.
- One example : of modern biotechnology is genetic engineering. Genetic engineering is the process of transferring individual genes between organisms or modifying the genes in an organism to remove or add a desired trait or characteristic.
- Examples of genetic engineering are described later in this document. Through genetic engineering, genetically modified crops or organisms are formed. These GM crops or GMOs are used to produce biotech-derived foods.
- It is this specific type of modern biotechnology, genetic engineering that seems to generate the most attention and concern by consumers and consumer groups. What is interesting is that modern biotechnology is far more precise than traditional forms of biotechnology and so is viewed by some as being far safer.)
- The wide concept of "biotech" or "biotechnology" encompasses a wide range of procedures for modifying living organisms according to human purposes, going back to domestication of animals, cultivation of plants, and "improvements" to these through breeding programs that employ artificial selection and hybridization.

6.3.1 Scope of Bioinformatics in Biotechnology

- Bioinformatics and Biotechnology is expected to substantially create an impact on scientific, engineering and economic development of the world. These are fast growing important disciplines for academic research and industrial applications.
- Career opportunities in Bioinformatics and Biotechnology will continue to expand on both the computer and biological science forefronts. For Computer Science, there are opportunities in academics, programming, database development, system analysis and software engineering.
- In the Biological Sciences, career opportunities exist in agricultural, animal, environmental, microbial and industrial research as well as academia.

6.3.2 Applications

Biotechnology has applications in four major industrial areas, including health care (medical), crop production and agriculture, non-food (industrial) uses of crops and other products (example : biodegradable plastics, vegetable oil, biofuels), and environmental uses. For example one application of biotechnology is the directed use of organisms for the manufacture of organic products (examples : include beer and milk products). Another example is using naturally present bacteria by the mining industry in bioleaching. Biotechnology is also used to recycle, treat waste, cleanup sites contaminated by industrial activities (bioremediation), and also to produce biological weapons.

Industrial Biotechnology

Industrial biotechnology applies the techniques of modern molecular biology to improve the efficiency and reduce the environmental impacts of industrial processes like textile, paper and pulp, and chemical manufacturing. For example : industrial biotechnology companies develop biocatalysts, such as enzymes, to synthesize chemicals. Enzymes are proteins produced by all organisms. Using biotechnology, the desired enzyme can be manufactured in commercial quantities.

Environmental Biotechnology

Environmental biotechnology is the used in waste treatment and pollution prevention. Environmental biotechnology can more efficiently clean up many wastes than conventional methods and greatly reduce our dependence on methods for land-based disposal.

Human Applications

- Biotechnical methods are now used to produce many proteins for pharmaceutical and other specialized purposes. A harmless strain of Escherichia coli bacteria, given a copy of the gene for human insulin, can make insulin.
- As these genetically modified (GM) bacterial cells age, they produce human insulin, which can be purified and used to treat diabetes in humans. Microorganisms can also be modified to produce digestive enzymes.
- In the future, these microorganisms could be colonized in the intestinal tract of persons with digestive enzyme insufficiencies. Products of modern biotechnology include artificial blood vessels from collagen tubes coated with a layer of the anticoagulant heparin.

Agriculture

Genetically modified crops ("GM crops", or "biotech crops") are plants used in agriculture, the DNA of which has been modified using genetic engineering techniques. In most cases the aim is to introduce a new trait to the plant which does not occur naturally in the species.

6.4 DEGRADATION IN THE ECOSYSTEM

- The degradation of ecosystems is an environmental problem that diminishes the capacity of species to survive. This degradation occurs in different ways and is manifested in a reduction in the richness of the ecosystems as well as their biological diversity, and in the goods and services they can offer, thereby affecting indigenous and/or migratory species.
- The degradation of ecosystems due to overexploitation of their resources, though serving a short-term economic goal, has had direct negative effects on social welfare in

the medium and long terms. As long as the ecosystem is not degraded, it represents a source of wealth for society, hence the importance of keeping it in good condition.

- One of the main causes that contribute to the degradation of ecosystems is the deforestation due to the advance of the agriculture frontier and inappropriate forest exploitation. More lands are deforested for commercial agriculture and live-stock rearing, and due to overexploitation of forest for wood and energy. In Nicaragua deforestation rates reach over 150,000 hectares per year and in Costa Rica over 18,500 hectares per year. At a lower scale, another problem is the uncontrolled fires used to prepare land for agricultural activities or to remove forest for the development of stock rearing areas. This practice eliminates the organic covering of the land, making it more susceptible to erosion by both wind and water.
- In addition, the fire's cause health problems and detract from the aesthetic value of the landscape. Accidental or natural fires are another case in point. They affect areas of natural forest.
- In the Upala and Los Chiles cantons, in Costa Rica, some 10,000 hectares were burned between 1998 and 1999. This problem is even more serious in the Nicaraguan territory of the basin. Equipment is lacking and communities need to be organized to control these fires as one of the main barriers to the burning of large areas.
- The construction of roads without proper drainage measures or in territories subject to penetration and settlement is high-stress factors for ecosystems, especially those which are highly fragile as a result of their weather conditions and the nature of their soil and water.
- Mining and the extraction of construction materials without taking measures to cushion the impact cause drastic changes in the natural landscape while degrading its valuable ecosystems.
- Wetlands are very fragile ecosystems that are being severely affected, causing a reduction in the number and diversity of the species of terrestrial flora, birds, reptiles, mammals, fish, and crustaceans.
- This problem results from excessive exploitation of wildlife species either to feed the population, to trade their furs, or to trade live species, and from sedimentation, which causes changes in water quality, thereby significantly affecting the reproduction of aquatic species that live and/or reproduce in the wetlands.
- The SJRB wetlands are very valuable ecosystems, which regulate the hydrological cycle and provide food and shelter for hundreds of species, including large quantities of migratory birds. One major cause of the deterioration of this ecosystem is the draining of wide areas of wetlands to give access to agricultural zones or human settlements.
- Aerial photographs of the Caño Negro sector show how the pools of water have diminished over time, due in part to the drainage of wetlands for agricultural purposes and to the sedimentation occurring in recent years in the basin.

- Owing to the deterioration of these areas and the pressure of the neighboring communities on the use of the natural resources of the wetlands, it is necessary to draw up management plans to outline the socioeconomic characteristics of users and guidelines for usage, since people are highly dependent on these resources for their survival.
- A large portion of the ecological problems of the wetlands is due to ignorance of their benefits. The use of inappropriate fishing techniques endangers the existence of certain species, altering the food chain of aquatic fauna and consequently deteriorating the aquatic ecosystems.
- This is the case of the bull shark that is now hard to find in Lake Nicaragua or in the San Juan River. In some cases, the introduction of exotic species endangers the existence of indigenous species with a high cultural value. Such is the case of the guapote, whose numbers are being reduced by the introduction of tilapias.
- The deterioration of ecosystems is exacerbated by the lack of an institutional presence in the territory, be it for technical or economic reasons, or a combination of both. As a result, laws on the regulation and control of natural resource use are not enforced.
- The participation of civil society in controlling the use and exploitation of natural resources is limited and, in many cases, very timid or markedly apathetic. The degradation of the ecosystems makes the economic and social infrastructure of the SJRB more vulnerable and increases the potential impact on the population.
- This vulnerability is reflected in shorter periods between the occurrence of floods or droughts and the soil becomes more unstable.
- Possible solutions to the problem of deterioration of the ecosystems include developing formal and informal environmental education programs to make farmers more aware of their actions; increasing enforcement of the existing legislation; promoting proper natural resource management; and promoting the organization of grassroots groups to control burning from the outset. To prevent or mitigate the damage caused by extreme conditions, such as flooding and droughts and other effects of natural phenomena, it is necessary to set up and early warning system about possible swelling of water bodies and to monitor hydro meteorological behavior.
- It is also necessary to set up a seismographic network to monitor the behavior of volcanoes and tectonic faults. Similarly, social organization is necessary to design and test emergency plans for natural phenomena, to reduce the damage they cause.

6.5 EARTHS FOUR SPHERE

The area near the surface of the earth can be divided up into four inter-connected "geo-spheres:" the lithosphere, hydrosphere, biosphere, and atmosphere. Scientists can classify life and material on or near the surface of the earth to be in any of these four spheres. The names of the four spheres are derived from the Greek words for stone (litho), air (atmo), water (hydro), and life (bio). The four spheres show how the four main components of Planet Earth form a complete system. These main components are land, air, water, and life.

Lithosphere

The lithosphere is the solid, rocky crust covering entire planet. This crust is inorganic and is composed of minerals. It covers the entire surface of the earth from the top of Mount Everest to the bottom of the Mariana Trench. Earth's crust and a portion of the upper mantle directly below the crust form the lithosphere. The lithosphere, also known as Geosphere is made of the earth's core, the mantle, crust, ocean floor, mountains, sand, rocks, alphalt, bricks, etc. Lithosphere of the earth is the outer solid crust on the earth's surface that surrounds the hot molten core of the earth. The lithosphere consists of about 30 small and large pieces called plates that are continuously but very slowly moving on the very hot rocks below it. These hot rocks constitute the athenosphere of the earth.

Pollutants in Lithosphere

Major problems of lithospheric pollution and environmental change

1. Soil erosion
2. Pesticides and herbicides
3. Hazardous industrial waste
4. Hazardous household and business waste
5. Nuclear waste

1. Soil Erosion

It is when particles of soil are transported (carried) by either water, or wind (two agents of erosion),

Four Principal Factors in Soil Erosion are

1. Climate
2. Soil Characteristics
3. Topography
4. Groundcover

Climate effects erosion principly in the area of precipitation. Soil Characteristics include soil texture, organic matter content, structure and permeability. Soils low in clay and organic matter, high in sand and silty are most erodible. Well drained sandy and rocky soils are the least erodible. Clayey soils are usually the worst polluters. Organic matter improves soil structure, increases permeability and water holding capacity and soil fertility. Soil structure is the organization of soil particles into aggregates. Soil structure effects the soils ability to absorb water. Compacted or crusted soils have low permeability. Soil Permeability is the ability of soil to allow air and water to move through the soil.

Impacts of Erosion

Topography refers to slope. Slope length and steepness are critical factors in erosion potential since they determine the velocity of runoff to a great extent. The energy of flowing water (and the erosion potential) increases as the square of the velocity Groundcover refers principally to vegetation. Vegetation shields the soil surface from the impact of falling rain, slows the velocity of runoff, holds soil particles in place and maintains the soils ability to absorb water.

Hydrosphere

The hydrosphere is composed of all of the water on or near the earth. This includes the oceans, rivers, lakes, and even the moisture in the air. Ninety-seven percent of the earth's water is in the oceans. The remaining three percent is fresh water; three-quarters of the fresh water is solid and exists in ice sheets. An abiotic (nonbiological) open system that includes all of the Earth's water. The hydrosphere is made of everything water such as oceans, rivers, lakes, rain, snow, and ice caps. Hydrosphere of the earth refers to all the bodies of water and ice on the surface of the earth as well as the water vapour in its atmosphere. Hydrosphere makes up about three fourths of the earth's surface.

Pollutants in Hydrosphere

- Industrial and communal waste products
- Petroleum and mineral oil
- Emissions of transport
- Waste products of agriculture
- Pesticides and mineral fertilizers, radioactive substances

Biosphere

The biosphere is composed of all living organisms. Plants, animals, and one-celled organisms are all part of the biosphere. Most of the planet's life is found from three meters below the ground to thirty meters above it and in the top 200 meters of the oceans and seas. The intricate, interconnected web that links all organisms with their physical environment. The biosphere is all that has life such as plants, animals, people, insects, microbes, etc. Biosphere of the earth refers to the regions of earth where life forms such as animals and plants live. These include the surface of the earth and areas close to the surface.

Pollutants in Biosphere

Pollutant	Sources	Effects
Ozone A colorless gas that is the major constituent of photochemical smog at the Earth's surface. In the upper atmosphere (stratosphere), however, ozone is beneficial, protecting us from the sun's harmful rays.	Ozone is formed in the lower atmosphere as a result of chemical reactions between oxygen, volatile organic compounds, and nitrogen oxides in the presence of sunlight. Sources: include vehicles, factories, landfills, industrial solvents.	It can irritate the respiratory system. It can also reduce the yield of agricultural crops and injure forests and other vegetation. Ozone is the most injurious pollutant to plant life.

(Contd.)

Pollutant	Sources	Effects
Carbon Monoxide Odorless and colorless gas emitted in the exhaust of motor vehicles and engines where there is incomplete fossil fuel combustion.	Automobiles, buses, trucks, small engines, and some industrial processes.	Reduces the ability of blood to deliver oxygen to vital tissues, affecting primarily the cardiovascular and nervous systems.
Nitrogen Dioxide Light brown gas at lower concentrations; in higher concentrations becomes a component of brown urban haze.	Result of burning fuels in utilities, industrial boilers, cars, and trucks.	One of the major pollutants that causes smog and acid rain. Can harm humans and vegetation when concentrations are sufficiently high.
Particulate Matter Solid matter or liquid droplets from smoke, dust, fly ash and condensing vapors that can be suspended in the air for long periods of time.	Industrial processes, smelters, automobiles, burning industrial fuels, woodsmoke, dust from paved and unpaved roads, construction, and agricultural ground breaking.	These microscopic particles can affect breathing and respiratory health, causing increased respiratory disease and lung damage, and possibly premature death.
Sulfur Dioxide Colorless gas, odorless at low concentrations but pungent at very high concentrations.	Emitted largely from industrial, institutional, utility and apartment-house furnaces and boilers, as well as petroleum refineries, smelters, paper mills, and chemical plants.	One of the major pollutants that cause smog. Can also, at high concentrations, affect human health, especially among asthmatics, and acidify lakes and streams.
Lead Lead and lead compounds can adversely affect human health through either ingestion of lead-contaminated soil, dust, paint, or direct inhalation.	Transportation sources using lead in their fuels, coal combustion, smelters, car battery plants, and combustion of garbage containing lead products.	Elevated lead levels can adversely affect mental development, kidney function, and blood chemistry. Young children are particularly at risk.
Toxic Air Pollutants Includes pollutants such as arsenic, asbestos, and benzenes.	Chemical plants, industrial processes, motor vehicle emissions and fuels, and building materials.	Known or suspected to cause cancer, respiratory effects, birth defects, and reproductive and other serious health effects.

(Contd.)

Pollutant	Sources	Effects
Stratospheric Ozone Depleters chlorofluorocarbons (CFCs), halons, carbon tetrachloride, and methyl chloroform rise to the upper atmosphere where they destroy the protective ozone layer.	Industrial household refrigeration, cooling and cleaning processes, car and home air conditioners, some fire extinguishers, and plastic foam products.	Increased exposure to UV radiation could potentially cause an increase in skin cancer, cataracts, suppression of the human immune response system, and environmental damage.
Greenhouse gases Gases that build up in the atmosphere that may induce global climate change or the "greenhouse effect."They include carbon dioxide, methane, and nitrous oxide.	Carbon dioxide emissions from fossil fuel combustion. Methane comes from landfills, livestock, coal mines, and rice paddies. Nitrous oxide results from industrial processes,	Increased global temperature, increased severity and frequency of storms and other "weather extremes," melting of the polar ice cap, and sea-level rise.

Atmosphere

- The atmosphere is the body of air which surrounds our planet. Most of our atmosphere is located close to the earth's surface where it is most dense. The air of our planet is 79% nitrogen and just under 21% oxygen; the small amount remaining is composed of carbon dioxide and other gasses.
- The atmosphere is a thin veil of gases surrounding the Earth, which form a protective boundary between outer space and the biosphere; generally considered to extend about 480 km from the surface.
- The atmosphere is made of gasses such as oxygen, hydrogen, water vapor, ozone, and the wind.
- All four spheres can be and often are present in a single location. For example, a piece of soil will of course have mineral material from the lithosphere. Additionally, there will be elements of the hydrosphere present as moisture within the soil, the biosphere as insects and plants, and even the atmosphere as pockets of air between soil pieces.
- The remaining part consists mainly of Argon and small amount of many other gases, water vapour and dust particles. The lower part of the atmosphere is called troposphere.
- All clouds exist in the troposphere, and various weather conditions like wind and storms also take place in it. At altitude of about 1600 kilometers the atmosphere gradually fades into empty space.

6.6 ROLE OF BIOINFORMATICS IN BIOTECHNOLOGY

- The term 'bioinformatics' is the short form of 'biological informatics', just as biotechnology is the short form of 'biological technology'. Anthony Kerlavage, of the Celera Genomics, defined bioinformatics as 'Any application of computation to the field of biology, including data management, algorithm development, and data mining'
- Clearly, a number of divergent areas, many of them outside biotechnology, come under bioinformatics. Bioinformatics is the field of science in which biology, computer science, and information technology merge to form a single discipline. The ultimate goal of the field is to enable the discovery of new biological insights as well as to create a global perspective from which unifying principles in biology can be discerned. Initial interest in bioinformatics was propelled by the necessity to create databases of biological sequences.
- The first database was created within a short period after the Insulin protein sequence was made available in 1956. The sequence information generated by the genome research, initiated in 1988 has now been stored as a primary information source for future applications in medicine. The available data is so huge that if compiled in books, the data would run into 200 volumes of 1000 pages each and reading alone (ignoring understanding factor) would require 26 years working around the clock.
- For the population of about 5 billion human beings with two individuals differing in three millions bases, the genomic sequence difference database would have about 15,000,000 billion entries.
- The present challenge to handle such a huge volume database design, develop software for database access and manipulation, and device data-entry procedures to compensate for the varied computer procedures and systems used in different laboratories.
- A single experiment can now yield data on the transcription level of 100,000 different mRNA species from a given tissue (Winzeler et al., 1998).

Applications of Bioinformatics

Genomics

- Genomics is an important area of modern biology, where the nucleotide sequences of all the chromosomes of an organism are mapped and thereby the location of different genes and their sequences are determined. Genomics involves extensive analysis of nucleic acids through molecular biological techniques, before the data are ready for processing by computers.
- Entire genomes of several organisms such as Escherichia coli, yeast, the malarial parasite, the nematode Caenorhabditis elegans, the angiosperm Arabidopsis thaliana, etc., have now been unravelled. The most significant recent advancement in modern biology is the mapping of the entire genomes of man and the rice plant.

- Estimating the number of genes in an organism basing on the number of nucleotide base pairs was not reliable, due to the presence of high numbers of redundant copies of many genes. Genomics has corrected this situation. It is now known that a human being has about 30,000 genes and not 1, 00,000, as estimated earlier. The rice plant contains about 50,000 genes, many thousands more than in the human being. It is also clear that several thousands of genes are common to different organisms, irrespective of their taxonomic closeness or otherwise. Information derived from genome analysis not only tells us on which chromosome specific genes reside but also helps in determining their function.
- Such knowledge is necessary to improve the economic potential of organisms, reduce susceptibility to parasites and diseases, transfer genes from one organism to a totally unrelated organism to produce improved varieties, etc. Useful genes can be selected from a gene library thus constructed and inserted into other organisms for improvement or harmful genes can be silenced.

Proteomics

- Proteomics involves the sequencing of amino acids in a protein, determining its three-dimensional structure and relating it to the function of the protein. Before computer processing comes into the picture, extensive data, particularly through crystallography and NMR, are required for this kind of a study. With such data on known proteins, the structure and its relationship to function of newly discovered proteins can be understood in a very short time. In such areas, bioinformatics has an enormous analytical and predictive potential. Protein folding alone of the most significant and fundamental problem in biological science realizing this, IBM in Dec 1999, had built a supercomputer, which is 2 million times faster than the today's fastest desktop PC. This new computer nicknamed "Blue Gene" by IBM researchers will be capable of performing more than one quadrillion operations per second. Better understanding of how proteins fold will give scientists and doctors better insight into diseases and ways to combat them.

Cheminformatics and Drug Design

- Drug design through bioinformatics is one of the most actively pursued areas of research. Since a great majority of drugs are LMW compounds and since many of them are primarily derived from biological sources, there has always been a great interest in the study of LMW compounds of biological origin. Cheminformatics (or chemoinformatics) deals with such compounds, the products of secondary metabolism, often called natural products. Over one million products of secondary metabolism are known. The physico-chemical properties and chemical structures for over 100,000 natural products are available in different databases. For most of them, the biological role in the organisms in which they are synthesized is not known, but they have some kind of bioactivity against others.

- This bioactivity can be turned to advantage for therapeutic purposes. Here the expertise of a pharmacologist is required. Several therapeutically active compounds are synthetic. Over a period of time, synthetic organic chemists have realized that it is no longer easy or possible, to continuously conceptualize new structures.
- The alternative is to use natural products with a desired and known activity and to use them directly or to structurally modify them for improved performance and lower levels of side effects. In this context, the natural products are of great importance to the field of drug design. Whether synthetic or structurally modified natural products, drug development is a time consuming and expensive process. It would take anything like 10 to 15 years and 100 to 150 million US dollars to develop a successful drug. At the end of this effort there is no guarantee that the drug would be as important as when it was conceived and/or that the market forces would accept it.
- It is now possible, through computer algorithm based bioinformatic procedures, to identify and structurally modify a natural product, to design a drug with the desired properties and to assess its therapeutic effects, theoretically. Such procedures, similar to an architect's on board plan before construction, are described as in silico (in the computer, based on silicon chip technology), as opposed to the earlier in vitro (in experimental models) and in vivo (in clinical trials) methods. In silico procedures take a surprisingly short time, and provide the drug designers all the information they need before actually synthesizing the drug.

  Cheminformatics involves organization of chemical data in a logical form to facilitate the process of understanding chemical properties, their relationship to structures and making inferences. Chemical structures are the input to identify similar compounds for screening for biological activity. It also helps to assess the properties of new compounds, by comparison with the known compounds.
- The risk involved in the earlier random processes of drug discovery methods is largely removed by bioinformatics.

Molecular Phylogenies

- Phylogeny is the origin and evolution of organisms. With an estimated four million organisms, though not even a quarter of them are currently known to science, it is necessary that they are properly classified and named. It will be of great advantage to understand the genetic and evolutionary relationships of organisms, in order to use them in a profitable manner, in biotechnology and elsewhere. Biologists have constructed very elegant systems of classifications for the known organisms, though problems persist. All this commendable work, with over three centuries of history, was done using externally visible, structural, chemical or functional attributes of organisms. This constitutes the field of taxonomy, which is called systematic when the theory of organic evolution is applied to it. With the advancements in molecular biology, biologists have used data from the genetic material to characterize organisms and to verify their classification and relationships, inferred on the basis of other evidence. Since it is impractical to use entire genomes for this purpose, nucleotide sequences of genes in the genomes from the mitochondria and chloroplasts are used. These nucleotide sequences are compared using complex computer software.

- Extensive work was carried out this way, comparing a very large number of organisms of plants and animals. A number of systematizes would be benefited if bioinformatists provide them with computer-based services to analyze their systematic data. Amino acid sequences and characteristics of proteins are also used in systematic. The metabolic protein enzyme cytochrome C, with 100 to 112 amino acids and a MW of about 12.59 kDa, was used to unravel phylogenetic relationships of a wide range of organisms. The protein is identified basing on its function, which is a certain guide of its nature and then the sequence comparisons are made. Study of amino acid sequences of insulin, the peptide/protein hormone, which is involved in the mammalian carbohydrate metabolism, is another example. Such a study has also helped in choosing non-homologous insulin closest to human insulin, for use in the management of diabetes.

Drug Modification

- Several synthetic products are quite useful but cannot be used by one and all for certain effects in some people. For example, aspartame (marketed under different trade names) is a dipeptide of aspartic acid and phenylalanine, and is 300 times sweeter than cane sugar. Aspartame is widely used as an alternate sweetener by diabetics and others who cannot take sweeteners loaded with calories. Unfortunately, pregnant women and people suffering from phenylketonuria, a disorder due to an impaired metabolism of phenylalanine, should not use aspartame. It would be useful if phenylalanine were submitted by some other amino acid without affecting it sweetness, to remove the restriction on its use. Cyclosporine A, an 11-amino acid cyclic peptide, is the most popular immunosuppressant widely used in tissue and organ transplantation to prevent tissue rejection.
- However, cyclosporine A has certain side effects and some antibiotic activity, which complicate post-transplant monitoring.
- It will be a great help if the side effects and antibiotic activity are removed through amino acid substitution, retaining immunosuppressant activity, to make the drug more reliable and safer.

Glycomics

- Glycobiology is the study of carbohydrates of biological origin. Monosaccharide's, the building blocks of complex polysaccharides, are LMW compounds like the nucleotides and amino acids. Polysaccharides are HMW compounds like nucleic acids and the proteins.
- There are iso- and heteropolymers of carbohydrates. Polysaccharides are involved in such biological functions as storage products (starch, glycans, arabans, galactans, and

mannans), structural components (cellulose, hemicelluloses, pectin, and chitin) and functional compounds (metabolic and nutritional). The structures of the monosaccharide's, their number and sequences in polysaccharides, are all genetically determined, as for nucleic acids and proteins. While four nucleotides offer only 64 triplet codes, the carbohydrates offer 34,625 combinations.

- With ever continuously discovered numerous biological roles of carbohydrates, glycobiology is a rapidly expanding are of biological research. Glycomics, the application of bioinformatic procedures to carbohydrates research, is the future field of bioinformatics.

L- AND D-AMINO ACIDS

- It is a much debated and yet unsolved perplexing feature that in nature all the carbohydrates are of the D-configuration and all the amino acids are of the L-configuration, although carbohydrates and amino acids of the alternative configuration do occur.

  The 'dermorphin gene associated peptide', that mimics morphin activity, is composed of 11 D-amino acids. An all L-amino acid structure has no activity. It is hard to explain why.

- It is also not understood why peptides formed of D-amino acids are more susceptible to protein degradation. It will be very helpful if search is made for peptide drugs with partially or wholly D-amino acids.

- There are several bioactive but toxic L-amino acid peptides, which can be modified to contain some or all D-amino acids to reduce toxicity and to even improve bioactivity.

  There is a D-amino acid hexapeptide combinational library with structures of over 52, 28,400 peptides, which is a very rich source of information for such research, in the very promising area of drug design.

SUMMARY

- **Biomass :** Material produced by or remaining after the death of organisms (e.g., bacteria, plants, and animals).
- **Biotechnology :** A collection of technologies that use living cells and/or biological molecules to solve problems and make useful products.
- **Bioremediation :** The use of organisms, usually microorganisms, to break down pollutants in soil, air or groundwater.
- **DNA (Deoxyribonucleic acid) :** The chemical molecule that is the basic genetic material found in all cells. Each unit of DNA is made of nucleotides: adenine (A), guanine (G), thymine (T) and cytosine (C), as well as a sugar and a phosphate. DNA is inherited. DNA is a very long, thin molecule; it is packaged into units called chromosomes.

- **Enzymes :** A protein that accelerates the rate of chemical reactions. Enzymes are catalysts that promote reactions repeatedly, without being damaged by the reactions.
- **Gene :** A unit of hereditary information. A gene is a section of a DNA molecule that specifies the production of a particular protein.
- **Genetic Engineering :** The technique of removing, modifying or adding genes to a DNA molecule in order to change the information it contains. By changing this information, genetic engineering changes the type or amount of proteins an organism is capable of producing.
- **Genetically Modified Organism :** An organism that has been modified, or transformed, using modern techniques of genetic exchange is commonly referred to as a genetically-modified organism (GMO).
- **Gene Therapy :** Altering DNA within cells in a living organism to treat or cure a disease. It is one of the most promising areas of biotechnology research. New genetic therapies are being developed to treat diseases such as cystic fibrosis, AIDS and cancer.
- **Genome :** The complete set of an organism's genetic information. In humans this corresponds to twenty-three pairs of chromosomes.
- **Molecular Biology :** A branch of biology concerned with studying the chemical structures and processes of biological phenomena at the molecular level
- **Plant Breeding :** It is the technique involving crossing plants to produce varieties with particular characteristics (traits) which are carried in the genes of the plants and passed on to future generations.
- **Recombinant DNA :** DNA that is formed by combining DNA from two different sources. Humans direct formation of recombinant DNA through selective breeding and genetic engineering
- **Recombinant DNA (rDNA) Technology :** The laboratory manipulation of DNA in which DNA, or fragments of DNA from different sources, is cut and recombined using enzymes. This recombinant DNA is then inserted into a living organism. rDNA technology is usually used synonymously with genetic engineering.
- **Transgenic Plant :** Genetically engineered plant or offspring of genetically engineered plants. Transgenic plants result from the insertion of genetic material from another organism so that the plant will exhibit a desired trait. Recombinant DNA techniques are usually used.

QUESTIONS

MAY 2012

1. (a) Discuss various factors responsible for degradation in the ecosystem. **[8]**

Ans. : Please refer Section 6.4.

(b) Explain how interchange and transformation of pollutants take place in atmosphere, hydrosphere and lithosphere. **[8]**

Ans. : Please refer Section 6.5.

OR

2. (a) Define genetic engineering. Explain any two techniques of genetic engineering in detail. **[8]**

Ans. : Please refer Section 6.2.1.

(b) Write short notes on:

(i) Significance of Biotechnology.

Ans. : Please refer Section 6.2.1.

(ii) Applications of genetic engineering.

Ans. : Please refer Section 6.2.2.

MAY 2013

1. (a) What is biotechnology? What is the scope of bioinformatics in biotechnology? **[8]**

Ans. : Please refer Section 6.3.2.

(b) What are the natural causes of degradation of ecosystem? **[8]**

Ans. : Please refer Section 6.4.

OR

2. (a) Define genetic engineering. Discuss current developments in genetic engineering. **[8]**

Ans. : Please refer Section 6.2.

(b) Write short notes on pollutants in Lithosphere, Hydrosphere and Atmosphere. **[8]**

Ans. : Please refer Section 6.5.

MAY 2014

1. (a) What is biotechnology? What is the scope of bioinformatics in biotechnology? **[8]**

Ans. : Please refer Section 6.2.1.

(b) Define genetic engineering. Explain any two techniques of genetic engineering in detail.

Ans. : Please refer Section 6.2.

OR

2. (a) What are various factors of degradation in the ecosystem. **[8]**

Ans. : Please refer Section 6.4.

(b) Write short notes on pollutants in Lithosphere, Hydrosphere and Atmosphere. **[8]**

Ans. : Please refer Section 6.5.

❍ ❍ ❍

UNIVERSITY QUESTION PAPERS

May 2012

Time : 3 Hours **Max. Marks : 100**

Instructions:

1. Answer Q. 1 or Q. 2, Q. 3 or Q. 4 and Q. 5 or Q. 6 from Section - I and Q. 7 or Q. 8, Q. 9 or Q. 10 and Q. 11 or Q. 12 from Section - II.
2. Answer 3 questions from Section - I and 3 questions from Section - II.
3. Answers to the two sections should be written in separate answer books.
4. Neat diagrams must be drawn wherever necessary.
5. Figures to the right indicate full marks.
6. Assume suitable data, if necessary.

SECTION - I

1. (a) Define bioinformatics. Explain bioinformatics applications related to the following areas : **[10]**

   (i) Phylogenetic Analysis.

   (ii) Genome Annotation.

   (iii) Proteomics.

   (iv) Drug Discovery.

   (b) Classify and explain major databases in bioinformatics giving examples of each database. **OR**

2. (a) Explain central dogma of molecular biology with neat diagram. Explain how is it an information science. **[8]**

   (b) State and explain various data retrieval tools in bioinformatics. Explain the steps for data mining and knowledge discovery of biological databases. **[10]**

3. (a) What is structure visualization? Explain the various rendering tools in structure visualization. **[8]**

   (b) Explain microarray spotting process flow in detail. How is microarray result analysis done ? **[8] OR**

4. (a) Explain in detail the various methods of data mining for extracting patterns from data. **[8]**

   (b) Differentiate between clustering and classification. Explain hierarchical and k-means clustering in brief. **[8]**

5. (a) Explain the basic machine learning process with neat diagram. Describe following machine learning processes in brief :

   (i) Neural networks.

   (ii) Decision Trees.

(b) What is text mining? Explain NLP approach of text mining in detail, giving significance of each stage.

OR

6. (a) Explain major steps in pattern recognition and discovery process. **[8]**

(b) Explain following methods of computational sequence alignment : **[8]**

(i) Dot MatrixAnalysis.

(ii) Word - based Method.

SECTION - II

7. (a) Explain modeling and simulation process along with the components involved in detail. **[8]**

(b) Differentiate between Ab-Initio and Heuristic methods of protein structure prediction. Explain the general ab-initio prediction process in detail with neat diagram. **[10]**

OR

8. (a)Draw the collaboration - communication model. Explain collaboration and communication hierarchy in detail with neat diagram and appropriate examples. **[10]**

(b) Explain synchronous and asynchronous collaboration.

9. (a) Explain similarities and differences between BLAST and FASTA tools for sequence alignment. **[8]**

(b) Explain FASTA algorithm in detail with recommended steps for similarity searching.

OR

10. (a) Explain BLAST algorithm. State the major refirements included in gapped BLAST. **[8]**

(b) Explain the significance of E( ) value with example. What is filtering in blast.

11. (a) Discuss various factors responsible for degradation in the ecosystem. **[8]**

(b) Explain how interchange and transformation of pollutants take place in atmosphere, hydrosphere and lithosphere. **OR**

12. (a) Define genetic engineering. Explain any two techniques of genetic Engineering in detail.

(b) Write short notes on :

(i) Significance of Biotechnology.

(ii) Applications of genetic engineering.

May 2013

SECTION - I

1. (a) What is the scope of bioinformatics? Explain bioinformatics applications related to the following areas : **[10]**

   (i) Information search & retrieval, (ii) Microarrays, (iii) Sequence Assembly, (iv) Pharmacogenomics

   (b) Explain with neat diagram the central dogma of molecular biology. **[8]**

   Explain the molecules participating in Information flow and the various functional sites. **OR**

2. (a) Discuss the public bioinformatics databases which are accessible via the internet with appropriate examples. **[10]**

   (b) Explain Data Life Cycle for clinical data management with respect to below steps : (i) Data creation and acquisition, (ii) Use, (iii) Modification, (iv) Archiving and data disposal.

3. (a) Define Micro-array. Explain the sources of variability in Micro-array preparation and reading. Explain how statistical analysis can be used to reduce variability. **[8]**

   (b) Explain in brief the data visualization techniques applicable to Bioinformatics. Discuss any two visualization tools with example. **[8] OR**

4. (a) Differentiate between clustering and classification. Discuss in brief the K-means clustering and Decision tree. **[8]**

   (b) List the various statistical analysis tools. What is meant by Sensitivity and Specificity of a tool? Explain in brief False Negative, True Negative, True Positive and False positive. **[8]**

5. (a) What are the types of machine processes? Explain any two machines learning processes. **[8]**

   (b) Write short notes on:

   (i) Pairwise Sequence Alignment (PSA)

   (ii) Multiple Sequence Alignment(MSA) **OR**

6. (a) Explain the text mining with NLP Process.

   (b) Explain computational methods of Sequence alignment : (i) Dynamic programming, (ii) Word method

SECTION - II

7. (a) Explain in detail Primary, Secondary, Tertiary and Quaternary structures of Proteins. **[10]**

   (b) Explain the process of Drug discovery. What high-throughput screening methods are employed in screening drugs? **[8] OR**

8. (a) Discuss in brief the components of a modeling and simulation system along with the process. **[8]**

   (b) Draw and explain Collaboration-Communication model with appropriate examples. **[10]**

9. (a) Explain in detail FASTA algorithm and the recommended steps for a FASTA search. **[8]**

   (b) Explain BLAST algorithm.

   Discuss Gapped BLAST with its major refinements. **[8] OR**

10. (a) Discuss Similarities & Differences of FASTA & BLAST tools for sequence alignment. **[8]**

    (b) Discuss the applications of PSI-BLAST program which explores protein family relationships. **[8]**

11. (a) What is biotechnology? What is the scope of bioinformatics in biotechnology? **[8]**

    (b) What are the natural causes of degradation of ecosystem? **[8]**

OR

12. (a) Define genetic engineering. Discuss current developments in genetic engineering. **[8]**

    (b) Write short notes on pollutants in Lithosphere, Hydrosphere and Atmosphere. **[8]**

❍ ❍ ❍

December 2013

SECTION - I

1. (a) Explain the Central Dogma of Molecular Biology. What is its significance in Bioinforamtics ? **[8]**

   (b) Discuss applications of bioinformatics in detail. **[8]**

OR

2. (a) The probability of a patient having a particular genetic disease is 0.6. Calculate the pretest odds ? If the likelihood ratio is given as 2.75, calculate the posttest odds ? Find the probability of the patient suffering from the genetic disease ? **[8]**

   (b) Explain any two limitations of Bayes' Theorem. **[8]**

3. (a) List different computational methods of sequence alignment and discuss any two in detail. **[8]**

   (b) What is Clustering ? Explain two methods of clustering gene expression data ? **[8]**

OR

4. (a) What is the role of microarray in bioinformatics ? Explain the stepwise spotting procedure of microarray in bioinformatics. **[8]**

   (b) Discuss difference between clustering and classification. **[8]**

5. (a) Define Data mining. State & explain various data retrieval tools in Bioinformatics ? **[10]**

   (b) Explain various representations of nucleotide sequence along with their particular uses and application. **[8]**

OR

6. (a) Explain following methods of computational sequence alignment : **[10]**

   (i) Dynamic programming.

   (ii) Dot matrix methods.

   (b) What is pattern matching ? Discuss different methods of pattern matching. **[8]**

SECTION - II

7. (a) Explain Modeling and Simulation process along with the components in detail. **[10]**

   (b) Differentiate between Ab-Initio and Heuristic methods of Protein structure prediction process. **[8]**

OR

8. (a) Draw and explain Collaboration-Communication model with appropriate examples and hierarchy. **[10]**

   (b) Explain the comparative modeling process of protein structure prediction. Discuss all its phases. **[8]**

9. (a) Explain in detail FASTA algorithm and the recommended steps for a FASTA search. **[8]**

   (b) What is Hashing ? How is it exploited in FASTA database algorithms ? **[8] OR**

10. (a) Discuss similarities and differences of FASTA and BLAST tools for sequence alignment. **[8]**

    (b) Explain steps followed by BLAST algorithm to find a matching sequence. **[8]**

11. (a) What is Biotechnology ? How Genetic engineering tools work in Biotechnology. **[8]**

    (b) Discuss the various factors responsible for degradation in the ecosystem. **[8] OR**

12. (a) Write short note on HMM, Neural Network. **[8]**

    (b) What is Genetic Engineering ? What is Genetic marker ? What are the dangers of GE ? **[8]**

May 2014

SECTION - I

1. (a) Define Bioinformatics. Discuss in detail any four Bioinformatics applications. **[10]**

   (b) Explain various protein databases used in Bioinformatics for analysis and developing applications. **[8]**

OR

2. (a) Discuss the application areas of computers in Bioinformatics with their associated technologies. **[8]**

   (b) Explain with neat diagram the Central dogma of molecular biology. How can molecular biology be considered as an information science ? **[10]**

3. (a) Discuss the statistical methods and tools used in data analysis of Bioinformatics.**[8]**

   (b) Explain in detail, how clustering and classification statistical operations are applied in Micro-array data. **[8]**

OR

4. (a) What are Micro-arrays ? Explain spotting with the help of process flow diagram for Micro-array analysis. **[8]**

   (b) List the different visualization techniques applicable to Bioinformatics. Explain any two visualization tools in detail. **[8]**

5. (a) Explain text mining with NLP process. **[8]**

   (b) Write short notes on : **[8]**

   (i) Pairwise Sequence Alignment (PSA), (ii) Multiple Sequence Alignment (MSA)

OR

6. (a) What are the various computational methods of Sequence Alignment ? Explain any two methods in detail. **[8]**

   (b) How the machine learning techniques are used in Bioinformatics ? Discuss any two machine learning methods with BI applications. **[8]**

SECTION - II

7. (a) Draw and explain Collaboration Communication model with appropriate examples. **[10]**

   (b) Explain with neat bock diagram the components of a modeling and simulation system. **[8] OR**

8. (a) What is the importance of protein structure in protein function ? Discuss the methods to predict the protein structures from sequence data. **[10]**

   (b) Explain the process of drug discovery. Which high throughput screening methods are employed in screening drugs ? **[8]**

9. (a) Define PSI BLAST. Explain its importance in Bioinformatics applications. **[8]**

   (b) Differentiate between FASTA and BLAST algorithms. **[8] OR**

10. (a) Explain in detail FASTA algorithm and the recommended steps for FASTA search. **[8]**

    (b) List the several implementations of FASTA algorithm. Explain any two in detail. **[8]**

11. (a) What is Biotechnology ? What is the scope of Bioinformatics in Biotechnology ? **[8]**

    (b) Define Genetic Engineering. Discuss current developments in genetic engineering. **[8]**

OR

12. (a) What are the various factors of degradation in the ecosystem ? **[8]**

    (b) Write a note on pollutants in Lithosphere, Hydrosphere and Atmosphere. **[8]**

❍ ❍ ❍

December 2014

SECTION - I

1. (a) Define bioinformatics. Discuss in detail any four bioinformatics applications. **[10]**

   (b) Explain various protein databases used in Bioinformatics for analysis and developing applications. **[8]**

OR

2. (a) Discuss the application areas of computers in Bioinformatics with their associated technologies. **[8]**

   (b) Explain with neat diagram the Central dogma of molecular biology. How can molecular biology be considered as an information science. **[10]**

3. (a) What is structure visualization? Explain the various rendering tools in structure visualization. **[8]**

   (b) Explain microarray spotting process flow in detail. How is microarray result analysis done? **[8] OR**

4. (a) Explain in detail the various methods of data mining for extracting patterns from data. **[8]**

   (b) Differentiate between clustering and classification. Explain hierarchical and k-means clustering in brief. **[8]**

5. (a) Explain text mining with NLP process. **[8]**

   (b) Write short notes on: **[8]**

   (i) Pairwise Sequence Alignment (PSA)

   (ii) Multiple Sequence Alignment (MSA)

OR

6. (a) What are the various computational methods of sequence alignment ? Explain any two methods in detail. **[8]**

   (b) How the machine learning techniques are used in bioinformatics ? Discuss any two machine learning methods with BI applications. **[8]**

SECTION - I

7. (a) Draw and explain Collaboration-Communication model with appropriate examples. **[10]**

   (b) Explain with neat block diagram the components of modeling and simulation systems. **[8]**

OR

8. (a) What is the importance of protein structure in protein function ? Discuss the method to predict the protein structures from sequence data. **[10]**

   (b) Explain the process of Drug discovery. What high-throughput screening methods are employed in screening drugs ? **[8]**

9. (a) Define PSI BLAST. Explain its importance in Bioinformatics application. **[8]**

   (b) Differentiate between FASTA and BLAST algorithms. **[8]**

OR

10. (a) Explain in detail FASTA algorithm and the recommended steps for FASTA Search. **[8]**

    (b) List several implementations of FASTA algorithm. Explain any two in detail. **[8]**

11. (a) What is biotechnology? What is the scope of bioinformatics in biotechnology? **[8]**

    (b) Define genetic engineering. Explain any two techniques of genetic engineering in detail. **[8]**

OR

12. (a) What are various factors of degradation in the ecosystem. **[8]**

    (b) Write short notes on pollutants in Lithosphere, Hydrosphere and Atmosphere. **[8]**